Happy 8th Birthday

♡ Juma & Jeepa

Happy 8th Birthday

♡ Juma & Jeepa

DOGS

The Illustrated Guide to Breeds

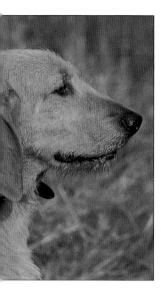

DOGS

The Illustrated Guide to Breeds

Joan Palmer

CHARTWELL
BOOKS

A QUARTO BOOK

This edition published in 2015 by
Chartwell Books
an imprint of Book Sales
a division of Quarto Publishing Group USA Inc.
142 West 36th Street, 4th Floor
New York, New York 10018
USA

ISBN: 978-0-7858-3278-2
QUAR.GUD

Conceived, designed,
and produced by
Quarto Publishing plc
The Old Brewery
6 Blundell Street
London N7 9BH

Typeset in Great Britain by Genesis Typesetters
Color separation in Singapore by Pica Digital Pte. Ltd
Reprinted in China by 1010 Printing Limited

10 9 8 7 6 5 4 3 2 1

This book was originally published as
The Illustrated Encyclopedia of Dog Breeds

CONTENTS

HISTORY AND ORIGINS

Before buying a dog, it is essential to get as much information as possible about all the different breeds, as this will help you select a dog that meets your requirements. This is important not only in terms of looks and size, but also character and temperament, so that the dog can fulfil the role you have in mind.

OWNERSHIP OF a dog is a serious undertaking. It requires a long-term commitment, bearing in mind that some breeds, the Miniature Poodle for instance, may live for 17 years or more. Twelve years is the average canine lifespan, during which time the dog must be fed, exercised and groomed, receive veterinary attention for accidents and illnesses and be taken into consideration whenever its owner is planning to be away from home for more than a matter of hours.

Owners should also consider their dog's welfare when making out their will. If a dog should survive its owner, clear instructions should be available stating whether the dog is bequeathed to an animal charity, with a suitable donation if possible, or to a named friend or relative.

A long-term commitment

Many dog owners do not take such a responsible attitude. This does not mean that they are bad or uncaring. More likely, they made the decision to buy a dog in the belief that the requirements and temperament of one canine were much the same as another, and that the only consideration was whether the dog looked big and tough or small, cute and cuddly. Yet some big, macho-looking dogs are great big softies, and some small breeds are famed for ill-humour. Only by studying the characteristics of

The surest way to develop a feel for dog psychology is by intelligent observation of puppies in the nest. For, even before they are weaned, puppies begin to display the characteristics which make canines uniquely useful to humans – or uniquely problematic. A successful relationship hinges on the owner learning to read the animal and to think like a dog.

The dog is a pack animal with a fundamental need for hierarchy. Already at four to five weeks it is obvious which of the litter is most dominant and how that dominance is asserted. This pup is the first to feed, to initiate play and to venture from the nest.

In leaving the litter, a puppy acquires a new pack consisting of all the members – human and animal – of its owner's household. Cast adrift from the security of the nest, it does not really begin to settle until it becomes familiar with its new territory and determines its status within the pack. It is at this time that the handler establishes himself as the pack-leader.

Canine language As a dog matures, it develops a full repertoire of postures and signals to do with behaviour. The confident dog conveys its non-aggressive dominance in its four-square posture, its ears erect and tail held high. On meeting it, a dog which is less robust psychologically signals its submission by lowering its tail, flattening its ears and perhaps turning its head to one side to avoid eye contact. In total submission it may lie on its back.

The relationship between human and dog is unique. If loved and well looked after, a dog will give its owner a lifetime of affection.

different breeds can you find out which ones are really suitable for you.

In addition, before buying a dog you must make sure, unless you own your home, that the landlord does not object to its presence. Most standard leases preclude the keeping of pets without the written consent of the landlord.

The therapeutic value of dogs is being increasingly recognized – indeed there is an International Association of Human-Animal Interaction Organizations – with dogs playing their part in comforting residents in hospices and nursing homes, as hospital visitors (Pro-Active Therapy Dogs), and as Hearing Dogs for the Deaf. At the same time, however, the laws concerning dogs are becoming ever more stringent, with some breeds being outlawed in certain states and countries. Laws relating to dog ownership vary from state to state in the US.

There is, for example, a very strict "poop and scoop" law in operation in New York State, and in others a limitation on the number of dogs that any individual may keep.

If you think much of this legislation is unnecessary, bear in mind that up to 10,000 cats and dogs are born every hour in the US and that 200,000 animals pass through the hands of the American Society for the Prevention of Cruelty to Animals each year. For this reason alone it is vital to make the right initial choice, so that the partnership between dog and owner is a happy and long-lasting one.

Miacis   *Tomarctus*

The first dogs

Canidae, the family of beasts of prey from which dogs and wolves are descended, first began evolving from prehistoric mammals some 60 million years ago. The Cynodictis, a strange-looking creature with a long body, sabre tail and short legs, is generally credited with being the original predecessor of the dog as well as other canines such as the wolf and fox. The dog

PSYCHOLOGY OF THE DOG

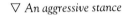
▽ An aggressive stance

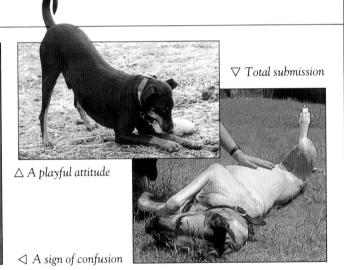

△ A playful attitude

▽ Total submission

◁ A sign of confusion

Most canine signals – from the gaily wagging tail to the fearsome snarl – are easily read, but there are some which may be misinterpreted. Yawning, for instance: this is not a sign of tiredness but of confusion. The dog yawns because it is receiving conflicting signals – usually from some owner who thinks he knows all there is to know about dog training. Staring is another example. To the dog staring is often a warning of impending attack and many people have provoked aggression by trying to master a dog with a stare.

Going on instinct Whatever its nature or disposition, a dog's behaviour is driven by instinct, not by intelligence as we understand it. The dog's intelligence

is to do with instant perception, not with planning and foresight, and the differences in performance between breeds reflect inbred traits rather than intelligence.

The Border Collie, for instance, is unrivalled as a herding dog – a role for which it has been selectively bred over many generations. There is no reason why the collie cannot also be taught to retrieve to the gun but it will never do so with the same style and consistency as the retriever bred for this purpose.

The dog is a predator and its instincts are to hunt, guard and reproduce. It is by channelling the first two of these drives (and controlling the third) that human beings have been able to forge such successful relationships with their dogs.

DESCENT OF THE MODERN DOG

All members of the species *Canis familiaris* are thought to descend from wolves as both animals are highly social and have many behavioural traits in common. Of 40 wolf races worldwide, four – *Canis lycaon* (eastern North America), *C. lupus* (Western Europe and central Asia), *C. pallipes* (Middle East and Indian subcontinent) and *C. lupus chanco* (south-east Asia) – are the most likely ancestors.

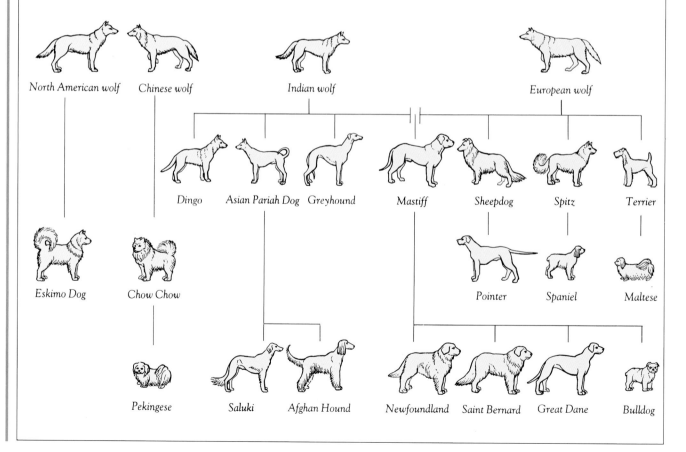

North American wolf   Chinese wolf   Indian wolf   European wolf

Dingo   Asian Pariah Dog   Greyhound   Mastiff   Sheepdog   Spitz   Terrier

Eskimo Dog   Chow Chow   Pointer   Spaniel   Maltese

Pekingese   Saluki   Afghan Hound   Newfoundland   Saint Bernard   Great Dane   Bulldog

family, *Canis familiaris*, can be traced back to the Miacis, a tree-climbing, weasel-like carnivore that lived around 50 million years ago. However, the Tomarctus, a fox-like animal that appeared 35 million years later, is believed to be the true ancestor.

The Tomarctus had disappeared by the middle of the Pleistocene age, 1 million years ago, and today it is agreed that the more recent ancestor of the dog is the social wolf, with which it shares both a great many characteristics and the same dental patterns.

Precisely how dogs became the companions of humans can only be surmised. Remains found in Denmark show that dogs were domesticated by the time of the Neolithic. Some say this came about when people threw scraps of meat to the wild dogs that crept up to their camp fires, and that later they recognized the value of dogs as hunters and protectors. Others believe that humans began the domestication and breeding of dogs by removing litters of pups from their lairs, irrespective of whether the young were wolves, jackals or wild dogs, all of which would interbreed in domestic conditions.

Breeding for diversity

Certainly, humans would have discovered that, by selective mating, certain traits could be bred in or perpetuated. In this way they were able to produce dogs that were not only a desired colour and size, but which had inbred characteristics: for example, strong guarding instincts or keen eyesight.

The first dogs were bred selectively for a specific purpose. The earliest recorded history of dogs, by the Greek Xenophon (*c.* 430–350 BC), was devoted to hunting and hunting dogs. Not until the Swedish naturalist Carolus Linnaeus (1707–73) produced his *Systema Natura* (*The Order of Nature*) in 1735 were dogs classified other than as workers.

By the middle of the 19th century, with interest in dogs steadily increasing, the need for a Group system became apparent. There were attempts at classification by appearance and according to archeological evidence for evolution of the species. The current, universally acknowledged, system has generally been developed to take into account the type of work, if any, and the size of breeds.

DOMESTICATION OF DOGS

The hunter and his dog setting off – an everyday picture, but one that reaches down 17,000 years, from the painters of the Lascaux caves of France.

Dogs were domesticted in many different parts of the prehistoric world. By the Bronze Age, it was possible to distinguish a number of groups by the work they did: *Canis familiaris intermedius* for hunting; *c. f. metris optimae* for herding; *c. f. inostranzevi*, the Mastiff type; *c. f. palustris*, the northern spitz type; and *c. f. leineri*, the greyhound type. Although this may be an oversimplification, there is ample pictorial evidence to prove the existence of a Mesopotamian Greyhound type in 6000 BC, which could run down prey.

By 2000 BC the Egyptians had produced a fast scent hunter by crossing the Greyhound with a Bloodhound. And the Syrian invaders brought their Mastiff and Saluki types from the Middle East to North Africa 200 years later. In Tibet, Mastiff dogs were already being bred and trained as guards, and the tiny "sleeve dogs" of the Chinese imperial household were being used as hand warmers. Homer immortalized the dog as man's most faithful companion in the Odyssey (*c.* 850 BC).

The Mastiff descends from the Molossus wardog of Rome.

The Pharaoh Hound, depicted in the tombs of the Pharaohs.

The Saluki, treasured by nomadic Bedouin tribes.

FORMATION AND TERMINOLOGY

If you take a random selection of pure-bred dogs, you will notice that their faces, ears, eyes, heads, colour, even the way in which they move – their gait – differ. As many new breeds have developed over the years, and continue to develop and become recognized as official breeds by the kennel clubs, it has become necessary to standardize the way in which all these differences are described.

TO THE inexperienced eye, or to the owner who buys a pure-bred dog purely as a pet, minor variations from the "standard" may be unimportant, but, for showing purposes, every detail counts in assessing a dog as a representative of its type. The special terminology used today has been developed to encompass all aspects of a dog's appearance and conformation, and makes interesting reading for any dog owner.

Buying a dog that will turn into a good show dog can never be guaranteed, as it is generally not possible to determine a dog's full potential until it is several months old. However, familiarity with the different characteristics required for the breed, and careful investigation into the dog's parents and background, should give you the best chance of obtaining a good show dog.

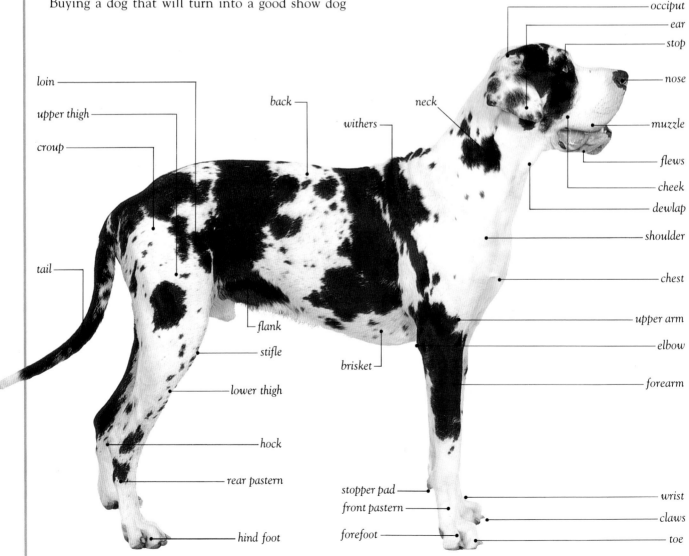

loin — back — withers — neck — occiput — ear — stop — nose — muzzle — flews — cheek — dewlap — shoulder — chest — upper arm — elbow — forearm — wrist — claws — toe — stopper pad — front pastern — forefoot — hind foot — rear pastern — hock — lower thigh — stifle — flank — brisket — tail — croup — upper thigh

BITE

A dog's bite is defined by the position of the lower jaw relative to the upper jaw. Not all dogs are required to have an even bite, but in some breeds, for example the Chihuahua, it is a show fault to be either over- or undershot.

NORMAL
Also called the scissor bite, where the upper and lower rows of teeth meet up

OVERSHOT
A short lower jaw, and where the lower incisors (front teeth) protrude beyond the inner surface of the upper incisors

UNDERSHOT
A long lower jaw, with the incisors projecting beyond those of the upper jaw

HEADS

There are three skull types. These describe the basic shape of the head, which comprises 50 bones. There are many subtypes that come within these basic groups. Heads lacking in refinement are said to be coarse.

MESOTICEPHALIC
Medium proportions of bone width to overall length of the skull (Irish Water Spaniel)

BRACHYCEPHALIC
Short, compressed head, with a rounded cranium (Pekingese)

DOLICHOCEPHALIC
Long narrow head, with shallow cranium (Borzoi)

APPLE
Domed and rounded (Chihuahua)

BALANCED
Skull and foreface equal in length to form a consistent whole (Springer Spaniel)

BLOCKY
Square or cube-like formation (Staffordshire Bull Terrier)

CLEAN
Free from wrinkles or bony or muscular lumps (Golden Retriever)

EGG-SHAPED
Strong and deep and free from hollowing, right to the end of the muzzle (Bull Terrier)

FOX-LIKE
Sharp expression, pointed nose, short foreface and pointed ears (Lapland Spitz)

OTTER
Head shaped like an otter's with broad, flat skull and short, strong muzzle (Border Terrier)

PEAR-SHAPED
Rounded, narrow skull with a tapering muzzle and no stop (Bedlington Terrier)

RECTANGULAR
Head slightly domed, a little narrower at the ears than the eyes (West Highland White Terrier)

FACES

The shapes of dogs' faces are influenced to a great extent by the basic skull type, but have changed and been refined over the years as the different breeds have developed.

The descriptive names used to classify the types of faces are derived both from the skeletal structure of the head, and from the coloration of the face.

BROKEN-UP

Has a receding, pushed-in nose, a deep stop, an undershot jaw and wrinkles (Pekingese)

CLOWN

Black and white or tan and white markings are more or less symmetrically divided by a line down the centre of the face and skull (Smooth-haired Fox Terrier)

DISH

The nose is higher at the tip than at the stop due to the nasal-bone formation, or the line of the stop to the tip of the nose is slightly concave (German Pointer)

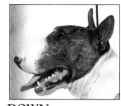

DOWN

Where the muzzle inclines downwards from the skull to the tip of the nose (Bull Terrier)

FROG

An extending nose combined with a receding jaw, usually overshot. It is a fault in some breeds, such as the French and British Bulldogs (Rottweiler)

EARS

Ears are described in terms of their shape and how they hang from the head. The phrase "set on" refers to the position of the ears in relation to eye level and/or the width of the skull. The ears may be set on high, like those of the Great Dane; set on low, like those of the King Charles Spaniel; or set on wide, as in the case of the German Shepherd Dog. There are two normal ear types and many variations.

Cropped ears involve cutting or trimming the ear leather so that the ears stand erect. It should only be carried out by a veterinary surgeon. In the US ear cropping is carried out on several breeds, including the Boxer, Doberman, Great Dane, Giant, Standard and Miniature Schnauzers, Griffon Bruxellois and Manchester Terrier. However, it is not allowed in the UK and a number of other countries.

BAT

Erect, somewhat broad at the base, rounded in outline at the tip, and with the orifice opening directly to the front (French Bulldog)

BUTTON

The ear flap folding forward and the tip lying close to the skull, covering the orifice and pointing towards the eye (Irish Terrier)

DROP

Where the ends of the ears are folded or droop forwards. They may be pendent or pendulous (English Cocker Spaniel)

FILBERT-SHAPED

Ears which are hazelnut-shaped (Bedlington Terrier)

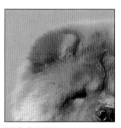

HEART-SHAPED

Shaped like a heart (Pekingese)

HOODED

Small, triangular and erect, but tilted forward slightly (Chow Chow)

HOUND

Triangular and rounded, the ear flap folding forwards and lying close to the head (Beagle)

PRICKED

Standing erect and generally pointed at the tips (German Shepherd Dog)

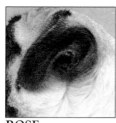

ROSE

A small drop ear that folds over and back so as to reveal the burr (Pug)

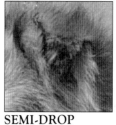

SEMI-DROP

Also called a Semi-prick Ear, where just the tip of the ears breaks and falls forwards (Shetland Sheepdog)

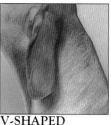

V-SHAPED

Usually, but not always, carried in the dropped position. Also known as Triangular Ears (Hungarian Vizsla)

EYES

The terminology for eyes is based on the shape of the eyes and how they are set in the skull. Because of the size of the muzzle, dogs have little overlapping sight, that is, they have only a small field of vision covered by both eyes. In breeds like the Bulldog, the eyes are positioned relatively far forward, limiting their total field of vision to 200 degrees. In other breeds, for example, the Coonhounds, the field of vision is much greater – 270 degrees – because the eyes are set further back on the head. Both glassy and beady eyes are regarded as a fault.

ALMOND

Almond-shaped (German Shepherd Dog)

CIRCULAR

As round as possible (Smooth-haired Fox Terrier)

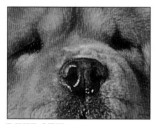

DEEP SET

Sunk well down in the eye sockets (Chow Chow)

GLOBULAR

Appearing to protrude, but in fact not bulging when viewed in profile (Chihuahua)

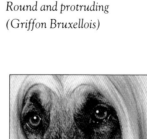

GOGGLY

Round and protruding (Griffon Bruxellois)

HAW

The term used for the third membrane in the inside corner of the eye. Its appearance is a fault in some breeds (Bloodhound)

OBLIQUE

Set in the head at an angle from the ear towards the muzzle (Miniature Wire-haired Dachshund)

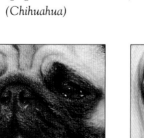

PIG

Very small and hard. Also describes eyes that are small and close together, a fault in the Miniature Pinscher (Pug)

TRIANGULAR

Set in triangular-shaped tissue (Afghan Hound)

TAILS

The names given to tails refer to their length, shape, position and the hair covering them. Retrievers use their tails as rudders when they are in the water, and Deerhounds use theirs to maintain their balance, but, for most breeds, the tail is most important as a means of communication.

The "tail set" refers to the way in which its base is set on the rump; whereas how the tail is "set on" refers to its placement: it may be high, low and so on.

Tails are docked in some breeds, such as the Doberman, to make them appear more aggressive. They also used to be docked in hunting breeds to prevent damage. About 45 breeds have docked tails. The operation is performed by a veterinary surgeon.

BOBTAIL
A dog that is naturally tail-less or a tail that is customarily docked very short (Old English Sheepdog)

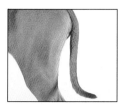

BRUSH
Tail like the brush of a fox (Alaskan Malamute)

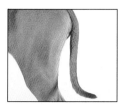

CRANK
Carried down and resembling a crank (Italian Short-haired Segugio)

CURLED
Tail set on high and curled over, either onto the spine or to one side. There may be single and double curls (Finnish Spitz)

FLAG
Long and carried high (Beagle)

KINK
Sharply bent (Lhasa Apso)

OTTER
Thick at the root, round and tapering towards tip, with short, thick hair, and used as a rudder when swimming (Labrador)

RING
Carried up and around, almost in a circle (Basenji)

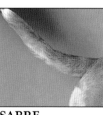

SABRE
Carried like a sabre (Basset Hound)

SCREW
Naturally short, twisted in a spiral fashion (French Bulldog)

SICKLE
Carried out and up in a semi-circle (Affenpinscher)

SPIKE
Short and thick, tapering quickly along its entire length (English Lakeland Terrier)

STERN
The technical term for the tail of a sporting dog or a hound (English Pointer)

SQUIRREL
Carried up and curving forward (Chow Chow)

WHIP
Carried stiffly straight and pointed (Bull Terrier)

COAT COLOURS

BELTON
(English Setter)

BLACK AND TAN
(Hamiltonstövare)

BLUE
(Blue Gascony Basset)

BRINDLE
(Greyhound)

GRIZZLE
(Old English Sheepdog)

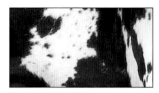

HARLEQUIN
(Great Dane)

PARTI-COLOUR
(Swedish Vallhund)

PIEBALD
(Dalmation)

RED
(Irish Setter)

ROAN
(Welsh Corgi)

TRICOLOUR
(Beagle)

WHEATEN
(Soft-coat Wheaten Terrier)

GAIT

The term gait refers to the pattern of a dog's footsteps at various speeds, and is distinguishable by a particular rhythm and footfall.

Gaiting a dog is a show term meaning to show off its paces.

There are a number of faults in movement. Crabbing is where the dog moves with its body at an angle to the line of travel. Other names for this type of action are sidewinding, sidewheeling and yawing. Cow-hocking is where the hocks turn inwards, facing one another. Dishing is similar to weaving in the horse, and is an unnatural movement of the forequarters.

The manner – and pace – at which dogs are gaited in the show ring differs from breed to breed. Some of the larger varieties are moved around the show ring at a fast pace; others are gaited fairly sedately. For this reason, it is important that the elderly exhibitor who may be new to the game does not select a breed that would prove too tiring to exhibit, as the dog cannot then be presented to its best advantage.

Amble A relaxed, easy movement, often seen as a transition between the walk and the faster movements. The front and hind legs on either side move in unison.

Trot A rhythmic, two-beat, diagonal gait during which the feet at diagonally opposite corners of the body strike the ground together – the right hind with the left front, and the left hind with the right front.

Canter A gait which has three beats to each stride. Two legs move separately and two as a diagonal pair. The movement is reminiscent of a rocking-horse, slower than a gallop and not nearly so fatiguing.

Gallop The fastest gait, during which all four feet are off the ground at the same time.

Pace Movement or gait during which the left foreleg and left hind leg go forward in unison, followed by the right foreleg and right hind leg.

Hackney Almost identical to the action of the Hackney horse or pony, with the same high lifting of the front feet. The Miniature Pinscher has a hackney gait.

BREED GROUPS

Dog breeds are divided into groups, and these are of considerable help and importance not only in categorizing the breeds for exhibition purposes, but also in aiding the purchaser to select the breed best suited to the purpose that he has in mind, be it a children's pet, hunting dog, or guard.

THERE ARE three official organizations involved in the classification of the dog groups. These are the United Kingdom Kennel Club, the oldest national kennel club in the world, which started in 1873 and recognizes 189 breeds; the American Kennel Club, which first began in 1884 and recognizes 135 breeds; and the Fédération Cynologique International (FCI), which was created in 1911, when the founder members were Austria, Belgium, France and the Netherlands. The FCI is divided into five regions: Europe, Latin and South America, Asia, Africa, Oceania and Australia. The Fédération recognizes a total of 340 different breeds, a number of which are little known, if at all, outside their country of origin.

The United Kingdom Kennel Club – the first of its kind in the world – led the way in introducing a registration system to determine the breeding of all pure-bred dogs, as well as an official "standard" for each recognized breed.

Listing the breeds in each group is a risky business in a book such as this, however, as there are always new breeds waiting in the wings for official recognition. This recognition can be granted between the time of a book being written and going to press. Listings need to be updated to keep pace with the ever-changing categories.

It will be apparent from studying the Groups how in fact a breed show is judged. The exhibits in a breed class (dog and bitch) have to beat others of their own kind in order to go forward into the group judging. Out of the group winners, the Best in Show is finally selected as the overall winner.

MAPS

The country of origin of the dog is given for each breed. This is shown on the small map at the top of the entry in every case.

FCI

- Sheepdogs and Cattle Dogs
- Guards and Working Breeds
- Terriers
- Dachshunds
- Spitz Types/ Hounds for Larger Game
- Scenthounds/ Hounds for Smaller Game
- Pointers
- Gundogs
- Companions and Toys
- Sighthounds/ Greyhounds

CKC

- Sporting Breeds
- Terriers
- Non-sporting Breeds
- Hounds
- Toy Breeds
- Working Breeds
- Herding Breeds
- Miscellaneous Class

AKC

- Non-sporting Breeds
- Working Breeds
- Herding Breeds
- Sporting Breeds
- Hounds
- Terriers
- Toy Breeds

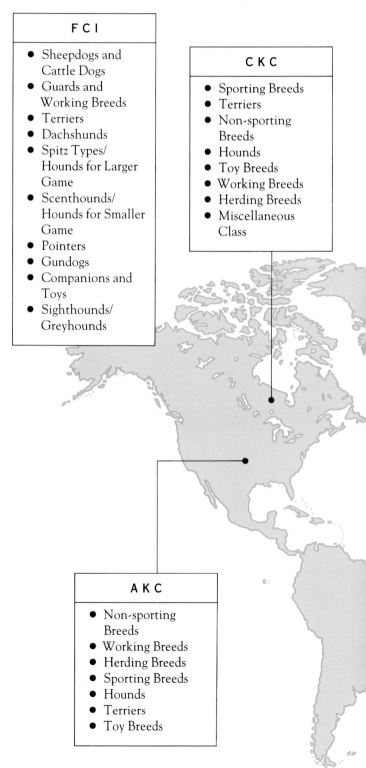

HOW STANDARDS ARE SET

The German Pointer is a long-established, recognized breed.

The American Cocker Spaniel has been bred with specific traits.

The Leonberger is in contention for kennel-club registration.

All breeds placed by their national kennel club within a specific group are given a breed standard. This sets out a standard of excellence for representatives of that breed, and includes such modifications as ideal height and/or weight, desirable colours, conformation points and so on. Again, there are slight differences in what is deemed ideal from country to country. For instance, while in America the height limit for the Beagle is 38cm at the shoulder, the English call for a height from ground to withers that should neither exceed 40.5cm nor fall below 33cm and they do not allow as great a tolerance in the case of the Kerry Blue Terrier. However, differences would not adversely influence an experienced judge adjudicating away from home.

For the older established breeds, standards were set by the appropriate fancier's club when they were founded, some as long ago as the 1870s. Today, when a new breed is accepted for registration, standards from the kennel club of the country of origin are examined by the standards committee, which may also consult with outside experts. An interim standard is used for an imported breed which is not on the full register.

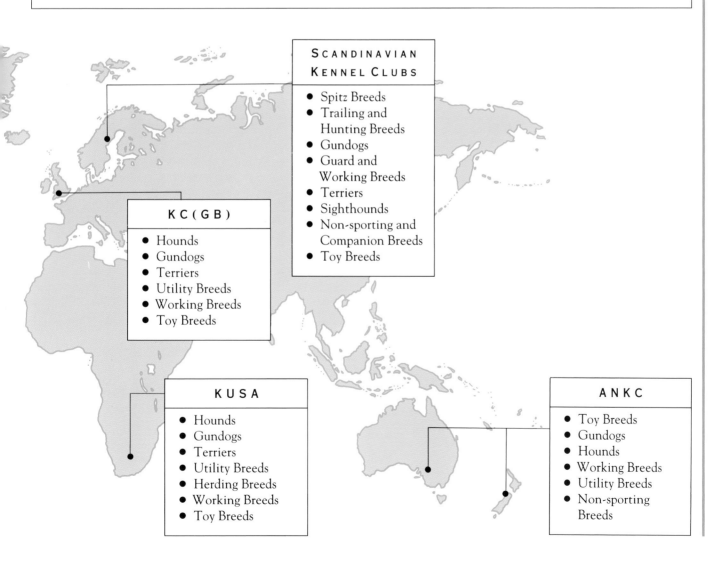

SCANDINAVIAN KENNEL CLUBS

- Spitz Breeds
- Trailing and Hunting Breeds
- Gundogs
- Guard and Working Breeds
- Terriers
- Sighthounds
- Non-sporting and Companion Breeds
- Toy Breeds

KC (GB)

- Hounds
- Gundogs
- Terriers
- Utility Breeds
- Working Breeds
- Toy Breeds

KUSA

- Hounds
- Gundogs
- Terriers
- Utility Breeds
- Herding Breeds
- Working Breeds
- Toy Breeds

ANKC

- Toy Breeds
- Gundogs
- Hounds
- Working Breeds
- Utility Breeds
- Non-sporting Breeds

BREEDING CHARACTERISTICS

Breeding for appearance was introduced in the 19th century. Up to that time, dog breeding concentrated on producing traits that were useful for work: vermin hunting (terriers), flushing and driving game (pointers, hounds), running down large and small quarry (mastiffs, greyhound) and guarding (mastiffs). From these basic types were derived more specialist breeds, each ideally suited to work a specific terrain (Saint Hubert Hound) or perform a particular job (Dogue de Bordeaux).

The interest in selective breeding was fostered by the Kennel Club, founded in London in 1873. It established a registration system which enabled breeders to record the lineage of each pure-bred animal, that is, one whose dam and sire were both off-spring of pure-bred animals as far back as could be traced.

Characteristics such as size, colour or set of tail can be introduced or altered by breeding from animals with those traits. It is also possible to introduce a feature from another breed – for example, Dingo blood added to the Smooth-coated Collie to produce the Australian Kelpie – and then to breed across enough generations for the trait to run "true". There is always a risk, however, that overbreeding can throw up inheritable weaknesses such as hip dysplasia (malformation) and progressive retinal atrophy (blindness). Congenital disorders can only be prevented by stopping all affected animals from breeding.

NON-SPORTING BREEDS

This is the category from which many pet dogs are selected. The breeds within this group may well have performed some task in the past, but in the main they are now the dogs whose sole purpose in life is to be a companion to their owners. There is a large choice, ranging from the lively Dalmatian, a former carriage dog, to the more sedate French Bulldog and the Chow Chow (shown above).

WORKING BREEDS

This group covers the traditional guards and workers – rescue, sled and draught dogs, and those favoured by the armed services, such as the Rottweiler (shown above). Bred to work, and in many cases fearsome, natural guards, most are happiest when they are doing the job for which they are bred or at least when in an environment where their abilities will not go to waste.

The Bullmastiff was created by crossing the Bulldog and English Mastiff in the 19th

HERDING BREEDS

The breeds in this group were originally developed to herd and protect sheep (such as the Maremma, Collie and German Shepherd Dog – the latter is shown above) and cattle (the Lancashire Heeler and Corgi) and other stock. Many are still used by shepherds and farmers, but they are also extremely adaptable as pets, often taking it upon themselves to herd the family together.

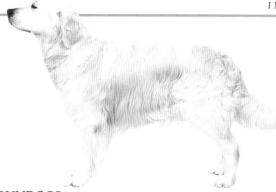

GUNDOGS

In this group are the pointers, retrievers (shown above is the Golden Retriever) and spaniels – all gundogs used variously to detect, flush out and retrieve game. Usually gentle natured, many dogs in this category have the dual role of huntsman's dog and family pet.

TERRIERS

These dogs were bred to go to ground, to hunt vermin and bolt the fox from its lair. Energetic, sporting and sometimes noisy, most terriers are affectionate by nature, but they can be nippy. The Yorkshire Terrier (shown above) is a friendly and very popular dog.

HOUNDS

Hounds are often divided into those that hunt by scent (scent hounds), for instance the Bloodhound, Basset and Beagle (the Beagle is shown above), and those that rely on their keen eyesight (sighthounds), such as the Greyhound and the Saluki. Hounds are good natured but have a propensity to roam. Many hounds are kept in packs, in outside kennels, rather than living indoors.

TOY BREEDS

Do not be fooled by the fact that the traditional ladies' lap dogs, such as the Pomeranian (shown above) come within this category. Many toy breeds would walk their owners off their feet, if given the chance to do so. Most are splendid guards, keenly intelligent, affectionate, if somewhat possessive, and courageous to the point of stupidity.

▷ *Chart showing the rates at which different breeds reach their mature size. The fastest growth occurs in the first six months of life, and continues more slowly for the next six months. The smaller breeds reach their full size by this time, although larger dogs continue to grow a little after this point.*

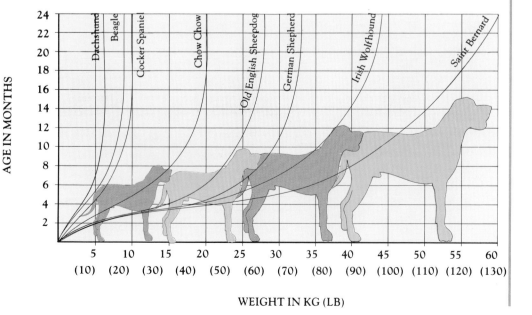

AGE IN MONTHS

Dachshund | Beagle | Cocker Spaniel | Chow Chow | Old English Sheepdog | German Shepherd | Irish Wolfhound | Saint Bernard

5 (10) 10 (20) 15 (30) 20 (40) 25 (50) 30 (60) 35 (70) 40 (80) 45 (90) 50 (100) 55 (120) 60 (130)

WEIGHT IN KG (LB)

CHOOSING A DOG

There is an old saying, "Buy in haste, repent at leisure", and this advice is certainly true in the case of buying a dog. Many people, on discovering that they have made a mistake, learn to love the dog just the same. However, with a little forethought, there would not have been any cause for regret.

FIRST OF all, it is important that the decision to buy a dog has the approval of both partners; likewise with the choice of breed. It is important that one member of the household, who may be closeted in an office every day, does not rush out and buy a large hunting dog, which they expect someone else to look after when they had been secretly yearning for a Pekingese.

Secondly, never buy a dog on face value. Always check whether its abilities, temperament and requirements are suitable for the role that you have in mind, and your circumstances. For instance, you may live in an apartment or in a house, in the town or in the country, and your choice of breed should take

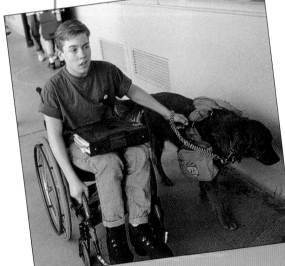

Today, dogs fulfil a wide range of working roles. The temperaments of certain breeds make them more or less suited to particular jobs, but good training will bring out the best in any dog.

this into account. In the case of a large, powerful breed and/or one that needs a great deal of exercise, you must be certain that you and/or your partner have the physical strength to control it.

By now you will have realized that study of the canine groups helps the dog buyer to fine down the choice to breeds that fall within the most suitable category. In each case, you should find a number of varieties from which to make a choice. It should not be too difficult to find several breeds which, for example, combine the role of sporting dog and/or guard with that of a family pet, or which could, if you wish, be kennelled out of doors, mindful that most pet dogs share their owners' home, but that many large, thick-coated dogs come to no harm outside. However, once having kept your dog indoors for any time, it would be unkind to reverse that decision and subject it to the rigours of kennel life.

A wise decision

In talking to breeders, you are bound to be told that their type of dog is the right one for you. Similarly, one person will tell you that he would never keep, for example, a German Shepherd Dog in the same house as a child, while someone else will say that he would trust that dog with the child's life.

It is important to bear in mind that, in common with a number of other working dogs such as the Doberman and the Rottweiler, the German Shepherd is a natural guard. Incidents reported in the media involving these breeds may well occur because these guarding breeds, which are naturally on the alert, misinterpreted a situation and sprang – as they saw it – to the defence of their charge. In other words, they did the job for which they were bred.

Study of the breed profiles will confirm that, because a dog is small or large, it does not necessarily need proportionately less or more exercise or floor space. The Greyhound, for example, is accustomed during its racing life to occupying a confined area away from the track, and will happily relax in its own corner when in a domestic situation.

Grooming

Most people have a preference for a long- or a short-coated animal, and even sometimes for a particular colour. Remember, however, that the long-coated animal is likely to need far more time spent on grooming than the short-coated one, and that the light-coloured dog, for instance the Dalmatian, is going to shed hairs that will be apparent on the sitting-room carpet.

What are the requirements of each breed of dog? The majority of fanciers are only expert in preparing their own chosen breed, and perhaps one or two

CARING FOR YOUR DOG

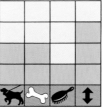

The care boxes located at the beginning of every entry in this book provide a ready reference for how to look after a dog. They show at a glance the basic requirements of each breed. The scales in the chart range from one shaded block (the least requirement) to four (the greatest requirement).

The first column indicates the amount of exercise a particular breed requires – in the case of the Bulldog, relatively little, whereas the Siberian Husky needs a great deal.

The second column shows the quantity of food that should be given – the Mastiff has a huge appetite, whereas the Sealyham Terrier has very modest requirements.

The third column gives an idea of the amount of grooming that is appropriate – the Bichon Frise should have daily, elaborate care, whereas the Bouvier de Flandres needs little grooming.

The fourth column is a guide to the suitability of the breed for a small house or apartment – with one block, the Dachshund is a good choice for limited living space; the Otterhound, with four blocks, needs a lot of room.

Many people choose long-coated dogs without considering the time that will need to be spent on grooming.

This "before and after" picture shows how much work is required even on a small dog like the Bichon Frise.

others. Only professional dog groomers could, for example, advise on the bathing, trimming, scissoring and grooming of all the breeds recognized by the American Kennel Club.

Special effects
While quite a number of breeds have to be hand-stripped, using fingers and/or a stripping knife, to give the coat the desired effect for the show ring, these same breeds are often clipped instead when they are kept solely as domestic pets.

Smooth-coated breeds such as the American Staffordshire Terrier, Coonhound, Boston Terrier and French Bulldog need only be groomed every day or two using a short, bristle brush; the German Shepherd Dog and many of the spaniels and retrievers need daily grooming using a bristle brush and a comb; those breeds that need particular coat

care and regular visits to the grooming parlour for clipping, stripping and, perhaps, scissoring, include the Airedale Terrier, Bichon Frise, the Schnauzers and the Poodles.

It must be emphasized, therefore, that, if time and expense are a consideration, you would be well advised to think in terms of a smooth, short-coated breed.

Feeding
The cost element does come into dog-keeping, the larger breeds costing considerably more to maintain, in food terms, than the smaller – a toy breed will eat approximately 25 per cent less than a Great Dane. The dog in regular work will also consume more food than its fellow that leads an indolent life, so this, too, must be taken into consideration. The breed standards laid down by national kennel clubs indicate, in many cases, the desired weight of the breed. If you are concerned that your dog falls below, or above, this ideal, you should consult your veterinarian, who may recommend a special diet.

Caring for a new puppy
When you collect your pup from the breeder, they will normally hand you a diet sheet, which you should observe for the first months of the pup's life. You may not wish to continue feeding the recommended products, but it would be foolish to deviate from the breeder's recommendations until the pup is well grown.

It is usual for a pup to require four small meals a day (five in the case of some of the larger breeds), reduced to two meals at six months of age, and one at

△ Young puppies have voracious appetites. Their growth rate is at its peak during the first six months of life, so a sufficient intake of food is essential to produce the energy required for healthy development.

▷ Table showing the quantity of food required by the different sizes of dog in the first 12 months of life.

NUMBER OF MEALS PER DAY AT AGE IN MONTHS	WEANING 0–3	3–6	6–12
TOY (less than 4.5kg/10lb)	90–150g (3–5oz)	200–600g (7–21oz)	300–800g (11–28oz)
SMALL (4.5–9kg/10–20lb)	200–350g (7–12oz)	350–800g (12–28oz)	750–95g (26–33oz)
MEDIUM (9–22kg/20–50lb)	350–600g (12–21oz)	700g–1kg (25–35oz)	850g–1.6kg (30–56oz)
LARGE (22–34kg/50–75lb)	600–850g (21–30oz)	800g–1.6kg (28–56oz)	1.6–2kg (56–70oz)

Teaching a puppy to use newspaper, in the first stage of house-training, and accustoming him to a new bed, are important steps in early training.

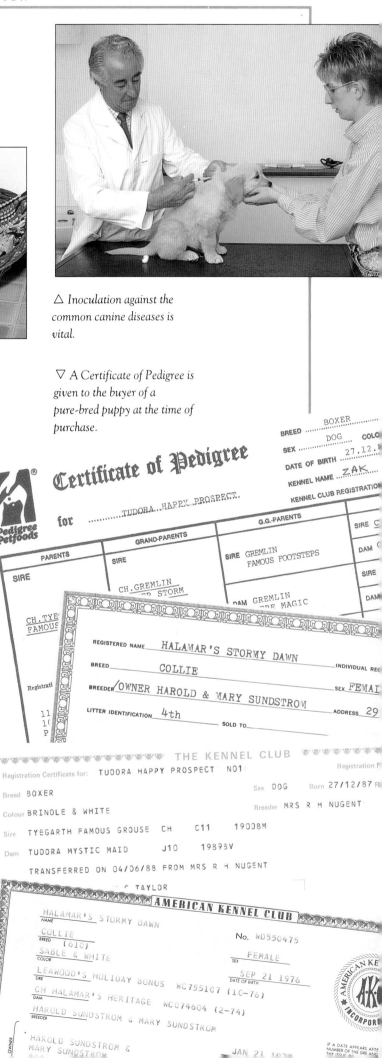

△ *Inoculation against the common canine diseases is vital.*

▽ *A Certificate of Pedigree is given to the buyer of a pure-bred puppy at the time of purchase.*

a year old, by which time it is deemed to be an adult. However, many owners, particularly in the case of toy breeds, prefer to continue giving their dog two meals a day, dividing the daily portion into two halves.

Veterinary care

You must remember to ask the breeder about the pup's worming programme, and to check whether it has had any inoculations against killer diseases such as canine distemper and parvo virus. If not, you will need to arrange for the necessary jabs with your veterinarian and to establish the routine for annual boosters thereafter.

Registration

Finally, if the pup that you have chosen is registered with its national kennel club, the breeder should give you its Certificate of Pedigree. Make sure that this has been duly signed and completed, so that you can arrange official transfer of ownership into your name. This is vital if you are intending to exhibit the animal, or to breed from it.

Because you are buying a dog with a Certificate of Pedigree, it does not mean that you are acquiring a show dog. The fact that the animal is of pure breeding does not necessarily mean that it is up to the standard of perfection laid down in its breed standard, although it may well be an attractive and healthy example of its kind. It is never possible even for a breeder to say with any degree of certainty that this or that puppy will become a champion. However, if you tell them at the outset of your ambitions to show, they will do their best, based on long experience, to pick out a show prospect for you. There are, however, no guarantees.

23

NON- SPORTING BREEDS

BOSTON TERRIER

The lively and intelligent Boston Terrier is a compactly built, well balanced dog with a rather short body. A joy to have around the house, it is nevertheless determined and self willed.

The Boston Terrier's head should be in proportion to its size; its teeth should be short and regular, with an even bite, and its neck of fair length, slightly arched, carrying the dog's head gracefully.

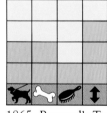

The Boston Terrier, formerly the American Bull Terrier, derives from a crossbred Bulldog/ Terrier that was imported into the United States from Britain in 1865. Barnard's Tom, the first example of the breed with the desired screw tail, was bred in Boston, Massachusetts, and registered with the American Kennel Club in 1893. The breed takes its name from the city where it was developed.

Character and care

It is a lively, intelligent dog and a loving family pet. It is easy to look after and requires little grooming. However, it is difficult to obtain a show specimen with the right markings – ideally, a white muzzle, even a white blaze over the head and down the collar, breast and forelegs below the elbows.

KEY CHARACTERISTICS
● **CLASS** Non-sporting. **Recognized** AKC, CKC, FCI, KC(GB).
● **SIZE** Weight not exceeding 11.4kg (25lb) divided by classes: *lightweight,* under 6.8kg (15lb); *middleweight,* under 9.1kg (20lb); *heavyweight,* under 11.4kg (25lb).
● **COAT** Short and smooth.
● **COLOUR** Brindle with white markings: brindle must show distinctly throughout body; black with white markings, but brindle with white markings preferred.
● **OTHER FEATURES** Square head, flat on top; round eyes set wide apart; broad, square jaw; ears erect at corners of head; broad chest; fine, low-set tail.

BULLDOG

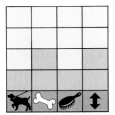

The Bulldog's proud ancestry can be traced back to the Molussus, the fighting dog named from an ancient Greek tribe, the Molossi. As its name suggests, it was bred to bait bulls. According to one story, this "sport" commenced in Britain in 1204 or thereabouts, when Lord Stamford of Lincolnshire in England was greatly amused by the sight of some butcher's dogs tormenting a bull. This gave his Lordship the idea of providing a field in which bull-baiting tournaments might take place on condition that the butcher would provide one bull a year for the "sport". Later, pits were set up in various parts of Britain where dogs would also fight other dogs.

When bull-baiting became illegal in 1835, the Bulldog was in danger of extinction. Fortunately, however, a Mr Bill George continued to breed Bulldogs and, in 1875, the first specialist club for the breed was formed, known as the Bulldog Club Incorporated. This was followed in 1891 by the London Bulldog Society, which still holds its annual meeting at Crufts Dog Show.

The Bulldog is not able to accompany its owner on long walks, but it does make a delightful companion.

The Bulldog's shoulders are broad, sloping and deep. They are also very powerful and muscular, giving the appearance of having been tacked on to its body.

Character and care

Despite its fearsome appearance, the Bulldog is now a gentle, good natured dog. It adores children and makes a delightful pet. The only grooming it requires is a daily run through with a stiff brush and a rub-down. Care must be taken that it is not over exerted in hot weather.

KEY CHARACTERISTICS
• **CLASS** Non-sporting. **Recognized** AKC, ANKC, CKC, FCI, KC(GB), KUSA.
• **SIZE** Weight: dogs 22.7–25kg (50–55lb), bitches 18–22.7kg (40–50lb).
• **COAT** Short, smooth and close, and finely textured.
• **COLOUR** Uniform colour or with black mask or muzzle; reds, red brindle, piebald; black undesirable.
• **OTHER FEATURES** Large skull; eyes set low; ears small and set high on head; broad, sloping shoulders; tail set low and can be either straight or screwed.

DALMATIAN

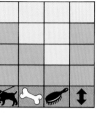

The nose of the black spotted Dalmatian is always black, but in the liver spotted variety it is brown.

The Dalmatian is named after Dalmatia on the Adriatic coast, but it is in Britain that the modern breed became well established. Heads would turn as a carriage of the British aristocracy went by with an elegant Dalmatian trotting alongside the horses. The breed still has an affinity with horses and will prove its worth as a ratter in the stables. Generally, however, the Dalmatian of today is kept solely as a pet and show dog.

Although already popular in Britain, the Dalmatian's registrations doubled following the filming in 1959 of Dodie Smith's book, *101 Dalmatians*. The breed received a further boost in 1978 when Mrs E. J. Woodyatt's Champion Fanhill Faune won the coveted Best in Show award at Crufts, in London. The breed's friendly character and elegant appearance have made it popular as a pet and show dog worldwide.

Character and care

This affectionate and energetic dog quickly becomes a family favourite. It requires plenty of exercise and a daily brushing but does tend to shed white hairs, which does not endear the breed to the houseproud. However, its intelligence and equable temperament should make up for this small failing.

KEY CHARACTERISTICS
• **CLASS** Non-sporting. **Recognized** AKC, ANKC, CKC, FCI, KC(GB), KUSA.
• **SIZE** Height at withers: 47.5–58.5cm (19–23in). Weight: 22.7–25kg (50–55lb).
• **COAT** Short, fine, dense and close; sleek and glossy in appearance.
• **COLOUR** Pure white ground colour with black or liver brown spots, not running together but round and well-defined, and as evenly distributed as possible; spots on extremities smaller than those on body.
• **OTHER FEATURES** Long head and flat skull; eyes set moderately far apart; medium-sized ears set high; deep chest; long tail that is carried with a slight upward curve.

A friendly, outgoing carriage dog capable of great speed, the Dalmatian should be free of any aggression or nervousness.

SCHIPPERKE

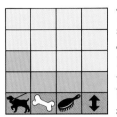

The Schipperke originated in Belgium but is often thought to be a Dutch dog, a confusion which may have arisen because the Netherlands and Belgium are relatively modern countries. The breed is thought by some to be 200 years old, although no records exist to prove this. It may have been established as long ago as the mid-1500s, because of a story that two black dogs without tails rescued Prince William of Orange (1533–84) from an assassin. Differences of opinion also exist on the breed's ancestry. Some think it arose from early northern spitz dogs, while others consider it a descendant of a now-extinct Belgian Sheepdog.

The Schipperke was once the most popular housepet and watchdog in Belgium. Traditionally its job there was to guard canal barges when they were tied up for the night, and it was this task that earned the breed its name. *Schipperke* is Flemish for "little captain", and has also been translated as "little skipper", "little boatman" and even "little corporal".

This breed was first exhibited in 1880. It was recognized by the Royal Schipperke Club of Brussels in 1886, and given an official standard in 1904. The Schipperke Club of England was formed in 1905 and the Schipperke Club of America in 1929. Miss F. Isabel Ormiston of Kelso Kennels is credited with being the greatest pioneer of the breed in the United States.

Character and care

The Schipperke is an affectionate dog which is good with children, usually very long lived, and an excellent watchdog. It is said to be able to walk up to 10km (6 miles) a day without tiring, but will make do with considerably less exercise. It should be housed indoors rather than in a kennel, and its coat needs very little attention.

Although other colours sometimes appear, the long lived and faithful Schipperke is generally pure black.

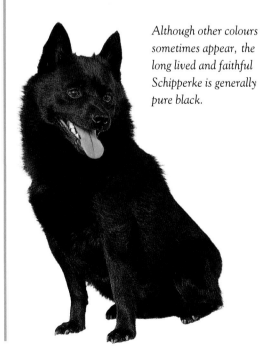

The Schipperke has a sharp, foxy expression; its back is short, straight and long; its feet are small and cat like.

KEY CHARACTERISTICS
● **CLASS** Non-sporting. **Recognized** AKC, ANKC, CKC, FCI, KC(GB), KUSA.
● **SIZE** Height at withers: dogs 27.5–32.5cm (11–13in), bitches 25–30cm (10–12in). Weight: 5.4–8.1kg (12–18lb).
● **COAT** Abundant and dense, with longer hair on the neck, shoulders, chest and backs of rear legs.
● **COLOUR** Black, but the undercoat can be slightly lighter. Outside the USA other solid colours are permissible.
● **OTHER FEATURES** Broad head with flat skull; eyes oval, dark brown; ears moderately long; chest broad and deep; the tail is docked.

FINNISH SPITZ

The Finnish Spitz is known in its native land as Suomenpystykorva, which means "cock-eared dog". It is the national dog of Finland, and is mentioned in a number of heroic Finnish national songs. It was once used by Lapp hunters to track elk and polar bears, but is now popular throughout Scandinavia for hunting grouse and other game birds. Related to the Russian Laika, the breed originated in the eastern area of Finland. It was introduced to and pioneered in Britain in the 1920s by the late Lady Kitty Ritson, who is responsible for the breed's nickname of Finkie.

Character and care

While still a favourite with hunters in Scandinavia, the Finnish Spitz is kept almost entirely as a companion and show dog elsewhere. It is appreciated as a faithful and home-loving pet, which is good with children and adept at guarding. It requires plenty of exercise and daily brushing.

KEY CHARACTERISTICS
● **CLASS** Non-sporting. **Recognized** AKC, CKC, FCI, KC(GB).
● **SIZE** Height at withers: dogs 43–50cm (17–20in), bitches 39–45cm (15–18in). Weight: 11.3–16kg (25–35lb).
● **COAT** Short and close on head and front of legs, longer on body and back of legs; semi-erect and stiff on neck and back.
● **COLOUR** Reddish-brown or red-gold on back, preferably bright; lighter shades permissible on the underside.
● **OTHER FEATURES** Medium-sized head and eyes; ears small and cocked, and sharply pointed; body almost square in outline; tail plumed, and curves vigorously from the root.

The Finnish Spitz is a breed that relishes being outdoors as much as it enjoys its home comforts.

FRENCH BULLDOG

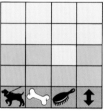

The French Bulldog is gentle and peace-loving. It has distinctive "bat" ears and a natural screw tail, which people often wrongly imagine is docked.

The French Bulldog, with its distinctive bat-like ears and screw tail, has had many famous owners, ranging from King Edward VII of England to the French novelist, Colette. It is obviously a descendant of small bulldogs, but it is not known whether these were English dogs taken to France by Nottingham laceworkers in the 19th century or dogs imported to France from Spain. Small English Bulldog ancestry is most generally accepted, despite the discovery of an ancient bronze plaque of a dog bearing an unmistakable likeness to the French Bulldog and inscribed: "Dogue de Burgos, España 1625".

A French Bulldog club was formed in Britain in 1902 and, in 1912, the breed was accepted by the British Kennel Club. By 1913, it had also achieved 100 entries at the Westminster Dog Show in New York.

Character and care

This breed is a popular and easy dog to show, and makes a delightful companion. It is good natured, affectionate and courageous, and usually gets on well with children and with other pets. Owners must become accustomed to its gentle snuffling, and be aware that it will invariably wander off and sulk on the rare occasions when it is in disgrace.

The "Frenchie" is easy to groom, requiring just a daily brush and a rub-down with a silk handkerchief, or piece of towelling, to make its coat shine. The facial creases should be lubricated to prevent soreness.

Warning This flat-nosed breed should not be exercised in hot weather.

KEY CHARACTERISTICS
• **CLASS** Non-sporting. **Recognized** AKC, ANKC, CKC, FCI, KC(GB), KUSA.
• **SIZE** Average height: 30cm (12in). Weight: dogs about 12.7kg (28lb), bitches 10.9kg (24lb).
• **COAT** Short, smooth, close and finely textured.
• **COLOUR** Brindle, pied or fawn.
• **OTHER FEATURES** Head square, large and broad; eyes dark and set wide apart; "bat ears", broad at base and rounded at tip, set high and carried upright; body short, muscular and cobby; tail very short.

SCHNAUZER

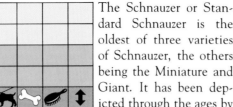

The Schnauzer or Standard Schnauzer is the oldest of three varieties of Schnauzer, the others being the Miniature and Giant. It has been depicted through the ages by artists including Albrecht Dürer (1471–1528), Rembrandt (1606–69) and Sir Joshua Reynolds (1723–92). The earliest likeness of the breed is probably that in Dürer's painting, *Madonna with the Many Animals* 1492.

Despite its many representations over the centuries, the Schnauzer's origin remains obscure. Some say that it was a cross between two now extinct breeds, the Beaver Dog of the Middle Ages and a rough-coated dog, perhaps a terrier, which was kept to dispel vermin. Others think that it evolved from the extinct Schafer Pudel and the Wire-haired German Pinscher. Still other researchers believe that the Schnauzer is descended entirely from drovers' dogs, including the Bouvier des Flandres to which it certainly bears a close resemblance. It was originally used as an all-purpose farm dog, and was a good ratter. It is also an excellent companion. The breed standard was first published in Germany in 1880. In 1918 the Bavarian Schnauzer Club united with the Pinscher Club of Cologne.

The Schnauzer's movement should be free, balanced and vigorous.

Character and care

The Schnauzer is an attractive, robust, intelligent and playful dog, which makes a good companion and is generally good with children. It enjoys plenty of exercise, and its hardy, harsh, wiry coat needs a certain amount of stripping and plucking. Pet dogs can be clipped but this will spoil the coat for showing, so owners wishing to exhibit are advised to discuss grooming with the breeder at the time of purchase.

KEY CHARACTERISTICS

- **CLASS** Non-sporting.
  Recognized AKC, ANKC, CKC, FCI, KC(GB), KUSA.

- **SIZE** *Standard* Height at shoulders: dogs 46–49cm (18½–19½in), bitches 44–46cm (17½–18½in). Weight: around 14.8kg (33lb). *Giant* Height at shoulders: dogs 65–70cm (25½–27¼in), bitches 60–65cm (23½–25½in). Weight: 32.8–34.6kg (73–77lb). *Miniature* Height: 30–35.5cm (12–14in). Weight 5.9–6.8kg (13–15lb).

- **COAT** Harsh and wiry, with a soft undercoat.

- **COLOUR** Pure black (white markings on head, chest and legs undesirable), or pepper and salt.

- **OTHER FEATURES** Strong head of a good length; dark, oval-shaped eyes; neat, pointed ears; chest moderately broad; tail set on and carried high, and is characteristically docked to three joints.

In this breed correct conformation is of more importance than colour or beauty points.

GIANT SCHNAUZER

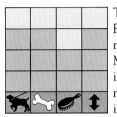

The Giant Schnauzer or Riesenschnauzer was for many years known as the Münchener Dog, because it originated from an area near Munich. It is believed to have evolved from crosses between smooth-coated drovers' dogs and rough-coated shepherd dogs, as well as black Great Danes and the Bouvier des Flandres. It worked as a cattle dog until the need for such an animal declined.

The Giant Schnauzer made its first appearance in the show ring at Munich in 1909, when it was listed in the catalogue as a Russian Bear Schnauzer. The 30 breed representatives created such an impression that the Munich Schnauzer Club was formed the following month. Not as popular as the Standard and Miniature varieties, the Giant Schnauzer might have become extinct had it not proved itself an excellent guard dog in the First World War. However, it was not until after the Second World War that dedicated fanciers in Germany worked hard to secure deserved popularity for this fine dog.

Character and care
This intelligent dog makes a reliable, good natured companion, which requires a fair amount of exercise. It needs little grooming other than stripping and plucking. The coat may also be clipped but this will spoil it for showing, so it is best to discuss grooming with the breeder at time of purchase.

Regular stripping prevents the prized "hard coat" of the Giant Schnauzer from becoming soft and woolly.

MINIATURE SCHNAUZER

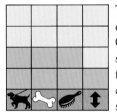

The Miniature Schnauzer, known in its native Germany as the Zwergschnauzer, was derived from crossing the Standard Schnauzer with smaller dogs – probably Affenpinschers. The breed was exhibited for the first time in 1899, and was established in Germany by the early 1920s. W. D. Goff is credited with taking the first breed member to the United States in 1923, while the first imports to the United Kingdom were made by a Mr W. H. Hancock in 1928.

In the United States and Canada, the Miniature Schnauzer is classed as a terrier and was at one time the most popular terrier there. In Britain, where it is regarded as a member of the utility group rather than a terrier, it is a popular family pet, and also does well in the obedience and show rings.

Character and care
The Miniature Schnauzer is a delightful small dog, which makes an excellent family pet and children's companion. Like its larger contem-

poraries, it needs a fair amount of exercise and its coat should be periodically stripped and plucked. The coat may also be clipped but this will spoil it for the show ring, so it is best to discuss grooming with the breeder at the time of purchase.

The Schnauzers are primarily companion dogs these days. They also make fine show dogs, but expert advice must be sought on how to trim them.

GERMAN SPITZ

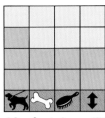

The confident German Spitz should never show any sign of nervousness or aggression. Indeed, its buoyancy, independence and devotion to its human family are the breed characteristics.

The only difference between the Small German Spitz (Kleinspitz) and Standard German Spitz (Mittelspitz) is size. Both are smaller versions of the Great German Spitz (Großspitz) or Wolfspitz. There are many varieties of spitz and, although it is difficult to pinpoint their origin, they were probably brought from Scandinavia by the Vikings. Spitz dogs were known as early as 1700 when white specimens were said to be kept in Pomerania and black ones in Württemberg. Some of the smaller varieties of the white spitz bred in Pomerania became known and established in Britain under the name Pomeranian (see page 224). In 1899, the German Spitz Club was formed, and standards were issued for the separate varieties.

Character and care

This active, intelligent and alert dog is independent, yet devotion to its human family is a breed characteristic. The German Spitz can adapt to life in the town or country, and needs vigorous daily brushing and an average amount of exercise. If unchecked, the breed does have a tendency to yap.

KEY CHARACTERISTICS
● **CLASS** Non-sporting. **Recognized** ANKC, FCI, KC(GB), KUSA.
● **SIZE** *Small* Height: 23–28cm (9–11in). Average weight: 3.1kg (7lb). *Standard* Height: 29–35.5cm (11½–13in). Average weight: 11.3kg (25lb).
● **COAT** Soft, woolly undercoat and long, dense, straight outer coat.
● **COLOUR** All solid colour varieties.
● **OTHER FEATURES** A broad head; oval-shaped eyes; small, triangular ears; compact body; tail set on high and carried curled over the body.

KEESHOND

The Keeshond (plural Keeshunden, which is pronounced "kayshond") has been known as the Fik, Foxdog, Dutch Barge Dog and even as the Overweight Pomeranian in Victorian England. Its modern name is after a dog of this breed owned by the 18th century Dutchman, Kees de Gyselaer.

Like other spitz breeds, the Keeshond is believed to derive from an Arctic breed. It became popular in Holland as the companion of bargees and as a watchdog.

In 1905, Miss Hamilton-Fletcher, later Mrs Wingfield-Digby, arranged to import some puppies into England. In 1923, two of her dogs were shown at the Birmingham National Dog Show as Dutch Barge Dogs. The Dutch Barge Dog Club (now the Keeshond Club) was formed in 1925 and, in 1928, challenge certificates were on offer for the breed. In 1920 Dutch fanciers again turned their attention to the breed. However, the FCI (Fédération Cynologique Internationale) has been reluctant to accept the standard that has been drawn up, believing that the Keeshond is identical to the German Wolfspitz.

Character and care

Good natured and long lived, the Keeshond tends to be a devoted one-person dog. It requires daily grooming using a stiff brush, and a fair amount of exercise. A choke chain will spoil the ruff.

JAPANESE SPITZ

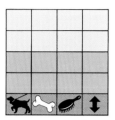

The Japanese Spitz shares a common ancestry with the Nordic Spitz. It is about half the size of the Samoyed, and is also closely related to the German Spitz and Pomeranian. Its ancestors are said to have been taken to Japan in the ships of traders many years ago, and there the breed was developed in isolation. The breed is a family favourite in Japan. It has only recently become known internationally, and is proving a popular show dog.

Character and care
Loyal to its owners but distrustful of strangers, this beautiful Spitz is alert, intelligent, lively and bold. It makes a fine small guard, and a number have been seen in Britain enjoying the role of companion and guard to long-distance lorry drivers. The breed requires daily brushing and, having an instinctive desire to herd other animals, enjoys a fair amount of exercise.

The Japanese Spitz has a snowy white coat, but its nose is black.

KEY CHARACTERISTICS

- **CLASS** Non-sporting.
  Recognized ANKC, CKC, FCI, KC(GB), KUSA.

- **SIZE** Height at shoulders: dogs 30–36cm (12–14in), bitches slightly smaller. Average weight: 5.9kg (13lb).

- **COAT** Straight, dense, stand-off outer coat; thick, short, dense undercoat.

- **COLOUR** Pure white.

- **OTHER FEATURES** Medium-sized head; dark eyes; small triangular ears standing erect; broad, deep chest; tail set on high and carried curled over back.

KEY CHARACTERISTICS

- **CLASS** Non-sporting.
  Recognized AKC, ANKC, CKC, KC(GB), KUSA.

- **SIZE** Height at shoulders: dogs, about 45.5cm (18in), bitches 43cm (17in). Weight: 25–29.7kg (55–66lb).

- **COAT** Long and straight with the hairs standing out; a dense ruff over the neck.

- **COLOUR** A mixture of grey, black and cream; undercoat pale.

- **OTHER FEATURES** Well-proportioned head that is wedge-shaped when seen from above; dark, medium-sized eyes; small, triangular ears; compact body; well-feathered, high-set tail that curls tightly over the back.

SHIBA INU

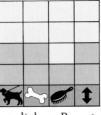

The Shiba Inu is an ancient breed associated with the prefectures of Gifu, Toyama and Nagano in central Japan ,and the name, in fact, means "little dog" in the Nagano dialect. Remains of a dog of this type were found in ruins dating back to the Joman era (500 BC). The Shiba Inu has, in recent years, become a firm favourite of exhibitors, following closely on the heels of the Japanese Akita (see page 64) onto the international scene. It is an excellent bird dog, guard and hunter of small game, with a considerable amount of native cunning.

Smallest of the spitz types, the fastidious, somewhat aloof Shiba is easily recognized by its deep set eyes and luxuriant coat.

Character and care
The Shiba is an affectionate, friendly and sensitive dog that makes a fine pet as well as a show dog and/or hunter. It needs a fair amount of exercise and a good daily brushing to keep it looking trim.

KEY CHARACTERISTICS
• **CLASS** Non-sporting. **Recognized** ANKC, FCI, KC(GB).
• **SIZE** Height at shoulders: dogs 37.5–40cm (15–16in), bitches 35–37.5cm (14–15in). Weight: 9–13.6kg (20–30lb).
• **COAT** Harsh, straight.
• **COLOUR** Red, salt and pepper, black, black and tan, or white.
• **OTHER FEATURES** Agile, sturdily built and well muscled; deep chest; long back; almond-shaped eyes; long sickle tail.

It is only in recent years that the Shiba Inu has been seen out of its native land. Now it has a growing band of devotees.

CHOW CHOW

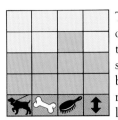

The Chow Chow is the only dog with a black tongue, a characteristic it shares with some small bears. This lion-like member of the spitz family has been known in its native China for more than 2000 years. It was bred variously for its flesh, its fur and as a hunter of game, its name possibly deriving from the Chinese Choo Hunting Dog. The Chow Chow is said to have been the original "Mastiff" of the Tibetan Lama, and is also referred to in early Chinese writings as the Tartar Dog and the Dog of the Barbarians.

The first Chow Chow imported into Britain in 1760 was exhibited in a zoo. In 1895, the Chow Chow Club was formed there, and in 1905 the first member of the breed was exported from Britain to America. This was Mrs Garnett Botfield's Chinese Chum which, in 1905, became the first American Chow Chow champion. In 1936, Mrs V. A. Mawnooch's Champion Choonam Hung Kwong won the Best in Show title at Crufts Dog Show. He was the recipient of 44 British Challenge certificates and was valued at the then immense sum of £5,250 (US$12,600).

Character and care

The Chow Chow has always had a reputation for ferocity but, although a formidable opponent, it is unlikely to attack unless provoked. It is a faithful, odour-free dog, which makes a good pet, but prefers to look to one person as its master and needs firm but gentle handling. A good daily walk will suffice, but the full coat requires considerable attention with a wire brush.

The Chow Chow is a good guard. Its tail, characteristic of the spitz breeds, is carried over its back.

A former hunter of wolves, today the Chow Chow is a successful show dog and companion.

KEY CHARACTERISTICS
● **CLASS** Non-sporting. **Recognized** AKC, ANKC, CKC, FCI, KC(GB), KUSA.
● **SIZE** Height at shoulders: dogs 48–56cm (19–22in), bitches 46–51cm (18–20in). Weight: 20.2–31.7kg (45–70lb).
● **COAT** Can be rough – abundant, dense and coarse textured, and varies in length, with pronounced ruff around head and neck and feathering on tail; or smooth – dense and hard, with no ruff or feathering.
● **COLOUR** Solid black, red, blue, fawn and cream.
● **OTHER FEATURES** Broad, flat head; dark, almond-shaped eyes; small ears slightly rounded at tips; long, nicely arched neck; broad, deep chest and compact body; tail set on high and carried curled over the back.

SHAR-PEI

The Shar-Pei's loose skin was an advantage in its fighting days. It is said that its opponents could not get a firm hold. No longer the rarest dog in the world, specimens still attract considerable attention.

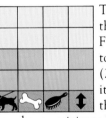

There are likenesses of the Shar-Pei or Chinese Fighting Dog dating back to the Han Dynasty (206BC to AD220), and it has been suggested that this loose-skinned breed may have originated in Tibet or China's Northern Province some 2000 years ago. Then it is likely to have been a larger dog, weighing some 39–75kg (85–165lb).

An unusual and attractive breed, the Shar-Pei was used to herd flocks and hunt wild boar in China. It was also matched against other dogs in trials of strength, although its nature is so affable that it may have had to be provoked to do so with the aid of drugs. It appears to have escaped the cooking pot, the fate of other Chinese breeds, because its flesh was not considered tasty.

It is not long since the Shar-Pei had the distinction of being the rarest dog in the world. Now it is drawing good entries in the show ring in the United Kingdom and elsewhere, and plans are afoot for breed members to be exported to Russia.

Character and care

A very affectionate dog with a frowning expression, the Shar-Pei is calm, independent and devoted. Its coat is never trimmed. It needs a reasonable amount of exercise.

KEY CHARACTERISTICS
● **CLASS** Non-sporting. **Recognized** AKC, ANKC, FCI, KC(GB), KUSA.
● **SIZE** Height at withers: 46–51cm (18–20in). Weight: 18–25kg (40–55lb).
● **COAT** Short, straight and bristly; no undercoat.
● **COLOUR** Solid colours only – black, red, light or dark fawn or cream.
● **OTHER FEATURES** Head rather large in proportion to body; dark, almond-shaped eyes; very small, triangular ears; broad, deep chest; rounded tail narrowing to a fine point, set on high and curling over to either side of the back.

LHASA APSO

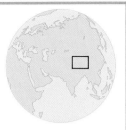

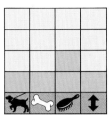

The Lhasa Apso originated in Tibet and is sometimes known as the Tibetan Apso. It is a small, indoor watchdog, possibly bred in the distant past from the Tibetan Mastiff. The word *apso* means goat-like, and the dog may have been so named because its coat resembled that of the goats kept by Tibetan herders. The breed was very highly regarded in its native land, and kept in temples and palaces. The Lhasa is often confused with the rather similar Shih Tzu from western China, but there are a number of physical differences between them, including the fact that the Lhasa Apso has a longer nose and its nose-tip is placed lower than that of the Shih Tzu. However, in the past there seems to have been some interbreeding between them outside their native lands, especially because it was the custom of the Dalai Lama of Tibet to give Lhasas from his court as gifts to visiting foreign dignitaries while, similarly, rulers in China gave the little Shih Tzu.

The Lhasa Apso first came to Britain in the 1930s, and the Tibetan Breeds Association was formed in 1934. The breed was recognized in America in 1935.

Character and care

The Lhasa Apso is happy, usually long lived, adaptable and good with children. It enjoys a good romp out of doors and has been seen in a stable yard, despite the need for careful daily grooming of its long coat.

KEY CHARACTERISTICS
● **CLASS** Non-sporting. **Recognized** AKC, ANKC, CKC, FCI, KC(GB), KUSA.
● **SIZE** Height at shoulders: dogs about 25.4cm (10in), bitches slightly smaller.
● **COAT** Top coat long, heavy, straight and hard; not woolly or silky. Moderate undercoat.
● **COLOUR** Solid golden, sandy, honey, dark grizzle, slate or smoke; black particolour, white or brown; all equally acceptable.
● **OTHER FEATURES** Long hair on head covering eyes and reaching towards floor; heavily feathered ears; dark eyes; compact, well-balanced body; tail set on high and carried over the back.

The Lhasa Apso is a firm family favourite, but its coat requires a great deal of grooming. Do not confuse it with the similar Shih Tsu, usually distinguished by its topknot.

SHIH TZU

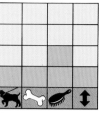

The upright head and round eyes are expressive of the Shih Tzu's alert, independent character. The nose should never be downpointed.

The Shih Tzu, whose Chinese name means "lion dog", is generally thought to have originated in western China. It resembles a Lhasa Apso except for its shortened face, and could be the result of crossing the Lhasa Apso and the Pekingese. Certainly it was the practice of the Dalai Lama of Tibet to give prize specimens of the Lhasa Apso to visiting dignitaries from foreign lands, including those from China.

An early standard for the breed written by the Peking Kennel Club, called the most flowery ever issued, reads: "should have lion head, bear torso, camel hoof, feather-duster tail, palm-leaf ears, rice teeth, pearly petal tongue and movement like a goldfish"!

The breed was first imported into England in 1930, but was not granted a breed register by the Kennel Club until 1946. The Shih Tzu was recognized by the American Kennel Club in 1969, and is now popular as a pet and as a show dog on both sides of the Atlantic.

Character and care

This happy, hardy little dog loves children and other animals and makes a good housepet suited to town or country living. It requires a good daily grooming using a bristle brush, and the topknot is usually tied with a bow.

KEY CHARACTERISTICS
• **CLASS** Non-sporting. **Recognized** AKC, ANKC, CKC, FCI, KC(GB), KUSA.
• **SIZE** Height at withers: 22.5–26.5cm (9–10½in). Weight: 4.1–8.1kg (9–18lb).
• **COAT** Long, dense, not curly, with a good undercoat.
• **COLOUR** All colours permissible; white blaze on forehead and white tip on tail highly desirable in parti-colours.
• **OTHER FEATURES** Broad, round head, wide between the eyes; large, dark, round eyes; large ears with long feathers, carried drooping; body longer between withers and root of tail than height at withers; tail heavily plumed and carried curved well over back.

Despite its elegant, slightly aloof bearing, the Shih Tzu is a courageous little dog that loves to play in the snow.

TIBETAN SPANIEL

Gentle and loving, the Tibetan Spaniel makes an ideal family pet, but tends to be fairly independent. It moves quickly on small, neat hare feet.

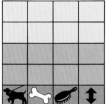

Despite its name, this breed is not related to the spaniels and is not known to have been used as a hunting companion or gundog. The Tibetan Spaniel is thought to have been in existence long before the history of Tibet started to be chronicled in the 7th century, and its origins are therefore obscure. The exchange of dogs between Tibet and China in ancient times means that Chinese dogs, such as early Shih Tzu or Pekingese-like dogs, could have contributed to it. It has also been said that the Tibetan Spaniel was crossed with the Pug to bring about the Pekingese. The Tibetan Spaniel was a favourite with monks, and was often kept in monasteries. It is said that it turned, and perhaps still turns, the prayer wheel of Tibetans. It is also said that, in common with the Hairless Dog in Mexico, it was used by humans for warmth.

The first Tibetan Spaniel recorded in the United Kingdom was brought by a Mr F. Wormald in 1905, but it seems to have been the late 1940s before the breed made any impact there.

Character and care

This charming, good natured dog is rarely seen outside the show ring. It is intelligent, good with children and makes a splendid housepet. It is energetic and enjoys a good romp, and its coat needs regular grooming.

KEY CHARACTERISTICS
• **CLASS** Non-sporting. **Recognized** AKC, ANKC, CKC, FCI, KC(GB), KUSA.
• **SIZE** Height: about 25.4cm (10in). Weight: about 4.1–6.8kg (9–15lb).
• **COAT** Moderately long and silky in texture; shorter on face and fronts of legs; feathering on ears, backs of legs and tail.
• **COLOUR** All solid colours and mixtures permissible.
• **OTHER FEATURES** Head small in proportion to body; dark brown, expressive eyes; medium-size pendant ears; tail set on high, richly plumed, and carried curled over the back.

This breed enjoys its daily walks. Watch that its collar does not mar the "shawl" of longer hair on its neck.

TIBETAN TERRIER

The Tibetan Terrier has a "resolute" expression and is intelligent and game. It looks like an Old English Sheepdog in miniature. Bred for farm work rather than going to earth, one wonders how it came to be called a terrier.

The Tibetan Terrier is not really a terrier at all, having no history of going to earth, but resembles a small Old English Sheepdog and, like those other little Tibetan dogs, the Tibetan Spaniel and Lhasa Apso, appears not to have been bred for any purpose other than that of companion dog.

Of ancient lineage, the Tibetan Terrier is said to have been bred in Tibetan monasteries, and specimens used to be presented to travellers as mascots and to bring luck. The breed was included in the Tibetan Breeds Association register in 1934 and now has its own standard. It has not yet become very popular in Britain and is even less well known in America, which may be to its advantage, as many breeds have been spoiled through over-popularization.

Character and care

The Tibetan Terrier might prove the ideal pet for those who admire the Old English Sheepdog but cannot house such a large animal. This appealing, shaggy little dog is also well worth choosing for its own sake. It is loyal, sturdy, a good walker, and devoted to its owners and to children, but a little apprehensive of strangers. Its long coat needs regular attention.

KEY CHARACTERISTICS
• **CLASS** Non-sporting. **Recognized** AKC, ANKC, CKC, FCI, KC(GB), KUSA.
• **SIZE** Height at shoulders: dogs 35.5–40.5cm (14–16in), bitches slightly smaller. Average weight: 9–10.8kg (20–24lb).
• **COAT** Soft, woolly undercoat; long, fine outer coat that can be straight or wavy.
• **COLOUR** Any colour or combination of colours permissible.
• **OTHER FEATURES** Large, round, dark eyes; pendant, feathered ears; compact and powerful body; medium-length tail set quite high and carried curled over the back.

BICHON FRISE

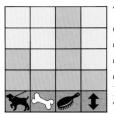

The word "bichon" is often used collectively to describe small, white dogs, such as the Coton de Tulear, Maltese, Frise, Bolognese and Havana. The Bichon Frise or Bichon à Poil Frise (curly haired bichon), or Tenerife Dog, is reputed to have been introduced to Tenerife in the Canary Islands by sailors in the 14th century. However, like the Poodle, it is thought to be a descendant of the French water dog, the Barbet, and its name comes from the diminutive, *barbichon.*

Similar in appearance to the Miniature Poodle, the Bichon Frise is recognized internationally as a Franco-Belgian breed. It was introduced into the United States in 1956 and registered by the American Kennel Club in 1972. A class for Bichon Frise was included at Crufts Dog Show in London in 1980.

Character and care

Happy, friendly and lively, this breed makes an attractive and cuddly small pet, which will enjoy as much exercise as most owners can provide. However, its long curly coat, resembling a powder puff, means that it is not the choice for anyone averse to grooming. The scissoring and trimming required to achieve this shape is intricate, and anyone intending to exhibit should discuss what is entailed with the breeder at the time of purchase.

KEY CHARACTERISTICS
● **CLASS** Non-sporting. **Recognized** AKC, ANKC, CKC, FCI, KC(GB), KUSA.
● **SIZE** Height at withers: 23–28cm (9–11in).
● **COAT** Long and loosely curling.
● **COLOUR** White, cream or apricot markings permissible up to 18 months. Dark skin desirable.
● **OTHER FEATURES** Long ears hanging close to head; dark, round eyes with black rims; relatively long, arched neck; tail carried gracefully curved over the body.

Friendly and outgoing, this little dog has grown steadily in popularity over the past 20 years.

The Bichon Frise has to have its coat regularly scissored. It is often to be seen in a canine beauty parlour.

STANDARD POODLE

Known in France as the Caniche, the Poodle was certainly favoured by the French Queen Marie Antoinette (1755–93). However, it originated in Germany as a water retriever, or Pudel in German. It resembles the Irish Water Spaniel, and both share common ancestors in the French Barbet.

The Poodle does not moult. Its woolly coat does not usually affect asthma sufferers, with whom it is naturally a favourite.

Character and care

The Standard Poodle still retains its ability as a gundog and swims well. Its intelligence and eagerness to learn mean that it is popular in obedience trials and as a circus dog.

This happy, good-tempered, lively dog makes a good family pet, enjoying a fair amount of exercise. It is also a fine show dog, provided you have the time for intricate preparation. While it is shown in the lion clip, many pet owners prefer the lamb clip (with hair uniform length). Whatever style you choose, you will need to use a wire-pin pneumatic brush and a wire-toothed metal comb for daily grooming. Even the pet Poodle must attend the canine beauty parlour every six weeks or so.

KEY CHARACTERISTICS
● **CLASS** Non-sporting. **Recognized** AKC, ANKC, CKC, FCI, KC(GB), KUSA.
● **SIZE** *Standard* Height at shoulders: over 38cm (15in). Weight: 20.2–31.7kg (45–70lb). *Miniature* Height: 25–37.5cm (10–15in). *Toy* Height at shoulders: under 25cm (10in).
● **COAT** Very profuse and dense; a good, harsh texture.
● **COLOUR** All solid colours, clear colours preferred.
● **OTHER FEATURES** Long, fine head; almond-shaped eyes; ears set on high and hanging close to head; chest deep and broad; tail set on high and carried up.

MINIATURE POODLE

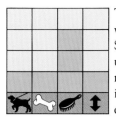

The Miniature Poodle was bred down from the Standard, presumably by using the smaller specimens, and in turn played its part in producing the even smaller Toy Poodle.

During the 1950s the Miniature Poodle became the most popular breed in many countries because it was believed, wrongly, that as more people migrated to the towns, interest in working breeds would lessen. This did not prove to be the case, and while there are those who say that it is not a proper dog at all – no doubt blissfully unaware of its origins as a gundog and water retriever – the Miniature Poodle remains a favourite.

Character and care
The Miniature Poodle has the same show standard as the larger and smaller breeds, except in the matter of size, and has similar characteristics. It requires frequent regular visits to the canine beauty parlour, even if it is not the intention to exhibit. Use a wire-pin pneumatic brush and a wire-toothed metal comb for daily grooming.

The intelligent and fun loving Miniature Poodle is often very long lived, and may survive for 17 years or more.

TOY POODLE

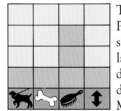

The origin of the Toy Poodle is exactly the same as that of its much larger relative, the Standard Poodle, for it is a descendant of the Miniature Poodle. The smaller specimens were so much in demand that, by the middle of the 1950s, the UK Kennel Club agreed to open a separate register for them. These are the least robust of the three varieties, however, so it is essential to select from sound stock.

Character and care
The Toy Poodle has the same characteristics and show standard as its larger contemporaries, except in the matter of size. It is happy and good tempered and makes a delightful pet that is ideal for the apartment dweller who nonetheless enjoys a canine companion. The Toy is exhibited in the same clips as the other two varieties. In any case it will require regular visits to the canine beauty parlour. Use a wire-pin pneumatic brush and a wire-toothed metal comb for daily grooming.

Even the Poodle kept solely as a pet companion must have its coat clipped about every six weeks.

45

WORKING BREEDS

MASTIFF

Of great strength and dignity, the Mastiff is normally gentle, but can be a formidable guard.

The Mastiff is among the most ancient breeds of dog. Mastiff-like dogs were treasured by the Babylonians over 4000 years ago, and the Mastiff has been resident in Britain since the time of Julius Caesar. The breed has proved its worth as a formidable guard and as a hunter. The Mastiff was depicted on the 12th century Bayeux Tapestry and in a painting by Van Dyck (1599–1641) of the children of King Charles I. Shakespeare's play, *Henry V*, mentions ". . . mastiffs of unmatchable courage".

In the 19th century Saint Bernard blood was introduced. There were less than a dozen Mastiffs left in Britain after the Second World War because many kennels had been disbanded, and numbers declined in America as well. The situation is gradually improving.

Character and care

The Mastiff is large and dignified. It is usually devoted to its owner. It needs regular walking to build up its muscles. Many do not complete growth until their second year.

KEY CHARACTERISTICS
• **CLASS** Working. **Recognized** AKC, ANKC, CKC, FCI, KC(GB), KUSA.
• **SIZE** Minimum height: dogs 75cm (30in), bitches 68.5cm (27½in). Weight: 78.7–85.5kg (175–190lb).
• **COAT** Outer coat short and straight; undercoat dense and close-lying.
• **COLOUR** Apricot, fawn or brindle; in all, the muzzle, ears and nose should be black, with black around the eyes and extending up between them.
• **OTHER FEATURES** Broad skull; small eyes set wide apart; small ears; long, broad body; legs squarely set; tail set on high.

PYRENEAN MASTIFF

The Pyrenean Mastiff or Mastin de los Pirineos is a Spanish breed native to the southern slopes of the Pyrenees, where it was used for centuries to guard flocks during the annual migrations. The Mastiff is heavily built, with a short, broad muzzle and a deep stop. It carries its tail high when aroused.

Character and care

The Pyrenean Mastiff is intelligent, loyal and generally good natured but is a formidable guard. It is not a good choice for the inexperienced dog owner. It needs plenty of exercise; and grooming with a bristle brush.

KEY CHARACTERISTICS
• **CLASS** Working. **Recognized** CKC, FCI.
• **SIZE** Height at withers: dogs 70–80cm (27½–31½in), bitches slightly less. Weight: 55–70kg (121–155lb).
• **COAT** Medium length, thick, dense and rough to the touch.
• **COLOUR** White with golden or grey markings on head; some markings on body.
• **OTHER FEATURES** Large head; small, dark eyes; small ears; long, robust body; supple tail with good feathering.

TIBETAN MASTIFF

The tail of the Tibetan Mastiff curls over its back in the same manner as that of the Chow Chow. Its broad skull is generally well wrinkled.

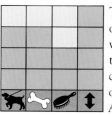

The Tibetan Mastiff is one of many breeds which is descended from the Molossus, a fighting dog of ancient Rome. It originated in central Asia, where it guarded flocks, and it can still be found in the central Asian steppes and around the Himalayan foothills performing the same task for nomadic shepherds. There is mention of the Tibetan Mastiff as early as the 13th century in the chronicles of the explorer Marco Polo, who referred to native mastiffs "as large as asses". This was possibly an exaggeration, but it is certainly imposing, as can be seen from the *New Book of the Dog* by Robert Leighton, in which he writes of the journey of "Bhotian", a Tibetan Mastiff exhibited at Crystal Palace, London in 1906: "Bhotian's journey through India was an expensive one as he had to have a carriage to himself. He effectively cleared the platform at all stations where he was given exercise."

The Tibetan Mastiff was imported into Britain by King George IV (reigned 1820–30) and reached America earlier this century, but is not numerous in either country. The breed was given an interim breed standard by the British Kennel Club in about 1986, and support for it appears to be growing.

Character and care

This breed makes a fine companion, watchdog and guard. It is aloof, protective and slow to mature, reaching its best at 2–3 years in females and at least 4 years in males. The Tibetan Mastiff has a reliable temperament unless provoked, and needs regular vigorous exercise on hard ground and daily brushing.

KEY CHARACTERISTICS
• **CLASS** Working. **Recognized** ANKC, FCI, KC(GB), KUSA.
• **SIZE** Minimum height: dogs 66cm (26in), bitches 61cm (24in). Minimum weight: 81.6kg (180lb).
• **COAT** Medium length, thicker on males than females, with a heavy undercoat.
• **COLOUR** Rich black, black and tan, brown, various shades of gold, various shades of grey, grey with gold markings.
• **OTHER FEATURES** Broad, heavy head; medium-sized, very expressive eyes; medium-sized ears; strong body with a straight back; tail medium length to long.

The lips of the Tibetan Mastiff are pendulous, and it often has tan markings over its eyes.

SPANISH MASTIFF

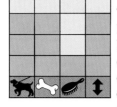

The Spanish Mastiff or Mastin de España (de Estremadura, de la Mancha) is an obvious descendant of the Molossus of ancient Rome. In common with many other mastiffs, this courageous and powerful animal was at one time used in organized dog fights, as a dog of war and as a hunter of wild boar. As a guard it protected stock during the traditional seasonal migrations across the mountains of southern Spain.

The Spanish Mastiff is not unlike the Neapolitan Mastiff in appearance, but has a longer coat and a more refined head. Traditionally, its ears were cropped and its tail docked to help reduce injuries in combat. These practices seem to be carried out less nowadays, greatly enhancing the appearance of this impressive animal.

Character and care
A superb guard of considerable strength and stamina, the Spanish Mastiff is loyal to its owner and responsive to training, but is not a suitable pet for the inexperienced dog owner. It needs wide open spaces and plenty of exercise. Groom with a bristle brush.

KEY CHARACTERISTICS
• **CLASS** Working. **Recognized** FCI.
• **SIZE** Height at shoulders: dogs 66–71cm (26–28in), bitches smaller. Weight: about 50–60kg (110–132lb).
• **COAT** Short, thick and coarse.
• **COLOUR** Wolf grey, fawn, brindle or white, with black, fawn or grey markings, grizzle.
• **OTHER FEATURES** Broad head with a rounded skull; small, dark eyes; pointed, pendant ears; powerful body; short thick tail carried low in repose and slightly curled in action.

NEAPOLITAN MASTIFF

The massive, imposing Neapolitan Mastiff is doubtless a descendant of the fighting mastiffs of ancient Rome and, in turn, of the Molossus dogs prized by Alexander the Great in Greece. Bred as a fighting dog, it has also been employed as a guard. It is majestic in appearance, being one of the largest and heaviest of dogs. In its native land, it often wears a spiked collar and its ears are cropped to add an air of ferocity.

The Neapolitan was first exhibited at a dog show in Naples in 1946 and has since become known in other parts of the world, although it is not yet recognized in the USA.

Character and care
The Neapolitan Mastiff is generally a friendly animal, which is only likely to attack on command and makes an affectionate companion. However, it does need space and does best when given a job to do. It requires plenty of exercise, and its short coat needs grooming every few days.

KEY CHARACTERISTICS
• **CLASS** Working. **Recognized** ANKC, FCI, KC(GB), KUSA.
• **SIZE** Height: Dogs 65–72cm (25½–28½in), bitches 60–68.5cm (23½–27in). Weight: 50–68kg (110–150lb).
• **COAT** Short, dense and smooth.
• **COLOUR** Black, lead or mouse grey; sometimes there are small white spots on the chest or the tips of the toes.
• **OTHER FEATURES** Heavy head with a broad skull; eyes set forward and well apart; ears small in proportion to head; long, thick-set body; tail thick at root and tapering towards tip.

BULLMASTIFF

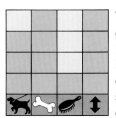

There have been bulldogs in Britain since the 13th century, but the Bullmastiff was developed some 200–300 years ago. It is the result of a cross between the Mastiff, an ancient breed which fought in the arenas of ancient Rome, and the British Bulldog. Like the Bulldog, it was used in bull-baiting until this "sport" was outlawed, and was a brave fighting dog, which could bear pain without flinching. It also had a considerable reputation for ferocity.

Later breeders worked towards a type which was 60 per cent Mastiff and 40 per cent Bulldog. The resultant Bullmastiff was registered by the Kennel Club in Britain in 1924.

Character and care

Despite its ferocious past, the Bullmastiff of today is a playful, loyal and gentle animal, an excellent guard and usually very dependable with children. However, it is too powerful for a child or slight adult to control, and should only be kept by experienced dog owners. It needs grooming every few days.

KEY CHARACTERISTICS
• **CLASS** Working. **Recognized** AKC, ANKC, CKC, FCI, KC(GB), KUSA.
• **SIZE** Height at shoulders: dogs 63.5–68.5cm (25–27in), bitches 61–66cm (24–26in). Weight: dogs 50–59kg (110–130lb), bitches 41–50kg (90–110lb).
• **COAT** Short, smooth and dense.
• **COLOUR** Any shade of brindle, fawn or red; a slight white marking on the chest is permissible, other white markings are undesirable; black muzzle.
• **OTHER FEATURES** Large, square, head; dark or hazel-coloured eyes; V-shaped ears set high and wide apart; strong, compact body; tail set on high.

This handsome breed was devised by crossing the Mastiff with the British Bulldog.

DOBERMAN

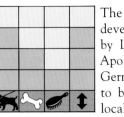

The Doberman was developed in the 1880s by Louis Dobermann of Apolda in Thuringia, Germany, who happened to be the keeper of the local dog pound. He wanted a ferocious, short-coated, medium- to large-sized dog with courage and stamina and developed his stock around the German Pinscher, which was both alert and aggressive. To this he introduced the Rottweiler with its stamina and tracking ability, the Manchester Terrier, then a much larger animal, from which the Doberman inherited its markings, and possibly also the Pointer.

The German National Doberman Pinscher Club was launched by Otto Göller in 1899, and the breed was given official recognition and a breed standard there in 1900. It was not until 1948 that the Doberman Pinscher Club was formed in Britain, and shortly afterwards the breed received recognition from the British Kennel Club.

BOXER

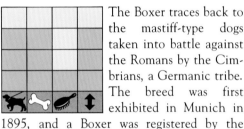

The Boxer traces back to the mastiff-type dogs taken into battle against the Romans by the Cimbrians, a Germanic tribe. The breed was first exhibited in Munich in 1895, and a Boxer was registered by the American Kennel Club as early as 1904. However, it was not until after the First World War that the Boxer was introduced into Britain. Within a few years, the breed had attained immense popularity worldwide.

The Boxer is an affectionate, playful breed which retains puppyish ways well into maturity. It is kind with children, but not averse to a scrap with its fellows.

Character and care

The Boxer is affectionate and usually good with children. This obedient and loyal dog also makes a good guard. It is, however, a very strong dog and is not averse to a scrap with its fellows. It needs a reasonable amount of exercise, and its short coat is easy to care for.

KEY CHARACTERISTICS
• **CLASS** Working. **Recognized** AKC, ANKC, CKC, FCI, KC(GB), KUSA.
• **SIZE** Height: dogs 57–63cm (22½–25in); bitches 53–59cm (21–23in). Weight: 23.8–31.9kg (53–71lb).
• **COAT** Short, glossy and smooth.
• **COLOUR** Fawn or brindle with any white markings, not exceeding one third of ground colour.
• **OTHER FEATURES** Dark brown, forward-looking eyes; moderate-sized ears set wide apart; body square in profile; tail set on high and characteristically docked.

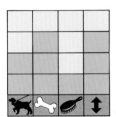

Character and care

The Doberman is a fine obedience and show dog and can make a good family pet, but it needs knowledgeable handling and training, being wary of strangers and constantly "on guard". It needs a lot of exercise, and should be groomed every couple of days.

The Doberman is constantly on the alert. It makes a first class companion and guard.

KEY CHARACTERISTICS
• **CLASS** Working. **Recognized** AKC, ANKC, CKC, FCI, KC(GB), KUSA.
• **SIZE** Height at withers: dogs 65–70cm (26–28in), bitches 60–65cm (24–26in). Weight: 29.7–39.6kg (66–88lb).
• **COAT** Smooth, short, thick and close.
• **COLOUR** Solid black, brown, blue or fawn (Isabella), with rust markings on head, body and legs.
• **OTHER FEATURES** Almond-shaped eyes; small neat ears set high on head; well-arched neck; square body; tail characteristically docked at second joint.

DOGUE DE BORDEAUX

The Dogue de Bordeaux or French Mastiff is also known as the Dogue de Burgos in Spain and the Mastino Napolitano in Italy. It has recently come to international prominence because of the appearance of a breed member in a tear-jerking Hollywood movie. However, it has long been prized in France, where it is the national watchdog.

Of ancient lineage, the Dogue de Bordeaux is thought to be a descendant of the Tibetan Mastiff and the Molossus dog brought by the ancient Romans.

This impressive and appealing breed was once used to guard flocks against bear and wolf, and later in bull- and dogfights. In more recent times it has been kept mainly as a guard and companion.

KEY CHARACTERISTICS
• **CLASS** Working. **Recognized** FCI.
• **SIZE** Height at withers: 69–75cm (27½–30in). Weight: 54.4–65.2kg (120–145lb).
• **COAT** Short and smooth.
• **COLOUR** Apricot, silver, fawn or brindle; muzzle, ears and nose can be black; nose can be lighter in dogs with a tan mask.
• **OTHER FEATURES** Massive head; large, wide-set eyes; pendant ears with slightly rounded tips; thick set body; tail carried low, but in line with back when on the alert.

Character and care

Of good and calm temperament, the Dogue de Bordeaux makes a first-class watchdog and guard, and an affectionate companion which is usually good with children. However, it is a powerful animal, and is not suitable for an inexperienced dog owner.

MUDI

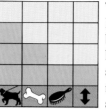

The Mudi originated in Hungary, where it has been used for centuries to herd sheep and cattle, and to hunt wild boar. In more recent times, it has also worked as a guard dog and as a dispeller of vermin. This versatile dog has something of the look of a Border Collie, but its tail, which hangs down, should be 5–7.5cm (2–3in) long – either by nature or by docking. The breed has only recently been recognized by the FCI and is rarely seen at dog shows.

Character and care

The Mudi is a brave, lively and intelligent animal, which is loyal and affectionate towards its human family and makes a good watchdog. It needs considerable exercise and daily brushing.

KEY CHARACTERISTICS
• **CLASS** Working. **Recognized** FCI.
• **SIZE** Height at shoulders: 35.5–48.5cm (14–19in). Weight: 8.1–13.1kg (18–29lb).
• **COAT** About 5cm (2in) long, shorter on head and front of legs; bristly and coarse, and tends to curl.
• **COLOUR** Black or white; sometimes a mixture of the two with scattered spots of more or less uniform size.
• **OTHER FEATURES** Dark brown oval eyes; erect, pointed ears; short, straight back; tail carried down.

GREAT DANE

One of the tallest dogs in the world, the Great Dane was a favourite of the German Chancellor Bismarck. A gentle giant which fits happily into its own special indoor space, the Great Dane sadly does not live much longer than 8 or 9 years.

BRAZILIAN GUARD DOG

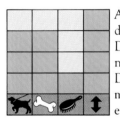

The Brazilian Guard Dog or Fila Brasileiro is descended from Spanish Mastiffs introduced into South America by the conquistadors in the 16th century. The Mastiffs were crossed with other dogs in Brazil to produce this mastiff-type breed, which has something of the expression of the Bloodhound about it. The Fila Brasileiro has been used as a drover, tracker and guard in its native land and is recognized by the FCI as a Brazilian breed.

Character and care

The Brazilian Guard Dog is obedient with its owner but distrustful of strangers, and makes a formidable guard. It needs firm training and handling to control its aggression. It should be groomed regularly with a hound glove.

KEY CHARACTERISTICS
• **CLASS** Working. **Recognized** CKC, FCI.
• **SIZE** Height: 60–74cm (24–29½in). Minimum weight: dogs 45kg (100lb), bitches 40.5kg (90lb).
• **COAT** Dense, soft and short; longer on throat.
• **COLOUR** Brindle or any solid colour except white; white allowed on tail tip and feet.
• **OTHER FEATURES** Large, heavy, square head; medium-sized, almond-shaped eyes; large ears; broad, deep chest; tail broad at the root and tapering to a point.

Among the tallest of the dog breeds, the Great Dane is known in its native Germany as the Deutsche Dogge. (German Mastiff). This statuesque dog, often referred to as the Apollo of the dog world, has existed in Britain for many centuries, and is said to be descended from the Molossus hounds of ancient Rome. In the Middle Ages, it was used as a wild boar hunter, companion and bodyguard, and the breed also played its part in bull-baiting.

In the 1800s the Chancellor of Germany, Bismarck, who had a particular interest in mastiffs, crossed the mastiff of southern Germany and the Great Dane of the north to produce dogs similar to the Dane we know today. They were first shown in Hamburg in 1863 under the separate varieties, Ulmer Dogge and Danisch Dogge. Then in 1876 it was decreed that the breed should be shown under the single heading Deutsche Dogge, and it was proclaimed the national dog of Germany. The Deutsche Doggen Klub was formed there in 1888. The Great Dane Club had already been formed in Britain, in 1882, and the breed has been in the British Kennel Club stud book since 1884.

member of the family. The Great Dane is good natured, playful and easy to train. However, it should not be teased lest an action be misinterpreted. It needs regular exercise on hard ground and daily grooming with a body brush. A sad fact for owners of this majestic breed is that it lives for only 8–9 years on average.

KEY CHARACTERISTICS
• **CLASS** Working. **Recognized** AKC, ANKC, CKC, FCI, KC(GB), KUSA.
• **SIZE** Minimum height over 18 months: dogs 76cm (30in), bitches 71cm (28in). Minimum weight over 18 months: dogs 54kg (120lb), bitches 46kg (100lb).
• **COAT** Short, dense and sleek.
• **COLOUR** Brindle, fawn, blue, black or harlequin (white, preferably with all black or all blue patches that have the appearance of being torn).
• **OTHER FEATURES** Large, wide and open nostrils; fairly deep-set eyes; triangular ears; very deep body; long tail, thick at the root and tapering towards the tip.

Character and care

Despite its size, this breed should not be kennelled out of doors, but kept indoors as a

55

CANAAN DOG

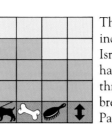

This breed has a long, bushy tail, pricked ears and an alert expression.

The Canaan Dog is an indigenous breed of Israel, which is said to have been developed through the selective breeding of the semi-wild Pariah dogs of the Middle East. A fine guard and protector of livestock, the Canaan has also proved its worth as a guard dog and as a messenger in the Israeli army. Other uses have been as a guide dog for the blind and as a search and rescue dog.

There are two varieties of Canaan Dog, one collie-like and the other Dingo-like, the latter being more heavily built.

Character and care

The Canaan is alert, home loving and loyal to its family. It has a distrust of strangers and will faithfully guard the humans and animals entrusted to its care, standing its ground if called upon to do so. It needs regular grooming with a brush and comb.

KEY CHARACTERISTICS
• **CLASS** Working. **Recognized** CKC, FCI, KC(GB), KUSA.
• **SIZE** Height at withers: 49.5–60cm (19½–23½in). Weight: 18–25kg (40–55lb).
• **COAT** Medium to long, straight and harsh; undercoat visible in winter.
• **COLOUR** Sandy to reddish brown, white or black; harlequin (black and/or blue-grey patches on a white background) also permissible.
• **OTHER FEATURES** Well-proportioned head; eyes slightly slanting, the darker the better; pricked ears; body generally strong but not massive; bushy tail set on high, carried curled over back when alert.

KOMONDOR

The Komondor was known as early as 1555, and has been used for centuries to guard flocks and property from predators and thieves on the Hungarian plains. It has worked with and without other dogs, first herding the semi-wild Hungarian sheep, and later protecting whatever required a large and commanding dog as guard. The breed was recognized in the United States in 1937, but is still comparatively rare in western Europe and has made its mark in the British show ring only over the last 10 years.

Very strong and agile for its size, the Komondor is hardy, healthy and tolerant of changing temperatures. It is a breed that can never be mistaken for any other because of its full white coat falling in tassels, or cords, which is thought by some to resemble an old-fashioned string mop. The cords of the coat form a kind of controlled matting which feels felty to the touch.

Character and care

The Komondor is a natural protector and will guard with its life sheep and cattle, or children and other pets if it is cast in the role of family companion. While it is utterly devoted to its human family, it is wary of strangers, does not take kindly to teasing and, if a warning growl goes unheeded, may attack without warning.

This breed needs plenty of exercise and meticulous grooming.

PINSCHER

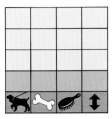

The Pinscher ("biter", in German) originated in Germany, where it has existed for several hundred years, as proved by likenesses in various works of art. The old Black and Tan Terrier may have contributed to its development at some stage.

Resembling the larger Doberman, to which it contributed, the Pinscher was officially recognized by the German Kennel Club as long ago as 1879. At the beginning of the 20th century, both smooth and coarse-haired puppies appeared in litters. However, the Pinscher Club ruled that a short-haired Pinscher would not be registered unless short-haired ancestors could be proved for three generations. However, it is only since 1988 that an interim breed standard has been set up for it by the British Kennel Club, and it will be interesting to see whether this good sporting and show breed makes an impact on the international show scene.

Character and care

The Pinscher's temperament has been described as high spirited and self possessed. It is a good natured, playful dog which is good with children and makes a fine guard, being alert, loyal, watchful and fearless. It needs exercise and grooming and can cope with life in an apartment.

KEY CHARACTERISTICS

- **CLASS** Working.
  Recognized FCI, KC(GB), KUSA.

- **SIZE** Height at withers: 43–48cm (17–19in).

- **COAT** Short and dense.

- **COLOUR** All colours from solid fawn (Isabella) to stag red; black or blue with reddish/tan markings.

- **OTHER FEATURES** Dark, medium-sized eyes; V-shaped ears set on high; wide chest; tail set on and carried high, and usually docked to three joints.

While sharing many characteristics with the Schnauzer, the Pinscher's smooth, glossy coat is similar to the Doberman's, to which this sturdily built dog contributed.

The Komondor's long, white, corded coat is a distinctive feature.

KEY CHARACTERISTICS

- **CLASS** Working.
  Recognized AKC, ANKC, CKC, FCI, KC(GB), KUSA.

- **SIZE** Minimum height at withers: dogs 63.5cm (25in), bitches 58.5cm (23½in). Weight: 36.3–68kg (80–150lb).

- **COAT** Long, coarse outer coat; may be curly or wavy; softer undercoat.

- **COLOUR** White.

- **OTHER FEATURES** Head is short in relation to its width; medium-sized eyes and ears; muscular, slightly arched neck; broad, deep body with a muscular chest; level back; tail continues line of rump, long and slightly curved at tip.

ROTTWEILER

Courageous and loyal, the Rottweiler can be a fearsome guard which will attack without warning, but many are gentle pets.

EURASIER

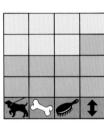

The Eurasier is a spitz breed, somewhere between the Chow Chow and Keeshond in appearance. It is a relative newcomer to the canine world, having emerged only in the 1950s as a separate breed. It was developed by a number of scientists, including the late Professor Konrad Lorenz, author of *Man Meets Dog*, who sought to revive what was once a Siberian dog. They did this by crossing the Chow Chow and the German Spitz, and then crossing again to another spitz, the Samoyed.

Character and care
This attractive, medium-sized dog has a good disposition, is easy to train and is relatively silent, barking only when provoked. It is also a vigilant and attentive guard, is loyal to its owner, hostile to intruders and needs time to accept newcomers. It has average exercise requirements and should be brushed regularly using a wire brush when necessary.

KEY CHARACTERISTICS
• **CLASS** Working. **Recognized** FCI.
• **SIZE** Height at shoulders: dogs about 60cm (23½in), bitches about 56cm (22in). Weight: dogs about 32kg (90lb), bitches about 26kg (57lb).
• **COAT** Abundant, short, dense undercoat and medium length top coat.
• **COLOUR** Red, wolf-grey, black, or black with fainter markings.
• **OTHER FEATURES** Fox-like head with flat skull and pronounced stop; almond-shaped eyes; erect ears; cat-like feet; tail reaching to hocks when resting, but carried curled over the back when on the move.

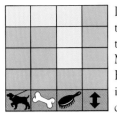

In its native Germany, this breed is still referred to as the Rottweiler Metzgerhund (Rottweil Butcher's Dog), because in the past it worked as a draught dog delivering the meat. It has also been used as a hunter of wild boar and a trusted cattle dog. Some fanciers believe that the Rottweiler is a descendant of the early German Shepherd Dog, while others consider that its ancestor was similar to the Tibetan Mastiff, brought as a guard by Roman soldiers. Certainly, this dog was prevalent from the Swiss canton of Argovie to the Nacker and Rottweil districts to the south of Württemberg, where the Romans had a military camp.

During the First World War, the Rottweiler proved itself to be an intelligent police dog and guard. It was recognized by the American Kennel Club in 1935, and the breed was introduced into Britain by the late Thelma Gray of the famous Rozavel Kennels in 1936. Surprisingly, another 30 years were to pass before the Rottweiler was given a separate register by the British Kennel Club. An inexperienced owner should never keep this breed. Nor should anyone who does not have considerable time to devote to its training.

Character and care
The Rottweiler is a large, courageous dog that makes an excellent companion-guard and responds to kindly but firm handling. It needs space and plenty of exercise. It also needs daily grooming with a bristle brush or hound glove and comb.

KEY CHARACTERISTICS
● **CLASS** Working. **Recognized** AKC, ANKC, CKC, FCI, KC(GB), KUSA.
● **SIZE** Height at shoulders: dogs 60–69cm (24–27in), bitches 55–63.5cm (22–25in). Weight: 40.5–48.6kg (90–110lb).
● **COAT** Medium length, coarse and lying flat, with undercoat on neck and thighs.
● **COLOUR** Black with clearly defined tan or deep brown markings.
● **OTHER FEATURES** Head broad between the ears; medium-sized, almond-shaped eyes; ears small in proportion to head; powerful, arched neck; broad, deep chest; tail docked at first joint and usually carried horizontally.

HUNGARIAN KUVASZ

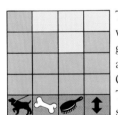

The Hungarian Kuvasz was established in Hungary many centuries ago, and has found its way to China, India, Tibet and Turkey. It bears a strong similarity to the Slovakian Kuvasz and, likewise, the Polish Sheepdog or Owczarek Podhalanski. These three, while regarded as separate breeds in their native lands, are in fact members of the same herding breed. The Polish and Slovakian types are sometimes called "Tatry" dogs after the mountain range that stretches between the two countries, and where each type has been long established.

Character and care
Brave, intelligent and lively, the Hungarian Kuvasz is an excellent guard – the name Kuvasz comes from the Turkish word *kavas* (guard). It has also been used to hunt big game. The Kuvasz may be kept as a pet, but it is wary of strangers. It needs plenty of exercise and a daily brushing to keep it looking trim.

KEY CHARACTERISTICS
● **CLASS** Working. **Recognized** AKC, CKC, FCI, KC(GB).
● **SIZE** Height at shoulders: dogs 70–73.75cm (28–29½in), bitches 65–68.75cm (26–27½in). Maximum weight: 50kg (110lb).
● **COAT** Harsh, wavy.
● **COLOUR** White or ivory.
● **OTHER FEATURES** Beautifully proportioned head; square in outline; almond-shaped eyes; tail set on fairly low, tip curving slightly upwards.

LEONBERGER

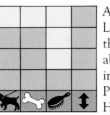

A German breed, the Leonberger is generally thought to have come about through the crossing of a Landseer and a Pyrenean Mountain Dog. However, some people believe that it is a descendant of the Tibetan Mastiff, while others consider it to be the product of selective breeding by Herr Essig of Leonberg. He is said to have used the Newfoundland, Saint Bernard and Pyrenean Mountain Dog to develop the breed. The breed was devastated by both World Wars and is considered a rare breed.

It was not until 1949 that a recognized standard for the breed clearly defined the differences between the Leonberger and the Saint Bernard. The Leonberger has worked in Germany, France, the Netherlands and Belgium as a watchdog, a protector of livestock, and as a draught dog, but has only become known outside these countries fairly recently.

Character and care

Good natured, intelligent and lively, the Leonberger is a fine-looking watchdog, produced from breeds of sound temperament. It is essentially a country dog, and needs daily brushing, regular exercise and plenty of space. It is very good with children, and has a great love of water.

KEY CHARACTERISTICS
• **CLASS** Working. **Recognized** ANKC, CKC, FCI, KC(GB), KUSA.
• **SIZE** Height at withers: dogs 72–80cm (28–32in), bitches 65–75cm (26–30in). Weight: 36.3–68kg (80–150lb).
• **COAT** Medium soft, fairly long and close to body.
• **COLOUR** Light yellow, golden to red-brown; preferably with black mask.
• **OTHER FEATURES** Top of head domed; eyes vary from light brown to brown; ears set high; long body; bushy tail carried at half-mast.

The Leonberger has a good natured expression. It is a strong, muscular dog, with webbed feet.

PORTUGUESE WATER DOG

Found mainly in the region of the Algarve, the Portuguese Water Dog is an invaluable member of the fisherman's crew. It is an exceptionally fine swimmer.

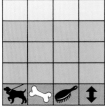

The Portuguese Water Dog (Cão d'Agua) was once a familiar sight throughout the fishing ports of the Iberian Peninsula, and is still commonly found in the Algarve region of Portugal. It is a fisherman's dog, a fine swimmer with great powers of endurance, and undertakes a wide variety of tasks. It will guard the catch, swim between boats, and dive and retrieve fish or objects lost overboard. It is also a good rabbiter.

There are two distinct varieties of the breed, one with a long, glossy, wavy coat and the other with a shorter, thicker, curlier coat, but conformation is identical. Although the Portuguese Water Dog was once a comparative rarity outside its native land, it is now a regular contender in the ring in Britain and elsewhere, and makes an attractive show dog.

Character and care

This intelligent and energetic dog is said to be self-willed but obedient to its owner, and somewhat apprehensive of strangers. It is a superlative swimmer and diver, needs ample exercise and regular brushing and combing. For exhibition purposes, the hindquarters are clipped from the last rib, and two-thirds of the tail are clipped.

KEY CHARACTERISTICS
• **CLASS** Working. **Recognized** AKC, ANKC, CKC, FCI, KC(GB), KUSA.
• **SIZE** Height at withers: dogs 50–57.5cm (19½–23in), bitches 43–52.5cm (17–21in). Weight: dogs 18.9–27kg (42–60lb), bitches 15.7–22.6kg (35–50lb).
• **COAT** Profuse and thick except under forelegs and thighs. There are two types, both without an undercoat: fairly long and loosely waved; and shortish with compact curls.
• **COLOUR** Solid black, white, or various shades of brown; black and white or brown and white; skin bluish under black, white, and black and white.
• **OTHER FEATURES** Large, well-proportioned head; round eyes set well apart; heart-shaped, dropped ears; wide, deep chest; tail thick at base and tapering towards point.

This dog's tail is set in line with its back and curls over. The tail is full and of natural length.

SWEDISH VALLHUND

The Swedish Vallhund is known in its native land as Västgötaspets, which means "spitz of the West Goths". It closely resembles the Welsh Corgis, although the Vallhund is somewhat higher in the leg and shorter in the back. Undoubtedly there is a connection between the breeds, but whether Corgis taken by the Vikings to Sweden developed into the Vallhund or Swedish dogs brought to Britain developed into Corgis is not known. Like the Corgi, the Vallhund is a splendid cattle dog. Much credit for the development of the modern breed must go to the Swedish fancier, Bjorn van Rosen. Despite its antiquity, the Vallhund did not win recognition by any kennel club until 1950, but it is now gaining popularity in the international show ring.

Character and care

The Swedish Vallhund is a friendly, loyal, affectionate little dog, described in its standard as active and eager to please. It makes a good family pet and needs plenty of exercise.

Less than 50 years ago this charming breed was almost extinct, but is now a popular contender in the show ring. It is similar to the Pembroke Welsh Corgi, but is higher in the leg and has a shorter back.

The Vallhund has a foxy head and medium sized hazel eyes.

KEY CHARACTERISTICS

- **CLASS** Working.
  Recognized ANKC, FCI, KC(GB), KUSA.

- **SIZE** Height at withers: dogs 33–35cm (13–13¾in), bitches 31–33cm (12–13in). Weight: 11.4–16kg (25–35lb).

- **COAT** Medium length, harsh and close, with a soft, woolly undercoat.

- **COLOUR** Steel grey, greyish brown, greyish yellow, reddish yellow or reddish brown; darker guard hairs on back, neck and sides of body; lighter shade of same colour desirable on muzzle, throat, chest, belly, buttocks, feet and hocks; white markings acceptable in place of these lighter shades but never in excess of one-third of coat.

- **OTHER FEATURES** Head rather long; medium-sized eyes; medium-sized pointed ears; back level and well muscled; tail – if present – should not exceed 10cm (4in) in adults – puppies born with tails may be docked.

LAPLAND SPITZ

The Lapland Spitz or Lapphund is an ancient breed which was developed north of the Arctic Circle by the Lapp people to herd reindeer. It spread from there through the rest of Sweden, where it also herded sheep and other livestock. Today, it is kept as a household companion and guard, and is used for security by the Swedish army.

The Lapland Spitz is a medium-sized dog with strong jaws, prick ears, a long, thick double coat and a tail curled over its back in the manner typical of the spitz varieties. The breed was not recognized by the FCI until 1944, when a standard drawn up for it by the National Association of Swedish Dog Fanciers was approved.

Character and care
Affectionate and loyal to its owners and gentle with children, the Lapland Spitz tends to be aggressive towards and suspicious of strangers, making it a good watchdog. It is happiest kept in an outdoor kennel. It needs plenty of exercise and regular brushing.

KEY CHARACTERISTICS

- **CLASS** Working.
  Recognized FCI.

- **SIZE** Height at shoulders: dogs 44.5–49.5cm (17½–19½in), bitches 39.5–44.5cm (15½–17½in). Weight: 20kg (44lb).

- **COAT** Long, thick double coat, standing off from body. Dense undercoat, fringed belly and back legs, heavily plumed tail.

- **COLOUR** Dark brown, black, brown-white; solid colours preferred.

- **OTHER FEATURES** Characteristic pricked ears, thick coat and tail curled over back, but coat longer than some other spitz varieties.

JAPANESE AKITA

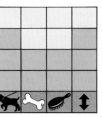

The Akita (or Akita Inu or Shishi Inu) is the largest and most well known internationally of the Japanese breeds. It originated in the Polar regions and has a history tracing back more than 300 years. The Akita was bred to hunt deer and wild boar, and has also, on occasion, hunted the Japanese black bear. It is an extremely swift-moving dog, which can work in deep snow. It also has webbed feet and is a strong swimmer, with the ability to retrieve wildfowl and to drive fish into fishermen's nets.

The Akita is revered in Japan, where it was officially appointed a national monument in 1931 in order to preserve the breed, and more recently was featured on a series of commemorative postage stamps. It is the recipient of a Japanese Dog Federation's "National Treasure" award, given under the auspices of the Japanese Government. Indeed, at one time this classic breed could only be owned by members of the Japanese nobility. The international popularity of the breed began when American servicemen took the Akita back to their homeland, after the Second World War.

AINU DOG

The Ainu Dog, also known as the Hokkaido, Kyushu or Ochi Dog, comes from the mountainous region of the Japanese island of Hokkaido and may have been taken there by the Ainu people when they emigrated thousands of years ago. The breed has changed little since its arrival, and with its smaller, heavy body it is said to resemble the Scandinavian spitz varieties more closely than other Japanese spitz breeds, such as the Akita. A medium-sized dog with a powerful physique, the Ainu is a guard and hunting dog, and is well behaved in the home.

Character and care

Despite its long history as a working breed, the Ainu Dog ideally combines the role of family pet and hunter. Intelligent and readily trained, it is fiercely loyal and affectionate towards an attentive master.

KEY CHARACTERISTICS
• **CLASS** Working. **Recognized** FCI.
• **SIZE** Height: dogs 49.5–53.5cm (19½–21in), bitches 42–48cm (16½–19in).
• **COAT** Double-coated: top coat medium short and dense, with dense undercoat.
• **COLOUR** Red, white, black, grizzle or black and tan.
• **OTHER FEATURES** Broad triangular head; ears upright and triangular; eyes dark and deep-set; muscular body; tail set on high, curling over back.

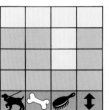

The dignified and courageous Akita tends to show dominance over other dogs. This breed has been popular in the United States since the 1970s, and now has an equally large following in the United Kingdom and elsewhere.

Character and care

The powerful but very trainable Akita is a versatile hunter and retriever, and a first class guard. It has a good temperament for a show dog and is now being kept widely as a pet. However, this alert and energetic dog should not be kept in confined conditions. It can be formidable if its hunting instincts become aroused and needs a good outlet, such as obedience classes, for its undoubted abilities. It also requires daily brushing and a reasonable amount of exercise.

KEY CHARACTERISTICS
• **CLASS** Working. **Recognized** AKC, ANKC, CKC, FCI, KC(GB).
• **SIZE** Height at withers: dogs 66–71cm (26–28in), bitches 61–66cm (24–26in). Weight: 33.7–48.6kg (75–101lb).
• **COAT** Outer coat coarse, straight and stand-off; soft, dense undercoat.
• **COLOUR** Any, including white, brindle and pinto (white with irregular black patches), with or without mask.
• **OTHER FEATURES** Large, flat skull; broad forehead; small eyes and ears; long body; large, full tail.

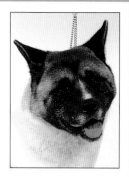

The almond shaped eyes of the Akita are typical of the spitz type breeds.

JAPANESE FIGHTING DOG

The Japanese Fighting Dog or Tosa was bred during the Meiji period (1867–1912), when dog fighting was a popular spectator sport in Japan. Local fighting dogs were crossed with the English Bulldog, English Bull Terrier, Saint Bernard and Great Dane, thus increasing height, strength and ferocity, and producing this massive, powerful yet agile dog. Named after Tosa on the Japanese island of Shikoku, the breed took on the roles of companion and guard when dog fighting was outlawed in Japan. It will fight to the death and is still reputed to take part in illegal fights in Japan.

Character and care

The Tosa can be fierce towards other dogs and needs experienced handling, but it is brave, patient and protective of its human family. Because of its aggressive past, people tend to regard this dog with caution and it is not permitted to be bred from in the United Kingdom. It should be groomed with a bristle brush and hound glove.

KEY CHARACTERISTICS
• **CLASS** Working. **Recognized** CKC, FCI.
• **SIZE** Minimum height at withers: 60cm (23½in). Weight: 45–90kg (100–200lb).
• **COAT** Short, smooth and hard.
• **COLOUR** Tan with or without markings in a different shade of tan; tan markings on white.
• **OTHER FEATURES** Large head; small amber-coloured eyes; small, high-set, dropped ears; powerful body; high-set tail reaching to the hocks.

ESTRELA MOUNTAIN DOG

A popular show dog in its native Portugal, the Estrela Mountain Dog is slowly but surely gaining international fame. It has great strength and is used for carting in its homeland.

The colour of the Estrela Mountain Dog is only seen when the young animal develops its outer coat. Its nose is always black.

The Estrela Mountain Dog, also known as the Portuguese Mountain Dog or Cão da Serra da Estrêla, originated many centuries ago in the Estrêla mountains of central Portugal. It was bred as a herding dog and has in its make-up something of the Mastiff, and of the Saint Bernard, to which it bears some resemblance.

It has always been popular in its native Portugal, where it is still used as a guard dog. The breed standard was first published there in 1933. The breed was first introduced into the United Kingdom in 1974, and it is shown there at larger shows.

Character and care
The Estrela Mountain Dog is an excellent guard, with immense stamina. It is very loyal and affectionate to its owners but indifferent to other humans. This intelligent dog is said to need a great deal of love and firm, kindly handling. It requires plenty of exercise, regular brushing and a light diet, which should be discussed with the breeder at time of purchase.

KEY CHARACTERISTICS

- **CLASS** Working.
  Recognized FCI, KC(GB), KUSA.

- **SIZE** Height at shoulders: dogs 58–68cm (23–27in), bitches 51–61cm (20–24in). Weight: dogs 34–48kg (75–105lb), bitches 27–41kg (60–90lb).

- **COAT** Two types: long – thick, moderately harsh outer coat with feathering on backs of legs and thighs, and dense undercoat; short – short, thick and moderately harsh outer coat, with shorter, dense undercoat.

- **COLOUR** All colours, or combinations of colours, permissible.

- **OTHER FEATURES** Long, powerful head; eyes should be neither deep nor prominent; ears small in proportion to body; short back, higher at withers than loins; long, thick tail.

PYRENEAN MOUNTAIN DOG

The Pyrenean Mountain Dog or Great Pyrenees probably originated in Asia before finding its way with immigrants to Europe. Its closest relatives are the Kuvasz and the Newfoundland to which it may have contributed. The breed has been used for centuries to guard flocks in the Pyrenean mountains bordering France and Spain, and throughout France. It was also a favourite at the French court prior to the French Revolution. A standard for this popular breed was approved in the mid-1960s.

Character and care

The Pyrenean can be kept in or out of doors, but must be well trained. It is a powerful dog, and I have witnessed one or two slight accidents when youngsters have thumped a strange Pyrenean on the head at dog shows. Generally, though, it is good natured, gets on with other pets and is a faithful protector. Provided you have sufficient space, food and time for regular exercise and brushing, the Pyrenean will make a good companion and/or show dog.

KEY CHARACTERISTICS
● **CLASS** Working. **Recognized** AKC, ANKC, CKC, FCI, KC(GB), KUSA.
● **SIZE** Height at withers: dogs 70–80cm (28–32in), bitches 65–72.5cm (26–29in). Minimum weight: dogs 50kg (110lb), bitches 40kg (90lb).
● **COAT** Long and coarse-textured, with a profuse undercoat of very fine hair.
● **COLOUR** White, with or without patches of badger, and wolf-grey or pale yellow equally acceptable.
● **OTHER FEATURES** Rounded crown; dark brown, almond-shaped eyes; small, triangular ears; broad chest; level back; tail thick at root and tapering towards tip.

The stately Pyrenean Mountain Dog was a favourite at the court of King Louis XIV of France.

The double dew claws in the Pyrenean's hindlegs are a distinguishing feature.

BERNESE MOUNTAIN DOG

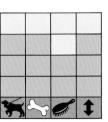

The Bernese Mountain Dog or Bernese Sennenhund is named after the canton of Berne in Switzerland, where it arrived with Caesar's army and was subsequently bred. Like other Swiss mountain dogs, such as the Great Swiss (see page 81), it has mastiff characteristics. The breed is believed to descend from the Molossus dog of ancient Greece and Rome, with some Rottweiler, Saint Bernard and Newfoundland blood discernible in its ancestry.

The Bernese has worked as herder and flock guardian in its native land, and is still used to pull milk carts up Swiss mountainsides. In Britain it frequently puts in an appearance, in harness, at fêtes and similar events in order to raise money for charity. This large, gentle dog has steadily gained popularity in the USA and Britain over the past few years, both as a pet and as a show dog, and is popular throughout Europe.

Character and care
The Bernese Mountain Dog makes a good pet for those with sufficient space, being amiable towards children and other pets. It needs regular brushing and plenty of exercise.

A capable worker, the Bernese Mountain Dog may also be kept as a loyal and affectionate pet.

KEY CHARACTERISTICS		
●	**CLASS** Working. **Recognized** AKC, ANKC, CKC, FCI, KC(GB), KUSA.	
●	**SIZE** Height at withers: dogs 64–70cm (25–27½in), bitches 58–66cm (23–26in). Weight: about 39.6kg (88lb).	
●	**COAT** Thick, moderately long, and straight or slightly wavy, with a bright, natural sheen.	
●	**COLOUR** Jet black, with rich, reddish brown markings on cheeks, over eyes, on legs and chest; some white markings on head, chest, tip of tail and feet are permissible.	
●	**OTHER FEATURES** Strong head with a flat skull; dark brown, almond-shaped eyes; medium-sized ears; compact body; bushy tail.	

There should be a distinctive tan brand marking on each of its paws.

SAINT BERNARD

The Saint Bernard is intelligent, faithful and extremely gentle. It loves children, too, but does require plenty of space and large food rations.

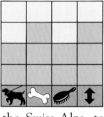

The Saint Bernard is a gentle giant, despite being descended from the fierce Molossus dogs of ancient Rome. It is named after the medieval Hospice of St Bernard in the Swiss Alps, to which it was introduced between 1660 and 1670. It became famous for rescuing travellers and climbers on the Swiss Alps. One dog, Barry, saved 40 lives during the period 1800–10.

Prior to 1830, all Saint Bernards were short-coated, but in that year Newfoundland blood was introduced in an attempt to give the breed added size and vitality. As a result the modern Saint Bernard may be long- or short-haired. In 1810, a Saint Bernard called "Lion" was introduced into England and the breed was first exhibited in Britain in 1863. An international standard for the Saint Bernard was drawn up in Berne in 1887.

Character and care

True to its past, the Saint Bernard is intelligent, eminently trainable, loves children and is a kindly dog. Because of this, it is, unfortunately, sometimes kept in conditions which do not allow it nearly enough space. Like many heavyweights, the breed should not be given too much exercise in the first year of life, short regular walks being better than long ones. It needs daily brushing and requires generous quantities of food. It also slobbers. Sadly, like the Great Dane, this lovable, large dog has only a limited lifespan.

KEY CHARACTERISTICS
● **CLASS** Working. **Recognized** AKC, ANKC, CKC, FCI, KC(GB), KUSA.
● **SIZE** Minimum height at shoulder: dogs 69cm (27½in), bitches 64cm (23½in). Weight: 48.6–90kg (110–200lb).
● **COAT** Dense, short, smooth and lying close to body.
● **COLOUR** Orange, mahogany-brindle, red-brindle or white, with patches on body in any of these colours; white blaze on face, and white on muzzle, collar, chest, forelegs, feet and end of tail; black shadings on face and ears.
● **OTHER FEATURES** Massive, wide head; medium-sized eyes and ears; broad, muscular shoulders; broad, straight back; tail set on high.

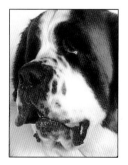

The white blaze that runs up the face of the Saint Bernard emphasizes its benevolent expression.

ESKIMO DOG

The Eskimo Dog, described by some as a miniature Husky.

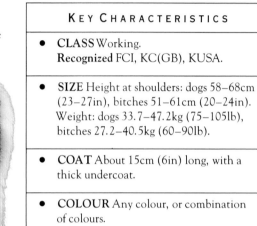

This hardy, strong spitz dog was developed to haul sleds in and around the Arctic Circle. The American polar explorer, Robert Peary (1856–1920), considered that there was only one breed of sled-dog with regional variations, but now a number of breeds are recognized. The beautiful Eskimo Dog probably originated in eastern Siberia, and shared common ancestry with the Alaskan Malamute, Siberian Husky and Samoyed. It bears a considerable resemblance to the Greenland Dog (which is not, at the time of writing, recognized in Britain), but the Eskimo Dog is shorter in the back and weightier.

Character and care

The Eskimo Dog is an excellent sled dog of remarkable endurance. It is a fine guard, which rarely lives indoors with its owners. It relishes vigorous outdoor exercise and a job of work, and benefits from regular brushing.

KEY CHARACTERISTICS
• **CLASS** Working. **Recognized** FCI, KC(GB), KUSA.
• **SIZE** Height at shoulders: dogs 58–68cm (23–27in), bitches 51–61cm (20–24in). Weight: dogs 33.7–47.2kg (75–105lb), bitches 27.2–40.5kg (60–90lb).
• **COAT** About 15cm (6in) long, with a thick undercoat.
• **COLOUR** Any colour, or combination of colours.
• **OTHER FEATURES** Well-proportioned head; dark brown or tawny eyes; short, firm ears set well apart; broad, deep chest; large, bushy tail.

GREENLAND DOG

The Greenland Dog or Grönlandshund, like all the spitz breeds, originated in the Arctic Circle, probably in eastern Siberia. It shares common ancestry with other sled dogs, such as the Alaskan Malamute, Siberian Husky and Samoyed, but particularly resembles the Eskimo Dog which many consider to be the same breed. The Greenland is usually a little longer in the back than the Eskimo Dog and somewhat lighter.

Character and care

This sled dog has considerable powers of endurance, is faithful and obedient to its owner and makes a fine guard and a good show dog. However, it generally lives outdoors and is not suited to the house. It needs vigorous exercise, and regular brushing.

KEY CHARACTERISTICS
• **CLASS** Working. **Recognized** CKC, FCI.
• **SIZE** Minimum height at shoulders: dogs 61cm (24in), bitches 55cm (22in). Minimum weight: 29.7kg (66lb).
• **COAT** Straight, coarse and rather long, with a heavy undercoat.
• **COLOUR** Any colour or combination of colours except albino.
• **OTHER FEATURES** Cone-shaped muzzle; dark, slightly oblique eyes; small, triangular, erect ears; tail carried rolled over the back.

ALASKAN MALAMUTE

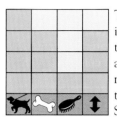

The Alaskan Malamute is a sociable member of the spitz family named after the Eskimo Mahle-mut people who reside by the shores of Kotzebue Sound, a mountainous region in the Arctic Circle. According to stories, this and other similar arctic dogs derive partly from wolves. Whether this is true or not, the Malamute has developed great stamina and speed. It is highly prized as a sled dog, being capable of surviving in arctic temperatures, and of hauling heavy loads over rough terrain. The American explorer, Robert Peary (1856–1920), was of the opinion that there was only one breed of sled dog, which varied in name purely according to the region from which it came. However, there are distinguishing features between sled dogs, and a number of breeds have been identified. The Alaskan Malamute, which is one of the larger sled dogs, now has a standard of its own.

Character and care

Despite its rather wolfish appearance the Alaskan Malamute is a gentle, kind-natured dog, and makes a loyal and devoted companion, but is not very good with other canines. It needs a daily brushing and lots of exercise.

KEY CHARACTERISTICS
• **CLASS** Working. **Recognized** AKC, ANKC, CKC, FCI, KC(GB), KUSA.
• **SIZE** Height: dogs 64–71cm (25–28in), bitches 58–66cm (23–26in). Weight: 38.5–57kg (85–125lb).
• **COAT** Thick, coarse guard coat; dense, oily, woolly undercoat.
• **COLOUR** From light grey through intermediate shadings to black, or from gold through shades of red to liver; always with white on underbody, parts of legs, feet and part of mask markings; also other specific markings.
• **OTHER FEATURES** Broad, powerful head; almond-shaped brown eyes; ears small in proportion to head, triangular; strong, powerful body; tail moderately high-set.

Gentle and kind with humans, the Alaskan Malamute can be quarrelsome with its own kind.

SAMOYED

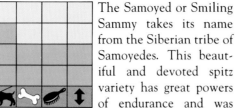

The Samoyed or Smiling Sammy takes its name from the Siberian tribe of Samoyedes. This beautiful and devoted spitz variety has great powers of endurance and was one of the breeds used by Fridtjof Nansen and Ernest Shackleton on their expeditions to the North Pole. It has also been used as a guard and to hunt reindeer. The Samoyed was introduced into Britain in 1889 by a Mr Kilburn Scott, who returned from the north coast of Russia with a pup. He subsequently mated a bitch "Whitey Pechora", said to have been obtained from a sailor in London, to a dog named "Musti" owned by Lady Sitwell, and many present-day Samoyeds descend from this pair. The standard originally drawn up by the Kilburn-Scotts has changed little over the years and British stock has been exported all over the world.

Character and care

Unlike many sled dogs, the Sammy lives in the homes of its owners in its native land. It is a devoted dog, which is good with children and makes an obedient, if slightly independent, housepet. Some breed members have excelled in obedience work. It revels in exercise, and its thick, water-resistant coat needs regular brushing and combing.

KEY CHARACTERISTICS
● **CLASS** Working. **Recognized** AKC, ANKC, CKC, FCI, KC(GB), KUSA.
● **SIZE** Height at withers: dogs 52.5–59cm (21–23½in), bitches 47.5–52.5cm (19–21in). Weight: 22.7–29.5kg (50–65lb).
● **COAT** Harsh, but not wiry, and straight, with thick, soft, short undercoat.
● **COLOUR** Pure white, white and biscuit, cream; outer coat silver-tipped.
● **OTHER FEATURES** Broad head; dark, almond-shaped eyes; thick ears, not too large, and slightly rounded at the tips; medium length back; long, profusely coated tail that is carried curled over the back.

The Samoyed's tail curls over its back in the characteristic manner of the spitz. Popular as a housepet, this dog has even made its mark in television and advertising.

SIBERIAN HUSKY

A dog of superb beauty, strength and stamina, the Siberian Husky has the Chukchi Sled Dog as an ancestor, and has a proud history of sled racing.

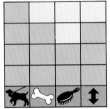

The Siberian Husky was developed in ancient times by the Chukchi people of north-east Asia who wanted a hardy sled dog with strength, speed and stamina. Wider recognition of its abilities came after the gold rush to Alaska at the turn of the century, when dog-hauled sleds were the only means of transportation available. There was considerable rivalry between the dog teams, and Huskies became famed sled racing dogs.

The breed became renowned, during the Second World War, for search and rescue work. In the following decade it gained considerable popularity in America, and by about 1960 had come into its own in the United Kingdom and elsewhere.

Character and care

The Siberian Husky is an intelligent and friendly animal with considerable stamina. It is not an aggressive dog and may be kept as a family pet, provided it is given some work and plenty of space and exercise.

KEY CHARACTERISTICS

- **CLASS** Working.
  Recognized AKC, ANKC, CKC, FCI, KC(GB), KUSA.

- **SIZE** Height at withers: dogs 53–60cm (21–23½in), bitches 51–56cm (20–22in). Weight: dogs 20–27kg (45–60lb), bitches 16–23kg (30–50lb).

- **COAT** Medium in length, giving a well-furred appearance; outer coat straight and lying smooth against body; undercoat soft and dense.

- **COLOUR** All colours and markings permissible; markings on head common, including striking ones not found on other breeds.

- **OTHER FEATURES** Medium-sized head in proportion to body; almond-shaped eyes; medium-sized ears; arched neck; strong body with a straight back; well-furred tail carried gracefully curled over back except when resting.

The Siberian Husky's head is rounded on top, and its ears – slightly rounded at the tips – are carried erect.

HERDING BREEDS

NEWFOUNDLAND

A gentle giant, the Newfoundland may seem ponderous on land but is in its element in water, swimming strongly and retrieving anything (or anyone) in its path.

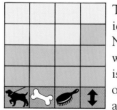

There are various theories on the origin of the Newfoundland, but that which seems most likely is that it is a descendant of the Tibetan Mastiff. In adapting to the rugged conditions in Newfoundland, eastern Canada, it developed webbed feet and an oily coat, which allows it to remain in the water for long periods of time. The breed aided fishermen and gained great fame as a life-saver. With the strong instinct to rescue anything, or anyone, in the water and retrieve it to safety, it became as valued by crews in Newfoundland waters as the Saint Bernard is by climbers in the Swiss Alps.

A particoloured variety of the Newfoundland, known as the Landseer, found fame in the paintings of Sir Edward Landseer (1802–73). The breed was also much admired by the English poet, Lord Byron.

Character and care

The large and beautiful Newfoundland is rarely bad tempered unless provoked. Indeed it is amazingly gentle with other breeds, one having been seen sitting quietly amid a bunch of squabbling Chihuahuas. It does, however, take up a fair amount of space, and needs regular exercise on hard ground and daily brushing using a hard brush.

KEY CHARACTERISTICS

- **CLASS** Herding.
  Recognized AKC, ANKC, CKC, FCI, KC(GB), KUSA.

- **SIZE** Average height at shoulders: dogs 71cm (28in), bitches 66cm (26in). Weight: dogs 64–69kg (130–150lb), bitches 50–54kg (110–120lb).

- **COAT** A double coat that is flat, dense and coarse textured; it is oily and water resistant. The outer coat is moderately long and can be straight or slightly wavy.

- **COLOUR** Black, brown, grey or Landseer (black head, black markings on a white ground).

- **OTHER FEATURES** Massive, broad head; small, dark brown eyes; small ears set well back; strong, broad, muscular body; thick tail.

The Newfoundland first began to appear in the show ring in the 1880s, its magnificent size and calm temperament soon attracting a loyal following.

LAPPONIAN HERDER

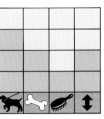

The Lapponian Herder, Lapponian Vallhund or Lapinporokoira is a Finnish breed which was developed by crossing the Lapphund with the German Shepherd Dog. Its task in life is to herd reindeer, which it is said to perform tirelessly, both guarding the herd against wolves and bears, and keeping the herd together. It is a medium-sized dog, strong-boned, muscular and longer than it is high. Its dense double coat, which is almost impervious to severe weather, may be medium length or short, but breeders are developing the short-haired type. The breed is recognized by the FCI but is not yet a contender in the European show ring.

Character and care

The Lapponian has strong herding instincts and is something of a barker, but is obedient and friendly and appears to make a good companion, provided that it receives vigorous exercise. It needs daily grooming with a bristle brush and slicker.

KEY CHARACTERISTICS

- **CLASS** Herding.
  Recognized FCI.

- **SIZE** Height at withers: dogs 48.5–56cm (19–22in), bitches 43–48.5cm (17–19in). Maximum weight: 29.7kg (66lb).

- **COAT** Long and glossy with a woolly undercoat.

- **COLOUR** Preferably black tinged with red, but also black and tan.

- **OTHER FEATURES** Pointed head; expressive eyes; erect ears; long in the back with a long tail.

BOUVIER DES FLANDRES

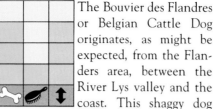

The Bouvier des Flandres or Belgian Cattle Dog originates, as might be expected, from the Flanders area, between the River Lys valley and the coast. This shaggy dog looks the picture of ferocity in its homeland, where its ears are traditionally cropped. It was bred as a farm dog from a multiplicity of working breeds with the purpose of producing a good all-rounder, and was used in the hunt over rough ground, and as a herder, drover, protector and guard.

A possible standard for the breed was discussed in 1912, but it was not until after the First World War that a standard was drawn up and finalized by the Club National Belge du Bouvier des Flandres.

Character and care

The Bouvier des Flandres can be rather fierce, but has a calm and sensible temperament, and is intelligent, hardy and trustworthy. It is extremely loyal to its family and is easily trained. The breed does, however, require a good deal of exercise and regular brushing. Its somewhat fearsome appearance belies its good nature. It is mainly kept as a pet or show dog.

Traditionally the ears of the Bouvier des Flandres are clipped in its homeland, perhaps to give it a more alert attitude for guarding.

KEY CHARACTERISTICS

- **CLASS** Herding.
  Recognized AKC, ANKC, CKC, FCI, KC(GB), KUSA.

- **SIZE** Height at withers: dogs 61–69cm (24½–27½in), bitches 59–66cm (23½–26½in). Average weight: 36kg (88lb).

- **COAT** Rough, thick and harsh with a soft dense undercoat.

- **COLOUR** From fawn to black, including brindle; white star on chest permissible; white predominating or chocolate brown highly undesirable; light, washed-out shades undesirable.

- **OTHER FEATURES** Eyes alert in expression; ears set on high; broad, deep chest and short, strong body; tail usually docked to 2–3 joints.

BOUVIER DES ARDENNES

The Bouvier des Ardennes or Ardennes Cattle Dog is one of a number of Bouviers or cattle dogs which were developed to guard herds of cattle and drive them to market. For many years, these rough-coated drovers were unclassified, but then they started to be selectively bred and became known by their district of origin. The Bouvier des Ardennes, named after a high forested area in south-east Belgium, also herded pigs and is still often used for this task.

Character and care

This tireless, intelligent working dog is happiest in the wide, open spaces. It is a severe, rough-and-ready looking animal that tends to keep strangers at bay, but is obedient and deeply affectionate towards its owner. It needs regular brushing with a bristle or pin brush. It has a massive, rather short head and yellow eyes.

Descended from ancient rough-coated stock, the breed has a steel wool, all weather coat.

KEY CHARACTERISTICS
● **CLASS** Herding. **Recognized** FCI.
● **SIZE** Height: about 61cm (24in).
● **COAT** Long and bushy with a thick undercoat.
● **COLOUR** All colours permissible.
● **OTHER FEATURES** Large head with a short muzzle; dark eyes; upright ears; rounded ribcage; usually born without a tail, otherwise tail is docked.

HOVAWART

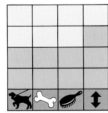

With roots in the farmyard, the Hovawart is an excellent watchdog and good with children and stock. The breed tends to require a firm hand in training.

The Hovawart has been described as a relative newcomer. In fact, the breed has been recognized by the German Kennel Club since 1936, having appeared in Württemburg towards the end of the 19th century. The name Hovawart comes from the German "Hofewart", meaning estate or watch dog, but its role, for many years, seems to have been simply that of a companion dog that will rise to the occasion if required to do so. It has appeared on the European show circuit in recent years and is recognized by the Kennel Club in Britain.

Character and care

An excellent guard dog that is home loving, fond of children and easy to train, the Hovawart tends to be a one-man dog. It is slow to mature and will respond aggressively when provoked.

KEY CHARACTERISTICS

- **CLASS** Herding.
  Recognized FCI, KC(GB), KUSA.

- **SIZE** Height: dogs 63–70cm (24–27½in); bitches 58–65cm (23–25½in). Weight: dogs 30–40kg (66–88lb); bitches 25–35kg (55–77lb).

- **COAT** Medium soft, fairly long and close to the body.

- **COLOUR** Black and gold, blond and black.

- **OTHER FEATURES** Strong head, broad, convex forehead; ears triangular and set on high, in proportion with head; body longer than height at withers; tail well feathered and carried low.

GREAT SWISS MOUNTAIN DOG

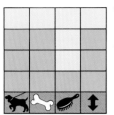

The Great Swiss Mountain Dog or Grosser Schweizer Sennenhund is the largest of four Swiss mountain dogs, of which the best known internationally is the Bernese (see page 68). All are thought to descend from Molossus dogs, brought north by ancient Roman armies, and local herding dogs, and they were used for guarding, herding and draught work. The Great Swiss, being an extremely robust dog with very strong hind-quarters, is capable of moving quite heavy loads. At the beginning of this century it was threatened with extinction, but it revived and today, like the Bernese, is used for pulling carts loaded with dairy produce. Many members of the breed have also been used for search and rescue work, particularly detecting lost people, and objects, in the mountains.

Character and care

The Great Swiss Mountain Dog is a faithful, gentle animal that is generally devoted to children. It is alert and highly intelligent and makes a fine watchdog, willing to protect its human family with its life. It is essentially a country dog that thrives in wide open spaces, and needs plenty of exercise. It requires regular grooming with a bristle brush.

KEY CHARACTERISTICS
• **CLASS** Herding. **Recognized** CKC, FCI.
• **SIZE** Height: dogs 65–70cm (25½–27½in), bitches 59.5–65cm (23½–25½in).
• **COAT** Stiff and short.
• **COLOUR** Black with bright, symmetrical russet and white markings.
• **OTHER FEATURES** Flat, broad head; brown, medium-sized eyes; triangular, medium-sized ears; moderately long, strong, straight back; tail fairly heavy and reaching to the hocks.

An attractive and easily groomed pet, the Great Swiss Mountain Dog still enjoys a return to one of its traditional duties – pulling a cart or sled.

81

APPENZELL MOUNTAIN DOG

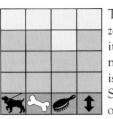

The Appenzell (Appenzeller Sennenhund) takes its name from a canton in northern Switzerland. It is one of four varieties of Swiss mountain dog, the others being the Entlebuch, the Great Swiss and, the best known internationally, the Bernese (see page 68). The Appenzell is similar in appearance to the Bernese but is generally smaller, more rectangular in shape and smooth coated.

Like all the Swiss mountain dogs, it is thought to descend from the Molossus dogs of ancient Rome, which were brought north with invading Roman soldiers, crossed with herding dogs. The Appenzell was used extensively at one time as a herding dog and to haul carts of produce to market. It is still fairly common in its native land, where there is a thriving Appenzell club, but is rarely seen in other countries.

Character and care
A resilient, intelligent dog that is easily trained, the adaptable Appenzell makes an excellent farm and rescue dog, companion and guard. It needs plenty of food and exercise, and a daily brushing.

Easily recognized by the tail curling over its back, the Appenzell is smaller and more rectangular than its cousin, the Bernese.

KEY CHARACTERISTICS
• **CLASS** Herding. **Recognized** FCI, KUSA.
• **SIZE** Height: dogs 56–58.5cm (22–23in), bitches 46–50cm (18½–20in). Weight: 22–25kg (49–55lb).
• **COAT** Short, dense and hard.
• **COLOUR** Black and tan with white markings on head, chest and feet; tail tip is always white.
• **OTHER FEATURES** Head flat, broadest between ears; brown, rather small eyes; fairly small ears set on high; strong, straight back; medium-length, strong tail carried curled over the back.

ENTLEBUCH MOUNTAIN DOG

The Entlebuch (Entlebucher Sennenhund) is named after the Swiss town and river of Entlebuch. The breed is mostly found around Lucerne and in the Bernese Emmenthal. It is the smallest of the four Swiss mountain dogs thought to be crosses between Molossus dogs, brought by the Romans, and local herding dogs.

The Entlebuch was bred to tend and drive cattle and is still sometimes used for herding.

Character and care
This good natured dog is intelligent and makes a good companion and obedience worker, provided that it has plenty of space. It needs regular grooming with a bristle brush.

KEY CHARACTERISTICS
• **CLASS** Herding. **Recognized** FCI.
• **SIZE** Height: about 51cm (20in). Weight: 25–29.7kg (55–66lb).
• **COAT** Smooth-coated, short, thick, hard and glossy.
• **COLOUR** Black, white and tan.
• **OTHER FEATURES** Top of head flat, and head in proportion to size of body; small, lively, chestnut-coloured eyes; V-shaped, pendant ears; broad, deep chest; short tail.

NORWEGIAN BUHUND

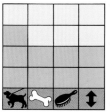

The Norwegian Buhund is a spitz type, and bears a strong resemblance to the Iceland Dog. The Icelandic Sagas (AD900–1300) record how dogs were brought to Iceland by Norwegian settlers in AD874.

In Norway, the Buhund is used as a guard and farm dog, for herding cattle, sheep and ponies, and is one of that country's national dogs. Despite its long history, it was little known outside its native land until 1920. Then it reached Britain, where it has never become really popular but does have a band of ardent devotees. It has been developing a following in other countries, but is not yet recognized in the USA.

Character and care

The Norwegian Buhund is a natural herder. It is also a gentle, friendly dog, and a natural guard and a reliable playmate for children. It needs a fair amount of exercise, and daily brushing and combing.

KEY CHARACTERISTICS
• **CLASS** Herding. **Recognized** ANKC, CKC, FCI, KC(GB), KUSA.
• **SIZE** Height: dogs about 42.5–45cm (17–18in), bitches smaller. Weight: 11.8–18.1kg (26–40lb).
• **COAT** Close, harsh and smooth, with a soft woolly undercoat.
• **COLOUR** Wheaten, black, red or wolf-sable; small symmetrical white markings permissible; black mask.
• **OTHER FEATURES** Light head, broad between the ears; ears set high; strong, short body; short, thick tail set high and carried tightly curled over back.

One of the earliest of the Nordic herding dogs, the Buhund is a good all-round working dog. It also makes an excellent pet.

The Australian Cattle Dog was purpose-bred from a number of breeds. A final cross was declared "pure" in 1893.

AUSTRALIAN KELPIE

The Australian Kelpie or Australian Sheepdog is descended from short-haired prick-eared collies imported from Scotland into Australia towards the end of the last century. The breed's ancestors are also thought to include the Old English Sheepdog. The mating of one pair of collies produced a bitch which became known as Gleeson's Kelpie. A dog called Caesar, also from imported stock, was bred to Gleeson's Kelpie and a pup from this litter was named King's Kelpie after the dam. The name Kelpie was thus adopted for the breed. In Scottish folklore, a "kelpie" is a water spirit in the form of a horse, and the Scottish writer, Robert Louis Stevenson,

refers to the "water kelpie" in his famous story *Kidnapped*, giving further credence to the breed's Scottish ancestry.

The Kelpie is a superb working sheepdog with the ability to sustain itself without water for considerable periods. It is also famed for running along the backs of the sheep to reach the head of the flock. Although it has always been well known in Australia it has come to the notice of fanciers during the 1980s, and the breed is now recognized in Britain and North America.

Character and care
The Kelpie is a fine sheepdog and makes a good, loyal companion. It requires considerable exercise and vigorous daily brushing.

AUSTRALIAN CATTLE DOG

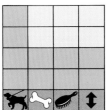

The Australian Cattle Dog is a superb worker which drives herds by nipping at the cattle's heels. The breed traces back to the now-extinct Black Bobtail, which has been described as large and rather clumsy. In 1840, new blood was introduced, including that of the extinct Smithfield, the native Dingo, the Kelpie, the Dalmatian and the blue merle Smooth Collie. The Dingo's contributions – its keen sense of smell and hearing, its stealth, speed and stamina, and its tolerance of a dry, hot climate – helped to create this unusual breed uniquely suited to the Australian outback. The addition of Kelpie made the AuCanDo an outstanding heeler as well. It has been said that ruthless culling took place during the early years of the breed, but the result has produced one of the most efficient herding dogs in the world.

At the beginning of this century, the first standard for the breed was drawn up by one Robert Kaleski and published in the *Agricultural Gazette* of New South Wales. This cattle dog was slow to become known internationally, but was recognized in the United States in 1980 and has made a welcome appearance in the British show ring over the past five years.

Character and care
The Australian Cattle Dog is intelligent and good tempered. This superlative working dog is capable of covering immense distances and so requires considerable exercise. It benefits from a vigorous daily brushing.

KEY CHARACTERISTICS
● **CLASS** Herding. **Recognized** AKC, ANKC, CKC, FCI, KC(GB), KUSA.
● **SIZE** Height at withers: dogs 46–51cm (18–20in), bitches 43–48cm (17–19in). Weight: 15.7–20.2kg (35–45lb).
● **COAT** Smooth, hard, straight, water-resistant top coat and short, dense undercoat.
● **COLOUR** Blue, blue mottled or blue speckled with or without black, blue or tan markings on head, evenly distributed for preference; there are other marking requirements; or red speckled with or without darker red markings on head.
● **OTHER FEATURES** Broad skull, slightly curved between the ears; alert, intelligent, oval-shaped eyes; moderate-sized to small ears; slightly long body; tail set low and follows slope of rump.

Born white, Australian Cattle puppies grow into medium height rangy creatures with blue or red speckled coats.

KEY CHARACTERISTICS
● **CLASS** Herding. **Recognized** AKC, ANKC, CKC, FCI, KC(GB), KUSA.
● **SIZE** Height at shoulders: about 51cm (20in). Weight: about 13.6kg (30lb).
● **COAT** A close outer coat and short, dense undercoat.
● **COLOUR** Black, black and tan, red, red and tan, fawn, chocolate and smoke blue, with or without tan.
● **OTHER FEATURES** Almond-shaped eyes; pricked ears; ribs well sprung; hindquarters show breadth and strength; at rest, tail hangs in very slight curve, when moving or excited it may be raised.

Unprepossessing to look at, the Australian Kelpie is an outstanding shepherd with strong natural herding and guarding instincts.

BEARDED COLLIE

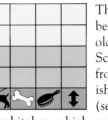

The Bearded Collie is believed to be one of the oldest herding dogs in Scotland. It is descended from three purebred Polish Lowland Sheepdogs (see page 102), a dog and two bitches, which were exchanged for a ram and a ewe brought by merchants on a trading voyage to Scotland in 1514.

A breed club was formed in Edinburgh, in 1912. Despite this, the Bearded Collie was in danger of extinction in the 1940s, but was saved by Mrs G. Willison of the former Bothkennar kennels in Ayrshire, Scotland. She obtained a Bearded bitch without pedigree in 1944 and started searching for a Bearded dog. Eventually she found one playing on the beach at Hove in East Sussex with his owners, who agreed to sell him to her. From this twosome, Jeannie and Baillie, all of today's Bearded Collies are descended.

The Bearded Collie, a delightful family dog, needs careful grooming to prevent moulting of the coat.

Character and care

The Beardie is an alert, self-confident and active dog, and is good natured and reliable with children. It makes a good pet and a first-class obedience and show dog. It enjoys plenty of exercise, and requires daily brushing, very little combing and the occasional bath.

KEY CHARACTERISTICS
• **CLASS** Herding. **Recognized** AKC, ANKC, CKC, FCI, KC(GB), KUSA.
• **SIZE** Height at withers: dogs 53–56cm (21–22in), bitches 51–53cm (20–21in). Weight: 18.1–27.2kg (40–60lb).
• **COAT** Flat, harsh and shaggy; can be slightly wavy but not curly; soft, furry, close undercoat.
• **COLOUR** Slate grey, reddish fawn, black, blue, all shades of grey, brown or sandy, with or without white markings.
• **OTHER FEATURES** Broad, flat head; eyes toning with coat colour; medium-sized, drooping ears; long body; tail set low, without a kink or twist.

BORDER COLLIE

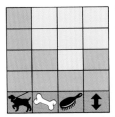

The present-day Border Collie is a descendant of working collies kept in the counties along the border of England and Scotland. It has participated in sheepdog trials since 1873, and has been exported as a working sheepdog all over the world. Bred for stamina and brains, the Border has the natural instinct to herd, and will crouch and circle from puppyhood and learn to work from more experienced dogs.

This collie has also made its mark as an unsurpassed contender in agility and obedience work. Prior to 1973, it was likely to be entered in the files of the International Sheepdog Society, and a standard for the breed was approved by the British Kennel Club in 1976. The popular Border now competes in both beauty and obedience classes in Britain.

Within the past 15 years, the Border Collie has been increasingly chosen as a domestic pet, despite being unsuited to an existence that does not offer sufficient outlet for its energy and intelligence.

Character and care

This loyal working dog requires considerable exercise but only a regular groom with a dandy brush and comb. It must be the ideal choice for anyone with their heart set on winning obedience competitions.

KEY CHARACTERISTICS
• **CLASS** Herding. **Recognized** ANKC, CKC, FCI, KC(GB), KUSA.
• **SIZE** Height: dogs about 53cm (21in), bitches slightly less. Weight: 13.6–20.2kg (30–45lb).
• **COAT** Two varieties: moderately long, and smooth; both are thick and straight.
• **COLOUR** Variety of colours permissible; white should never predominate.
• **OTHER FEATURES** Oval-shaped eyes set wide apart; medium-sized ears set wide apart; body athletic in appearance; tail moderately long.

The Border Collie is still predominantly a working dog, much in demand to herd cattle and sheep. It also excels at obedience competitions.

LANCASHIRE HEELER

The Lancashire Heeler has been known in its native county of England for many years as a sporting dog and dispeller of vermin. As its name suggests, it was developed to herd cattle by nipping at their heels, but also has strong terrier instincts and is an excellent rabbiter and ratter. It is a small dog, and its coat is black with tan markings. The breed was little known outside the north of England

The Lancashire Heeler is a small black and tan dog bred from Corgis and Manchester Terriers for its cattle-driving potential.

prior to the 1980s. It was granted an interim standard by the British Kennel Club in 1986, and happily, breed members are now beginning to appear at dog training classes and in local exemption shows as well as at championship events.

Character and care
The Lancashire Heeler is a happy, affectionate little dog, which gets on well with humans and other pets. It requires an average amount of exercise and daily brushing.

KEY CHARACTERISTICS
• **CLASS** Herding. **Recognized** FCI, KC(GB), KUSA.
• **SIZE** Height at shoulders: dogs 30cm (12in), bitches 25cm (10in). Average weight: 3.5–5.4kg (8–12lb).
• **COAT** Short and smooth.
• **COLOUR** Black and tan, with rich tan markings on muzzle, in spots on cheeks and often above eyes, from knees downwards, with desirable thumb-mark above feet, inside legs and under tail.
• **OTHER FEATURES** Richness of tan may fade with age. White to be discouraged, except for a very small white spot on forechest which is permitted but not desirable.

OLD ENGLISH SHEEPDOG

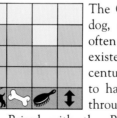

The Old English Sheepdog, or Bobtail as it is often called, has been in existence in Britain for centuries. It is believed to have been developed through the crossing of the Briard with the Russian Owtcharka, which in turn is related to the Hungarian sheepdogs. An early example is portrayed in a painting of 1771 by Gainsborough. The breed club for the Bobtail was set up in Britain as long ago as 1888, and its standard has altered little since then. In the past it was used as a drover's dog and for defending flocks of sheep. In the early 18th century in Britain drovers' dogs were exempt from taxes, and their tails were docked as a means of identification,

hence the name Bobtail. In recent years the breed has enjoyed overwhelming popularity as a pet and show dog, owed in part to its frequent appearances in advertisements.

Character and care
The Old English Sheepdog is a kindly dog, which gets on well with people, children and other animals. The breed is of sound temperament and, provided that it has sufficient space and is adequately exercised, makes a splendid pet. However, parents of young children who wanted a dog "like the one on television" have sometimes found the breed too much to handle because it is fairly large, heavy and exuberant. Bobtails are also popular show dogs but do require many hours of grooming in preparation for exhibition.

SHETLAND SHEEPDOG

A small Collie-type dog with a handsome ruff, the Shetland Sheepdog, or "Sheltie", makes a most agreeable family pet.

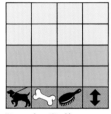

The Shetland Sheepdog or Sheltie originated in the Shetland islands off the north coast of Scotland where it has bred true for more than 135 years. It resembles a Rough Collie in miniature, with its thick double coat to protect it from the elements in its rigorous native habitat. It is believed to descend from working collies, the Iceland or Yakki Dogs which sometimes reached these islands on whalers and, possibly, the black and tan King Charles Spaniel.

The Sheltie was recognized by the British Kennel Club in 1909 and a breed club was formed in 1914.

Character and care

The Shetland Sheepdog is an excellent choice of family pet for those seeking an intelligent, faithful dog which enjoys exercise, gets on well with children and makes a fine show and obedience animal. It requires daily grooming using a stiff bristled brush and a comb. Despite having originated in cold climes, it should not be kennelled outside.

KEY CHARACTERISTICS
• **CLASS** Herding. **Recognized** AKC, ANKC, CKC, FCI, KC(GB), KUSA.
• **SIZE** Height at withers: dogs about 37cm (14½in), bitches about 35.5cm (14in).
• **COAT** Outer coat of long, straight, harsh-textured hair; soft, short-haired, close undercoat.
• **COLOUR** Sable, tricolour, blue merle, black and white, and black and tan.
• **OTHER FEATURES** Refined head, with medium-sized, almond-shaped eyes, obliquely set; ears small and moderately wide at base; muscular, arched neck; back level; tail set low and tapering towards tip.

KEY CHARACTERISTICS
• **CLASS** Herding. **Recognized** AKC, ANKC, CKC, FCI, KC(GB), KUSA.
• **SIZE** Height at withers: dogs 55.8cm (22in), bitches 53.3cm (21in). Minimum weight: 29.7kg (66lb).
• **COAT** Profuse but not excessive, and a good harsh texture.
• **COLOUR** Any shade of grey, grizzle or blue is acceptable.
• **OTHER FEATURES** Head in proportion to body; eyes set well apart; small ears carried flat to the side of the head; short, compact body; tail docked close to body.

SMOOTH COLLIE

The Smooth Collie is identical to the Rough Collie except in coat, that of the Smooth being short and flat, with a harsh-textured top coat and a very dense under-coat. Both Collies' ancestors were brought over 400 years ago from Iceland to Scotland, where the breed worked as a sheepdog. Like the Roughs, the modern Smooth Collie can trace its ancestry to a tricolour dog called "Trefoil", which was born in 1873. The breed was exhibited alongside its more glamorous long-haired relative in the show ring until 1974, when the Smooth Collie was eventually given a separate standard.

Sadly, although the Smooth Collie has all the attributes of the Rough, it is seldom seen. However, the variety does have a dedicated small band of followers and there are many excellent examples with first-class temperament in the beauty and obedience rings.

Character and care

The Smooth Collie has the same character and temperament as the Rough, and its care requirements are also the same.

KEY CHARACTERISTICS
● **CLASS** Herding. **Recognized** AKC, ANKC, CKC, FCI, KC(GB), KUSA.
● **SIZE** Height at the shoulders: dogs 56–65cm (22–26in), bitches 51–60cm (20–24in). Weight: dogs 20.5–33.7kg (45–75lb), bitches 18–29.5kg (40–65lb).
● **COAT** Short, harsh and smooth with a dense undercoat.
● **COLOUR** Sable and white, tricolour, blue merle (not permissible in UK).
● **OTHER FEATURES** Head should appear light in proportion to body; medium-sized, almond-shaped eyes; ears small and not too close together; body slightly long in relation to height; long tail usually carried low.

Rough and Smooth Collies – both sometimes referred to as Scotch Collies – are really the same breed, and are identical except for their coats. The Smooth Collie is today much rarer than its long-haired stablemate.

ROUGH COLLIE

More challenging to groom, the Rough Collie rose to fame on the strength of the Lassie films.

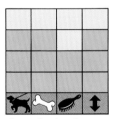

The Rough Collie, sometimes called the Scots or Scottish Collie, is still best known as the star of the "Lassie" films. This breed's ancestors were introduced into Britain from Iceland more than 400 years ago. The word "colley" is a Scottish term for a sheep with a black face and legs, and the breed worked as a sheepdog in the Highlands of Scotland for centuries.

In 1860, Queen Victoria admired the Rough Collie while on a visit to Balmoral, Scotland, and installed some breed members in the royal kennels at Windsor. In that same year, a Rough Collie was exhibited at a show in Birmingham, England, but its finer points were not agreed upon until some 25 years later. The beauty of the breed was enhanced, perhaps by the introduction of some Borzoi and Gordon Setter blood. The breed is no longer required to work, although it retains its intelligence, hardiness and keen eyesight.

Character and care

The Rough Collie makes an excellent guard, being suspicious of strangers. It is supremely loyal and affectionate to its owners, a joy to train and usually reliable with children. The breed needs a lot of exercise but, despite its thick coat, it is not difficult to groom.

KEY CHARACTERISTICS
• **CLASS** Herding. **Recognized** AKC, ANKC, CKC, FCI, KC(GB), KUSA.
• **SIZE** Height at shoulders: dogs 56–65cm (22–26in), bitches 51–60cm (20–24in). Weight: dogs 20.5–33.7kg (45–75lb), bitches 18–29.5kg (40–65lb).
• **COAT** Very dense, straight outer coat harsh to touch, with soft, furry, very close undercoat.
• **COLOUR** Sable and white, tricolour, blue merle (not permissible in UK).
• **OTHER FEATURES** Head should appear light in proportion to body; medium-sized, almond-shaped eyes; ears small, not too close together; body slightly long in relation to height; long tail.

WELSH CORGIS (PEMBROKE AND CARDIGAN)

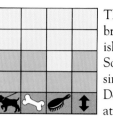

The Welsh Corgi Pembroke, a favourite of British royalty, has worked in South Wales at least since the time of the Domesday Book, instigated by William the Conqueror in the 11th century. Its job was to control the movement of cattle by nipping their ankles, which is an inherent characteristic as many protectors of the British royal family have discovered to their cost. The breed may have been introduced to Wales by Flemish weavers who settled in the area and crossed their own dogs with local stock, or it may descend from the Swedish Vallhund.

The rarer Welsh Corgi Cardigan, which has a similar history to the more popular Pembroke, is said to have a slightly more equable temperament. It is readily distinguishable from the tailless or docked Pembroke by its

Until the 1930s the two Welsh Corgis were inter-bred, and there is still today little difference between them. The better known Pembroke has straighter legs and a foxy face.

fox-like brush. The Welsh Corgis were first exhibited in Britain in 1925 and the Pembroke and Cardigan received separate classification in 1934. Both have among the keenest and most dedicated groups of exhibitors in the United Kingdom, and their classes are almost invariably of high standard.

Character and care

Corgis are extremely active and devoted little dogs, and are usually good with children. They make fine guards, and excellent show and obedience dogs. They have a tendency to put on weight if under-exercised, and their water-resistant coats need daily brushing.

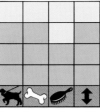

The Cardigan is heavier boned and larger bodied than the Pembroke, and easily distinguished by its long, bushy tail.

KEY CHARACTERISTICS
● **CLASS** Herding.   **Recognized** AKC, ANKC, CKC, FCI, KC(GB), KUSA.
● **SIZE** *Pembroke* Height at shoulders: about 25.5–30.5cm (10–12in). Weight: dogs about 12kg (27lb), bitches about 11.3kg (25lb). *Cardigan* Height at withers: 26–31cm (10½–12½in). Weight: dogs 13.6–17.2kg (30–38lb), bitches 11.3–15.3kg (25–34lb).
● **COAT** *Pembroke* Medium length and straight, with a dense undercoat; never soft, wavy or wiry. *Cardigan* Short or medium length, with a hard texture, and weatherproof; short, thick undercoat.
● **COLOUR** *Pembroke* Red, sable, fawn or black and tan, with or without white markings on legs, brisket and neck; some white on head and foreface permissible. *Cardigan* Any, with or without white markings, but white should not predominate.
● **OTHER FEATURES** *Pembroke* Head foxy in shape and appearance; firm, upright ears with slightly rounded points; deep chest and moderately long body; short tail, docked if necessary. *Cardigan* Head foxy in shape and appearance; medium-sized eyes; upright ears; chest moderately broad with prominent breast bone; tail bushy and set in line with body.

PYRENEAN SHEPHERDS

The Pyrenean Shepherds or Bergers des Pyrénées may be indigenous to the area, or are descendants of the Catalonian Shepherd. However, it is generally thought that they derive from Eastern shepherd dogs whose coats and abilities were adapted to the harsh conditions in the Pyrenean mountains on the border between France and Spain. The task of these sheepdogs was to herd flocks, while the much larger and heavier Pyrenean Mountain Dog or Great Pyrenees defended the flocks against predators. These lively herders are also protective of owners' property.

There are two varieties of Pyrenean Shepherd: one with long to medium-length hair all over, and the Smooth-faced Shepherd (Berger des Pyrénées à Face Rase), which has medium-length hair over most of its body but short hair on its face and the front of its legs. Both are still used for herding and are kept as companion dogs and watchdogs.

Character and care
These intelligent workers have a considerable amount of nervous energy and can be kept as pets, but are best given a job to do. The Smooth-faced Shepherd is easier to train, and likely to be more companionable and less aggressive to strangers. They require daily brushing and very little combing.

KEY CHARACTERISTICS
● **CLASS** Herding.   **Recognized** FCI, KC(GB), KUSA.
● **SIZE** *Pyrenean Shepherd* Height: dogs 39.5–49.5cm (15½–19½in), bitches 38–49.5cm (15–19½in). *Smooth-faced Shepherd* Height: dogs 40.5–53.5cm (16–21in), bitches 40.5–52cm (16–20½in). Weight: 8.2–13.6kg (18–30lb).
● **COAT** Short or medium length.
● **COLOUR** Harlequin, black, salt and pepper, fawn in various shades.
● **OTHER FEATURES** Head strong; dark eyes; ears set on fairly high; body square; tail may be docked.

The Briard – official dog of the French army – developed as a large herding dog which could also protect livestock.

PICARDY SHEPHERD

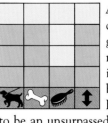

Also known as the Berger de Picard, this breed has guarded flocks in its native France since time immemorial. It is said to be probably the oldest French herding dog and to be an unsurpassed worker with both sheep and cattle. It is a medium-sized, shaggy, somewhat rustic-looking dog and, when 12 Picards were entered in a dog show in Amiens in 1899, the eminent judge of sheepdogs refused to recognize them. Despite this the breed flourished until the First World War when its numbers were seriously depleted.

They built up again in the 1920s, only to have a further setback during the Second World War. In the 1950s, the breed finally revived and since then some fine examples have appeared in the show ring.

Character and care
The Picardy is an energetic, affectionate animal which superbly combines the role of working dog with that of family companion, and is almost always trustworthy with and devoted to children. It requires plenty of space and exercise, and regular brushing.

BRIARD

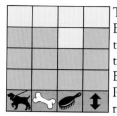

The Briard, or Berger de Brie, is the best known of the French sheepdogs, the others being the Beauce, Picardy and Pyrenean. The Briard is reputed to have come to Europe with Asian invaders before the end of the Middle Ages, along with other breeds of sheepdog such as the Hungarian Komondor and Kuvasz and the Russian Owtcharka, which have similar conformation.

"Les Amis du Briard" was formed around 1900 when a standard of sorts was drawn up. However, it was not approved until 1925 and then was amended in 1930. The Briard Club was formed in about 1928. By this time the breed had already become known in other parts of the world, partly through its work in the French Army during the First World War, when it carried ammunition and was employed by the Red Cross.

It is widely believed to have been introduced into the US during the 18th century, possibly by the Marquis de Lafayette or Thomas Jefferson. The first litter was registered with the AKC in 1922.

Character and care

The Briard has a gentle nature and makes a good family pet or farm dog, provided sufficient space is available. It is good with children, intelligent and fearless. It is a breed that takes pride in cleaning itself, but needs regular brushing. Like all sheepdogs, it requires plenty of exercise, and is not suited to a cramped environment.

KEY CHARACTERISTICS
• **CLASS** Herder. **Recognized** AKC, ANKC, CKC, FCI, KC(GB), KUSA.
• **SIZE** Height at withers: dogs 57.5–67.5cm (23–27in), bitches 55–64cm (22–25½in). Weight: about 33.7kg (75lb).
• **COAT** Long and slightly wavy, and dry to the touch, with a fine, dense undercoat.
• **COLOUR** Solid black, or with white hairs scattered through black coat; fawn in all its shades, darker shades preferred; fawns may have dark shading on ears, muzzle, back and tail.
• **OTHER FEATURES** Strong, slightly rounded skull; dark eyes, set wide apart and horizontally placed; ears set on high; back firm and level; broad chest; long well-feathered tail that has an upward hook at the tip.

With its rounded head and widely set eyes, the Briard looks out through a dense curtain of hair.

KEY CHARACTERISTICS
• **CLASS** Herding. **Recognized** FCI.
• **SIZE** Height at withers: dogs 61–66cm (24–26in), bitches 5cm (2in) less. Weight: 22.6–31.7kg (50–70lb).
• **COAT** Hard and moderate in length, with a heavy undercoat.
• **COLOUR** All shades of grey and fawn; white allowed only in spot on the chest and toes.
• **OTHER FEATURES** Large head with strong muzzle; dark eyes; ears carried erect; sturdy body; tail curved at the tip.

BELGIAN SHEPHERD DOGS

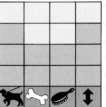

This breed includes four varieties: the Groenendael (long-coated black), the Tervueren (long-coated other than black), the Malinois (smooth-coated) and the Laekenois (wire-coated). All were developed from the many sheepdogs of varying colours and sizes that existed in Belgium towards the end of the 19th century. In about 1890, Monsieur Rose of the Café du Groenendael discovered a black, long-coated bitch in a litter. He bought a similar dog and, by selective breeding and considerable culling, produced the Groenendael, the most popular variety of Belgian Shepherd Dog. Further work began in 1891, when a collection of Belgian Sheepdogs was gathered at the Brussels Veterinary University. There it was agreed to recognize and develop three varieties and a fourth was subsequently added. They are recognized as separate breeds everywhere except in the UK.

First to establish type among the motley of Belgian Shepherd Dogs was the Malinois, which is named after its region of origin, Malines.

Character and care

The medium-sized, well-proportioned, intelligent and attentive Belgian Shepherd Dog works well in obedience trials and makes an excellent guard. It is very protective, and can be kept in the home provided time is set aside for early training. It needs plenty of exercise and regular grooming.

The Laekenois, today the rarest of the four breeds, comes from the district of Boom, near Antwerp, which is noted for its fine linens.

The long-haired Tervueren, also named after its region of origin, was developed by a local breeder. The Tervueren fawn factor occasionally occurs in a litter of light coloured Groenendaels, yielding a cuckoo in the nest.

With its distinguished war history, the Groenendael is today the most numerous and popular of the Belgian Shepherd Dogs.

KEY CHARACTERISTICS

- **CLASS** Herding.
  Recognized AKC, ANKC, CKC, FCI, KC(GB), KUSA.

- **SIZE** Height: dogs 61–66cm (24–26in), bitches 56–61cm (22–24in). Weight: about 27.9kg (62lb).

- **COAT** *Groenendael* Long, straight and abundant, with an extremely dense undercoat. *Tervueren* Long, straight and abundant, with an extremely dense undercoat. *Malinois* Very short on head, exterior of ears and lower parts of legs, short on rest of body. *Laekenois* Harsh, wiry and dry.

- **COLOUR** *Groenendael* Black; black with limited white – small to moderate patch or strip on chest, between pads of feet and on tips of hind toes; frosting (white or grey) on muzzle. *Tervueren* All shades of red, fawn, grey, with black overlap. *Malinois* All shades of red, fawn, grey, with black overlap. *Laekenois* Reddish fawn with black shading, principally on muzzle and tail.

- **OTHER FEATURES** Finely chiselled head; medium-sized eyes; ears distinctly triangular in appearance, stiff and erect; powerful but elegant body, broad-chested; medium-length tail, firmly set on and strong at the base.

97

BERGAMASCO

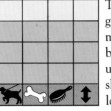

The Bergamasco or Bergamese Shepherd is a medium-sized, squarely built dog with soft, pendulous ears, almond-shaped slanted eyes and a long, rather harsh, wavy coat. Its ancestors almost certainly include the rather similar French Briard. Named after the city of Bergamo in northern Italy, the Bergamasco has worked for centuries in Italy, herding and guarding flocks. Unfortunately, relatively few Italian livestock keepers still use, or attempt to perpetuate, this fine sheepdog and its numbers are small. The breed is not well known outside its native country and it has yet really to make its mark upon the show rings of the world.

Character and care

The Bergamasco is a courageous, docile and loyal working dog. In common with all sheepdogs, it needs plenty of exercise. The cords of its coat need to be separated by hand and brushed and combed.

KEY CHARACTERISTICS
• **CLASS** Herding. **Recognized** FCI, KC(GB).
• **SIZE** Height: dogs about 61cm (24in), bitches about 56cm (22in). Weight: dogs 32–38kg (70–84lb), bitches 26–32kg (57–70lb).
• **COAT** Wiry at front, soft at back, very long with matted curls.
• **COLOUR** Solid shades of grey from light to almost black; solid white is not allowed, and white markings should not cover more than 20% of the coat.
• **OTHER FEATURES** Long head; large eyes; soft, thin ears; large chest; tail set on in last third of the rump, thick and robust at root.

BEAUCE SHEPHERD

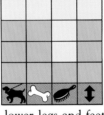

The Beauce Shepherd, also known as the Beauceron, Berger de Beauce, French Short-haired Shepherd or the Red Stocking (because of the tan markings on its lower legs and feet), could be mistaken for a Doberman and may have played a part in the development of that breed.

The Beauce is an ancient French breed, thought to have evolved from fiercer rough-coated stock, and bred to form the modern type. First used as a hunter of wild boar and later as a herder and guard of livestock, today it is often kept solely as a companion and guard. It has been exhibited since 1897 and is one of the most popular dogs in France.

Character and care

While retaining its herding instincts, the Beauce Shepherd is easily trained, good tempered but distrustful of strangers. It is not a house dog. It requires plenty of exercise and its short, smooth coat needs daily brushing. Its ears are cropped in its country of origin.

KEY CHARACTERISTICS
• **CLASS** Herding. **Recognized** FCI.
• **SIZE** Height: dogs 63.5–71cm (25–28in), bitches 61–68.5cm (24–27in). Weight: 29.7–38kg (66–85lb).
• **COAT** Reasonably short, close and dense.
• **COLOUR** Black with rich tan markings on face and legs and under tail; harlequin; or tricolour – grey with black patches and tan markings.
• **OTHER FEATURES** Long, flat head; blackish-brown eyes; ears set on high, pendant or, most usually, cropped; straight back; broad, well-arched loins; long tail curving slightly towards the end.

MAREMMA SHEEPDOG

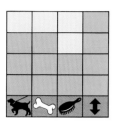

The Maremma Sheepdog has two names in its native Italy because for centuries the shepherd dogs spent from June until October in the Abruzzi, where there was good summer grazing, and from October until June in the Maremma. Called both Pastore Abruzzese and Pastore Maremmano, some people thought that they were two different breeds. Then, about 25 years ago at a meeting in Florence, the eminent judge, Professor Giuseppe Solaro, drew up a single breed standard under the name of Pastore Maremmano Abruzzese.

The Maremma has never worked sheep like the Border Collie, but defended the flock against wolves and bears. The first record of a Maremma Sheepdog appeared 2000 years ago when Columella (c. AD65) made reference to a white dog and Marcus Varro (116–27BC) produced a standard for a sheepdog almost identical to that for the Maremma of today. The breed has been known in the United Kingdom since 1872.

Character and care

The Maremma is a natural guard that will never forget a kindness or an injury. To quote an Italian expert, "If you want obedience and submission keep away from our breed, but if you appreciate friendship given and received, a trace of humour and much teaching of the lore of the wild, a typical Maremmano is the best you can have." The Maremma should be regularly groomed using a wire dog brush and, occasionally, a good cleansing powder.

KEY CHARACTERISTICS
• **CLASS** Herding. **Recognized** ANKC, CKC, FCI, KC(GB), KUSA.
• **SIZE** Height: dogs 65–73cm (25½–28½in), bitches 60–68cm (23½–26½in). Weight: dogs 35–45kg (77–99lb), bitches 30–40kg (66–88lb).
• **COAT** Long, plentiful and rather harsh; never curly.
• **COLOUR** All white.
• **OTHER FEATURES** Head conical in shape and appears large in proportion to body; bold eyes; ears small in proportion to head; strong, well-muscled body; tail set on low.

The Maremma is the serene master of all he surveys.

The Maremma is an ancient breed, descended from the original flock guarding dogs of the Middle East.

GERMAN SHEPHERD DOG

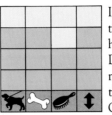

It has been suggested that the German Shepherd Dog (Alsatian or Deutscher Schäferhund) may be a descendant of the Bronze Age wolf. Certainly, around the 7th century AD, there existed in Germany a shepherd dog of similar type but with a lighter coat. By the 16th century, the coat is said to have darkened appreciably.

The German Shepherd was first exhibited at a dog show in Hanover in 1882. Credit for the formation of the modern breed is generally attributed to the German fancier, Rittmeister von Stephanitz, who worked tirelessly in the early 1900s to improve its temperament and conformation. The breed won dedicated fanciers in other countries, including Britain and America, among those who had seen the breed working in Germany in the First World War. It was at that time thought inappropriate to call the breed by a name that included the word "German", and it became known in the United Kingdom, and elsewhere, as the Alsatian because it had originated in the Alsace. In 1971, the British Kennel Club finally relented and the name German Shepherd Dog was restored.

Character and care

The popular German Shepherd is extremely intelligent and makes a first-class companion, show dog, obedience worker and guard. It is eminently trainable and so works as a police dog, in the armed services, as a guide dog for the blind, and in numerous other capacities. Its superior guarding ability can get it into trouble, because it may misread a sign and spring to its owner's defence. However, with knowledgeable handling and training it is a splendid canine companion. It needs vigorous daily grooming, plenty of exercise and, above all, a job to do, even if this only entails competing in obedience or agility tests. It is unfair and unwise for this intelligent animal to be subjected to a life of boredom.

Perhaps the most widely recognized of all breeds, the German Shepherd Dog is a versatile worker, renowned for its strength and agility.

KEY CHARACTERISTICS

- **CLASS** Herding.
  Recognized AKC, ANKC, CKC, FCI, KC(GB), KUSA.

- **SIZE** Height at top of shoulders: dogs 60–65cm (24–26in), bitches 55–60cm (22–24in). Weight: 33.7–42.7kg (75–95lb).

- **COAT** Medium length, straight, hard and close-lying, with a dense, thick undercoat.

- **COLOUR** Solid black or grey; black saddle with tan or gold to light grey markings; grey with lighter or brown markings (referred to as sables). Blues, livers, albinos and whites highly undesirable (a light-coated German Shepherd is included in the breed standards of some overseas countries).

- **OTHER FEATURES** Strong head; medium-sized eyes and ears; relatively long neck; long shoulder blades; straight back; strong hindquarters, broad and well muscled; long, bushy tail.

There is some colour variation among German Shepherd Dogs, with the familiar sable background with a black saddle being most prevalent. All white coloration is not acceptable in the show ring.

DUTCH SHEPHERDS

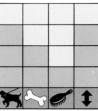

There are three varieties of Dutch Shepherd or Hollandse Herdershond, which differ only in coat and colour: the Short-haired, Long-haired and Wire-haired. Anatomically they are close to the Belgian Shepherd dogs, and, like them, probably descend from a variety of sheepdog breeds. They are recognized as separate breeds in their native Holland, but are rare elsewhere.

The Dutch Shepherds worked for many years as herding dogs. When the demand for this work lessened, they declined, but have now become quite popular again. They are kept as housepets, utilized as guard dogs, for police work, as guide dogs for the blind, and are known to be worthy retrievers.

Character and care

These obedient, hardy and trustworthy dogs make excellent guards, and are impervious to bad weather. They may be kept as pets, but preferably in rural surroundings, and are best kennelled out of doors. The Wire-haired's coat moults twice a year and must then be stripped, or plucked, using finger and thumb. All three types need daily brushing.

KEY CHARACTERISTICS

- **CLASS** Herding.
  Recognized FCI.

- **SIZE** Height at withers: dogs 58.5–63.5cm (23–25in), bitches 54.5–62cm (21½–24½in). Weight: about 29.7kg (66lb).

- **COAT** *Short-haired* Hard, woolly and not too short. *Long-haired* Long and rather stiff, lying close to the body. *Wire-haired* Hard and wiry all over body with little waviness, and close, woolly undercoat except on head.

- **COLOUR** *Short-haired* and *Long-haired* Gold or silver with streaks of black. *Wire-haired* Blue-black or grey-black.

- **OTHER FEATURES** Head in proportion to body and not coarse; dark, medium-sized, almond-shaped eyes; ears small in proportion to head, stiff and erect; solid body; tail carried low, with slight curve in it in repose, high in action.

HUNGARIAN PULI

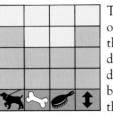

The Puli (plural Pulik), one of the best known of the Hungarian sheep-dogs, is said to be a descendant of sheepdogs brought to Hungary by the Magyars over 1000 years ago. It has herded sheep on the edge of the Hungarian plain for many centuries and, more recently, has been used for police work. In 1935, the Puli was imported into the United States by the Department of Agriculture with the aim of improving local sheep- and cattle-herding breeds. However, the Puli was not recognized by the American Kennel Club until 1936. The breed has been in Britain for the past 20 years and now attracts a reasonable number of show entries.

Character and care

The Puli is a loyal, devoted, obedient and intelligent dog, which is good with other pets and slow to anger. It is, however, reserved with humans outside its own family. The breed requires a good amount of exercise and the cords of its coat, which give it a somewhat unkempt look, have to be separated by hand, brushed and combed.

KEY CHARACTERISTICS
• **CLASS** Herding. **Recognized** AKC, ANKC, CKC, FCI, KC(GB), KUSA.
• **SIZE** Height at withers: dogs 40–44cm (16–17½in), bitches 37–41cm (14½–16in). Weight: dogs 13–15kg (28½–33lb), bitches 10–13kg (22–28½lb).
• **COAT** Dense and weatherproof; outer coat wavy or curly, undercoat soft and woolly; correct proportion of each creates the desired cords.
• **COLOUR** Black, rusty black, white or various shades of grey and apricot, overall appearance of solid colour.
• **OTHER FEATURES** Small, fine head with slightly domed skull; medium-sized eyes; ears set slightly below top of skull; withers slightly higher than level of back; medium-length tail curling over loins.

POLISH LOWLAND SHEEPDOG

The Polish Lowland Sheepdog is also known as the Valee Shepherd Dog and the Owczarek Nizinny. It looks very much like the Old English Sheepdog and the Bearded Collie, which is descended from it. It probably resulted from crossing the Hungarian Puli with other herding breeds during the 16th century, with the aim of producing a natural herder and an animal with a tough, weather-resistant coat suitable for the harsh Polish climate. This sheepdog has been granted an interim breed standard by the British Kennel Club within the past five years and has begun to make its mark on the European show scene.

Character and care

This efficient herding dog is easily trained and generally good natured. A reasonable amount of exercise is essential, as is daily grooming with a brush and a steel comb.

KEY CHARACTERISTICS
• **CLASS** Herder. **Recognized** ANKC, FCI, KC(GB), KUSA.
• **SIZE** Height at withers: dogs 43–52cm (17–20in), bitches 40–46cm (16–18½in).
• **COAT** Long, dense, thick and shaggy with a harsh texture; soft undercoat.
• **COLOUR** All colours and markings are acceptable.
• **OTHER FEATURES** Medium-sized head and eyes; body rectangular in shape rather than square when viewed from side; often born without a tail, otherwise tail docked.

Still seen with flocks in present-day Hungary, the Puli is ideally clad for herding in Central Europe.

PUMI

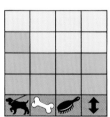

A Hungarian breed, the Pumi was developed by crossing the Hungarian Puli with straight-eared French and German herding dogs in the 17th and 18th centuries. It also has some ancient terrier blood, which is apparent in its looks and temperament. It was originally bred to drive cattle, but is now used mainly as a herder and often as a guard. The Pumi looks unkempt but appealing, with semi-erect ears and a long, shaggy coat. Its eyes and muzzle are barely visible and the tail, which curls over the back, is naturally short or docked. It is rarely seen outside its country of origin.

Character and care

The Pumi is a lively, high-spirited, rather noisy dog, which is loyal to its owner and makes a good herder and watchdog. It can be very aggressive with strangers. It should be groomed with a slicker brush.

KEY CHARACTERISTICS
• **CLASS** Herding. **Recognized** FCI.
• **SIZE** Height at withers: 33–44.5cm (13–17½in). Weight: 8–13kg (17½–28½lb).
• **COAT** Medium-length and curling, tangled but not matted.
• **COLOUR** All shades of grey, also black or chestnut.
• **OTHER FEATURES** Muzzle small in proportion to head; ears like upside-down Vs; coffee-coloured eyes; square body; tail customarily docked.

ANATOLIAN SHEPHERD DOG

The Anatolian Shepherd Dog, previously known as the Anatolian Karabash, has existed for centuries, from the Anatolian plateau of Turkey right across Afghanistan. Such large, powerful and heavy headed dogs have lived in the area since Babylonian times (2800–1800BC) and were once used as war dogs and to hunt big game such as lions and even horses. However, their more usual job was to guard sheep, and shepherds would crop their ears and fit them with spiked collars to help them defend flocks from predators. They still perform this task today, watching flocks from high ground and then, at the slightest suspicion of trouble, splitting up and converging silently upon the scene at great speed.

Character and care
This powerful, loyal and loving dog is good with children, makes a fine watchdog and is eminently trainable. However, it cannot be kept in a confined space, is not suited to town life and does not take kindly to strangers. It requires considerable exercise and, although the breed has a natural ability to keep itself clean, it should be brushed regularly.

A black mask and black-fringed ears are identifying features in a breed which varies considerably in colour.

KEY CHARACTERISTICS
• **CLASS** Herding. **Recognized** ANKC, FCI, KC(GB), KUSA.
• **SIZE** Height at shoulders: dogs 74–81cm (29–32in), bitches 71–79cm (28–31in). Weight: dogs 50–64kg (110–141lb), bitches 41–59kg (90½–130lb).
• **COAT** Short and dense, with a thick undercoat.
• **COLOUR** All colours acceptable, but most desirable is solid cream to fawn with black mask and ears.
• **OTHER FEATURES** Large, broad head, flat between the ears; small eyes; medium-sized, triangular ears rounded at the tips; deep chest; long tail.

A big, powerful breed, the Anatolian Shepherd Dog will guard flocks tirelessly in extremes of heat or cold.

RUSSIAN SHEEPDOG

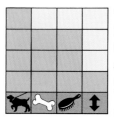

There are four breeds of Russian Sheepdog or Owtcharka: the Mid-Asian, the South Russian, the Steppe and the Transcaucasian. All are descendants of spitz breeds crossed with local dogs to produce types suited to the requirements and climatic conditions of the area in which they were bred. They are all excellent herding and guarding dogs, and are also often employed to protect military camps and installations. The Owtcharka are rarely seen outside their country of origin, and particularly little is known about the rare Steppe Owtcharka.

The South Russian Owtcharka, which originated in the Crimean area, resembles an Old English Sheepdog. The Mid-Asian Owtcharka is a more powerful animal, designed to defend the herd against wolves and robbers, and likely to have Mastiff blood in its ancestry. The Transcaucasian comes from around the Caucasus Mountains, and, like the Mid-Asian, it has Mastiff ancestors. Its long tail is rarely docked. The Steppe (North Caucasian) is found in the desert regions of North Caucasia and the low country round the Caspian Sea. It is a squarely built dog, lighter in the body and longer in the leg than the Transcaucasian.

Character and care
Although said to be easy to train and intelligent, these dogs are strong-willed, fearless guards and are unlikely to be suitable as pets. The South Russian is reputed to be the most biddable of the four. All need abundant exercise and regular brushing.

KEY CHARACTERISTICS
• **CLASS** Herding. **Recognized** FCI.
• **SIZE** Height at withers: *South Russian* about 51cm (20in); *Mid-Asian* 61–66cm (24–26in); *Transcaucasian* about 66cm (26in); *Steppe* no height recorded.
• **COAT** *South Russian* Long and dense. *Mid-Asian* Hard and straight. *Transcaucasian* Long, dense and rough. *Steppe* Short.
• **COLOUR** *South Russian* White or pale grey, with or without small white or fawn spots. *Mid-Asian* black white, grey, fawn or brindle. *Transcaucasian* White, fawn, grey, tan or brindle, solid or combination of colours. *Steppe* Various.
• **OTHER FEATURES** *Mid-Asian* often has ears cropped and tail docked.

RUMANIAN SHEPHERD DOG

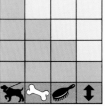

This breed is reputed to be descended from the Greek Simocyon which, in turn, is related to the ancient Molossus. Large and powerful with a massive head, the Rumanian Shepherd looks rather like a Saint Bernard. It has been used to hunt wolf and bear, and is still kept extensively in its native land as a flock guard. It was recognized by the Rumanian Kennel Club in 1937, but is little known outside its country of origin.

Character and care
The Rumanian Shepherd is kept for its working abilities rather than as a domestic pet. It makes a fine guard, being loyal to its owner and distrustful of strangers. It needs regular exercise, and its heavy coat requires regular brushing.

KEY CHARACTERISTICS
• **CLASS** Herding. **Recognized** AKC, ANKC, CKC, FCI, KC(GB), KUSA
• **SIZE** Height at shoulders: 63.5–66cm (25–26in). Weight: 50kg (110lb).
• **COAT** Medium-length, soft and smooth; onger on flanks and hindquarters.
• **COLOUR** White, or tricolour, sable with darker head points, black and tan, and various brindles.
• **OTHER FEATURES** Distinct stoop and slightly domed skull; dark amber eyes; small ears set wide apart, rather low and folded back; tail usually medium length, but may be docked very short.

GUNDOGS

CHESAPEAKE BAY RETRIEVER

The ancestry of the Chesapeake Bay Retriever is less obscure than that of many breeds. Indeed, its origins can be pinpointed to 1807, when an English brig was shipwrecked off the coast of Maryland. An American ship, the *Canton*, rescued the English crew and two Newfoundland puppies. One puppy was a male called Sinbad, which has been described as dingy red in colour, while the other was a black bitch, which became known as Canton after the rescue ship. The pups were presented to the families that had given shelter to the English sailors and were trained as duck retrievers. In time, they mated with various working breeds in the Chesapeake Bay area. It is likely that the cross bloods added were those of the Otterhound and the Curly-coated and Flat-coated Retrievers. The matings produced a variety with the swimming ability of the Newfoundland and the duck retrieving abilities of local dogs.

Until fairly recently, the Chesapeake Bay Retriever was kept strictly as a sporting dog. However, it is now finding its way into the family home and becoming a contender in the show ring.

Character and care

The Chesapeake is good natured and does well in field trials. It has an oily coat which needs regular brushing and gives off a slight, but not unpleasant, odour. It has yellow-orange eyes. Like all gundogs it needs plenty of exercise and does best in an environment where it has space to roam freely.

The reddish-brown coat of this Chesapeake Bay Retriever clearly shows the typical waviness on the neck, back and loins.

Yellow-amber eyes are a characteristic of this retriever.

KEY CHARACTERISTICS

- **CLASS** Gundog.
  Recognized AKC, ANKC, CKC, FCI, KC(GB), KUSA.

- **SIZE** Height: dogs 58.4–66cm (23–26in), bitches 53.3–60.9cm (21–24in). Weight: dogs 29.5–36.3kg (65–80lb), bitches 25–31.75kg (55–70lb).

- **COAT** A distinctive feature: thick and reasonably short (not over 3.8cm (1½in) long), with harsh, oily outercoat and dense, fine, woolly undercoat.

- **COLOUR** Dead grass (straw to bracken), sedge (red-gold), or any shade of brown; white spots (the smaller the better) on chest, toes and belly permissible.

- **OTHER FEATURES** Broad, round head; medium-sized eyes; small ears; strong, deep, broad chest; tail should extend to hock.

NOVA SCOTIA DUCK TOLLING RETRIEVER

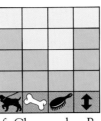

The Nova Scotia Duck Tolling Retriever originated in the Maritime Provinces of Canada and has only recently become known outside its native area. It is believed to be of Chesapeake Bay and Golden Retriever stock. With the head of the Golden it is well boned down to its strong webbed feet. Although the breed has been set for over 100 years, it only received a breed standard in the 1940s. It was given full international recognition by the FCI in 1982. This dog's job in life is to thrash about at the water's edge in order to attract the attention of wildfowl, a performance known as tolling. Eventually the wildfowl become curious or angry enough to swim within range of the hunter on the bank. The dog will retrieve the fowl shot down.

Character and care

The Nova Scotia Duck Tolling Retriever is quiet and easy to train. Like many gundogs it makes a good family pet provided that it receives plenty of exercise. It needs regular grooming with a bristle brush and comb.

KEY CHARACTERISTICS

- **CLASS** Gundog.
  Recognized ANKC, CKC, FCI, KC(GB).

- **SIZE** Height at shoulders: 41–52cm (17–21in). Weight: 16.6–23kg (37–51lb).

- **COAT** Moderately long and close lying, with a thick, wavy undercoat.

- **COLOUR** Red fox, with white marking on chest, feet and tip of tail, and sometimes on face.

- **OTHER FEATURES** Broad head with well-defined stop; webbed feet.

The sleek, slightly wavy coat of this dog is a feature of the breed. White markings on the face, feet and/or the tip of the tail are common.

CURLY-COATED RETRIEVER

Everything about the Curly-coated Retriever points to the Irish Water Spaniel or the Standard Poodle contributing to its ancestry. The Labrador Retriever obviously also played some part in producing this fine breed, of which far too little is seen.

The Curly-coated was first exhibited at dog shows in the United Kingdom as long ago as 1860, and one of the first breeds to be used seriously for retrieving purposes in England. However, despite its attractive appearance, stamina and working ability, it is now rarely seen outside the show ring. It has been said that its popularity as a sporting dog declined because of its reputation of being hard-mouthed, a fault that certainly does not exist in the breed today.

Character and care

The Curly-coated Retriever has an excellent nose and a good memory. It is a better guard than other retrievers, and while a little anti-social with its canine colleagues in the shooting field, it generally combines its working life admirably with that of a reliable family dog. It requires vigorous exercise, and fares best in a country environment with plenty of opportunities to run free. Its curly coat does not need to be brushed or combed, just dampened down and massaged with circular movements. Advice should be sought on the necessary trimming if it is the intention to exhibit.

KEY CHARACTERISTICS
• **CLASS** Gundog. **Recognized** AKC, ANKC, CKC, FCI, KC(GB), KUSA.
• **SIZE** Height at withers: dogs about 67cm (27in), bitches about 62cm (25in). Weight: 31.7–36.3kg (70–80lb).
• **COAT** A mass of crisp, small curls all over, except on face.
• **COLOUR** Black or liver.
• **OTHER FEATURES** Long, well-proportioned head; black or dark brown eyes; small ears, set on low; muscular shoulders and deep chest; moderately short tail.

FLAT-COATED RETRIEVER

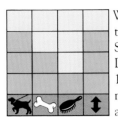

When a Flat-coated Retriever won the Best in Show award at Crufts Dog Show in London in 1980, reporters clamoured around its owner anxious to know what the breed did. "Picking up," they were told. In fact, the Flat-coat is superlative at picking up game, and it is an excellent wildfowler and water dog. It is loyal and affectionate, and although it can be kept as a pet, most Flat-coats are maintained for the job for which the breed was originally bred and they are happiest when doing this.

Once known as the Wavy-coated Retriever, the breed is thought to have evolved from the Labrador Retriever and spaniels. It is likely that Collie blood was introduced to produce the flat coat. This was achieved around the 1800s, when a Mr Shirley of Ettington Park, Warwickshire (now the West Midlands), in England, made tremendous efforts on the breed's behalf. The Flat-coat went on to become the most popular retriever in Britain, a position it held until after the Second World War when it was eclipsed by the Golden and Labrador Retrievers.

Character and care

An intelligent and sound dog with a kindly temperament, it is a hardy breed and many owners choose to keep their Flat-coats in outside kennels, although this is a matter of preference. Like most gundogs, Flat-coats need plenty of exercise and a daily brushing.

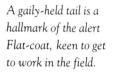

KEY CHARACTERISTICS
• **CLASS** Gundog. **Recognized** AKC, ANKC, CKC, FCI, KC(GB), KUSA.
• **SIZE** Height: dogs 58–61cm (23–24in), bitches 56–59cm (22–23in). Weight: dogs 25–35kg (60–80lb), bitches 25–34kg (55–70lb).
• **COAT** Dense, fine to medium texture, medium length and lying flat.
• **COLOUR** Solid black or solid liver.
• **OTHER FEATURES** Long, clean head; medium-sized eyes; small ears well set on, lying close to side of head; deep chest and strong body; tail short, straight and well set on.

A gaily-held tail is a hallmark of the alert Flat-coat, keen to get to work in the field.

LABRADOR RETRIEVER

Originally from Canada, the Labrador Retriever was developed in Britain from the late 19th century onwards to its present pre-eminence as a gundog. Always a popular pet, it is also a show favourite.

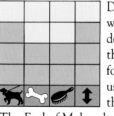

Despite its association with Britain, the Labrador Retriever arrived in the 1830s with Newfoundland fishermen who used the dogs to help them land their nets. The Earl of Malmesbury, who appears to have named the breed, bought his first Labrador in 1870 from a fisherman plying between Newfoundland and Poole, Dorset. A great authority on the Labrador was the late Countess Howe, whose dog, Champion Bramshaw Bob, became a UK field trials champion and then went on to win Best in Show at Crufts on two occasions.

At one time, Labrador Retrievers were invariably black. Yellow Labradors are now much more popular, though a good black is a joy to behold in the field. Unfortunately, there are so many crossbred blacks that the beauty of the purebred black Labrador is now little seen outside show and sporting circles.

This breed remains among the most popular of dogs. A first-class gundog and fine swimmer, it ideally combines the role of family pet and sporting companion. It is also a worthy contender in obedience competitions, draws large entries in the show ring and works as a guide dog for the blind.

Character and care

Exuberant in youth, but easy to train, the Labrador is good with children and rarely seems to get itself into any kind of trouble. It needs plenty of exercise and regular brushing. It can be kept indoors as a family pet or in an outdoor kennel.

KEY CHARACTERISTICS
• **CLASS** Gundog. **Recognized** AKC, ANKC, CKC, FCI, KC(GB), KUSA.
• **SIZE** Height at shoulders: dogs 56–61cm (22½–24½in), bitches 54–59cm (21½–23½in). Weight: dogs 27.2–33.7kg (60–75lb), bitches 25–33.7kg (55–70lb).
• **COAT** Short and dense, without wave or feathering; weather-resistant undercoat.
• **COLOUR** Wholly black, yellow or liver/chocolate; yellows range from light cream to red fox; small white spot on chest permissible.
• **OTHER FEATURES** Head broad with defined stop; medium-sized eyes; ears not large or heavy; chest of good width and depth; distinctive "otter" tail.

GOLDEN RETRIEVER

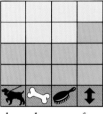

Some controversy surrounds the Golden's origin. One tale tells that, in 1858, Sir Dudley Marjoribanks (later Lord Tweedmouth) saw a troupe of eight Russian sheepdogs performing in a circus in the seaside resort of Brighton in England. So impressed with them was Sir Dudley that, following the show, he approached the owner and offered to buy two of them. The offer was declined on the grounds that the circus act would be spoilt if the troupe was split up, whereupon Sir Dudley agreed to buy all eight dogs. According to this tale, the troupe provided the foundation stock for the Golden Retriever breed to which Bloodhound blood was introduced. Although this story still persists, it is more generally believed that the Golden Retriever was the progeny of retriever/spaniel stock born on His Lordship's Scottish estate.

Character and care
The Golden Retriever ideally combines the role of sportsman's companion and family pet, being an excellent gundog, of sound temperament and gentle with children. This beautiful animal also makes a popular show dog and works well in obedience competitions. Requiring regular brushing and ample exercise, the Golden Retriever is best suited to a country environment. It will, however, adapt to suburban conditions provided that good walks and a garden are available.

KEY CHARACTERISTICS
● **CLASS** Gundog. **Recognized** AKC, ANKC, CKC, FCI, KC(GB), KUSA.
● **SIZE** Height at withers: dogs 56–61cm (22–24in), bitches 51–56cm (20–22in). Weight: dogs 29.5–33.7kg (65–75lb), bitches 25–29.5kg (55–65lb).
● **COAT** Flat or wavy with good feathering; dense, water-resistant undercoat.
● **COLOUR** Any shade of gold or cream, but neither red nor mahogany; a few white hairs on chest only are permissible.
● **OTHER FEATURES** Head balanced and well chiselled; dark brown eyes; moderate-sized ears; deep chest and well balanced body; tail set on and carried level with back.

Varying in colour from cream to warm gold, the Golden Retriever is an excellent family dog with a kind, brown eye.

AMERICAN COCKER SPANIEL

The name of the American Cocker Spaniel is derived from the predilection of the English Cockers for "cocking", or hunting woodcock. The breed was of Spanish origin, but the American Cocker can be traced back to an English-bred bitch, Obo Obo, brought over from Britain in the 1880s.

The English Cocker Spaniel Club of America, formed in 1935, helped establish the breed. It is distinguished by its small stature – suited to the lighter New World game birds – shorter head and extremely dense coat. This smallest of American gundogs, and the most popular breed in the country, was recognized by the AKC in 1946 as the American Cocker Spaniel.

For many years the American Cocker was shown exclusively in the ring. Recently, however, field trials have been reintroduced.

No longer bearing much resemblance to its English cousins, the American Cocker Spaniel ranks among top dog breeds in the United States.

Character and care

The American Cocker has a much thicker coat than the English Cocker and elegant trousers. It is a useful, all-purpose gundog, able both to flush out and retrieve. It is a popular show dog, makes a fine housepet and is usually good with children. The American Cocker needs plenty of exercise, daily brushing and combing, and, if it is the desire to exhibit, fairly intricate trimming using scissors and electric clippers.

Careful attention is needed to the American Cocker Spaniel's long, silky coat, which is much thicker than that of the English Cocker.

KEY CHARACTERISTICS
• **CLASS** Gundog. **Recognized** AKC, ANKC, CKC, FCI, KC(GB), KUSA.
• **SIZE** Height: dogs 36.25–38.75cm (14½–15½in), bitches 33.75–36.25cm (13½–14½in). Weight: 10.8–12.5kg (24–28lb).
• **COAT** Short and fine on head, medium length on body, with enough undercoat to give protection.
• **COLOUR** Black, jet black, shadings of brown or liver in sheen of coat undesirable; black and tan and brown and tan, with definite tan markings on jet black or brown body; particolours and tricolours (those wishing to exhibit are advised to check breed standard for lengthy colour requirements).
• **OTHER FEATURES** Head rounded and well developed; eyes full and looking directly forwards; back slopes slightly downwards from shoulders to tail; tail characteristically docked.

AMERICAN WATER SPANIEL

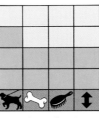

The American Water Spaniel is a comparatively modern breed. It was officially recognized by the American Kennel Club in 1940, and, while its development can be traced to the American Midwest, it probably descends from the Irish Water Spaniel, which owes its ancestry to crosses with the Poodle and the Curly-coated Retriever and in its present form dates from the late 1800s. The American Water Spaniel, which is a fine swimmer and bird dog, is smaller than its Irish counterpart. However, like the latter, it has a good nose and will work and quarter much like a Springer Spaniel.

Character and care

The American Water Spaniel is an affectionate, hardy and intelligent dog, much esteemed by huntsmen. It makes a good pet, but can be too boisterous with other animals. It needs regular combing, using a steel comb, and occasional stripping and trimming.

KEY CHARACTERISTICS
• **CLASS** Gundog. **Recognized** AKC, CKC, FCI, KC(GB).
• **SIZE** Height at shoulders: 37.5–45cm (15–18in). Weight: dogs 12.7–20.4kg (28–45lb), bitches 11.3lb–18.2kg (25–40lb).
• **COAT** Tightly curled.
• **COLOUR** Solid liver or dark chocolate (a small amount of white on chest or toes is permissible).
• **OTHER FEATURES** Body sturdy, not too compact; head of moderate length; skull quite broad; ears lobular; eye colour should tone with coat; tail moderately long.

CLUMBER SPANIEL

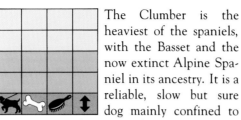

The Clumber's silky coat is free of markings, except for some freckling on the ears and face.

The Clumber is the heaviest of the spaniels, with the Basset and the now extinct Alpine Spaniel in its ancestry. It is a reliable, slow but sure dog mainly confined to country areas where it excels in flushing game over rough ground and as a retriever.

A favourite of British royalty, the Clumber has a romantic history. In the years just prior to the French Revolution it was promoted by the Duc de Noailles and became renowned as a beater and retriever. At the beginning of hostilities, the French Duke brought his dogs to England and entrusted them to the Duke of Newcastle at Clumber Park, near Nottingham, from which the breed gets its name. The French Duke met his death in the Revolution but the breed lived on, a fitting memorial to its aristocratic master.

Character and care

The Clumber is of good temperament and may be kept as a pet but its ideal role is as a working gundog in the countryside. It needs a fair amount of brushing, and care must be taken that mud does not become lodged in between its toes.

KEY CHARACTERISTICS
● **CLASS** Gundog. **Recognized** AKC, ANKC, CKC, FCI, KC(GB), KUSA.
● **SIZE** Height at withers: dogs 48–50cm (19–20in), bitches 42.5–48cm (17–19in). Weight: dogs 31.7–38kg (70–85lb), bitches 25–31.7kg (55–70lb).
● **COAT** Abundant, close and silky.
● **COLOUR** Plain white body with lemon markings preferred; orange permissible; slight head markings and freckled muzzle.
● **OTHER FEATURES** Massive, square, medium-length head; clean dark amber eyes, slightly sunk; large, vine-leaf shaped ears; long, heavy body close to ground; chest deep; tail set low and well feathered.

A favourite of royalty, the Clumber is slower than lighter-boned dogs in the field, but is nevertheless a good, steady gundog.

ENGLISH COCKER SPANIEL

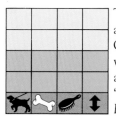

The Cocker Spaniel is also called the Merry Cocker because of its wagging tail. It originated in Spain (the word "spaniel" comes from *Espagnol*, meaning Spanish). Spaniels have been known since the 14th century and were used in falconry.

In the 19th century, the breed came into its own in the task of flushing out woodcock and small game, and became known as the cocking or Cocker Spaniel.

Recognized by the British Kennel Club in 1892, the English Cocker Spaniel is still the smallest spaniel in the gundog group. It is a favourite contender in obedience and working trials as well as in the show ring. The breed soared in popularity in the years leading up to the Second World War when Mr H. S. Lloyd's famous "Of Ware" Kennels won the coveted Best in Show Award at Crufts in London on no less than six occasions. These kennels continue under his daughter today.

Character and care

It is a gentle and popular pet, as well as being a first-class gundog, which is able both to flush out and retrieve. It needs careful brushing and combing every day, and immense care must be taken to dislodge any mud that may have become caked in its paws or its ears. Some owners gently peg back their spaniel's ears when it is eating.

KEY CHARACTERISTICS
● **CLASS** Gundog. **Recognized** AKC, ANKC, CKC, FCI, KC(GB), KUSA.
● **SIZE** Height: dogs approx. 39–42.5cm (15½–17in), bitches approx. 38–41cm (15–16in). Weight: approx. 12.7–14.5kg (28–32lb).
● **COAT** Flat and silky in texture.
● **COLOUR** Various; self (pure) colours, no white allowed on chest.
● **OTHER FEATURES** Square muzzle; eyes full but not prominent; strong, compact body; tail set on slightly lower than line of back.

Long, silky ears frame the English Cocker Spaniel's square muzzle.

The English Cocker is the smallest spaniel in the gundog group, but is excellent in the field, tending to work close to the guns.

ENGLISH SPRINGER SPANIEL

The English Springer is one of the oldest of the British spaniels, with the exception of the Clumber. The land spaniel written about in 1570 by the historian Dr Caius was obviously a forerunner of the Springer. It was originally used for flushing or springing game from cover before shotguns were in use. For a time it was known as the Norfolk Spaniel, named after either a Norfolk family that kept a strain of "springing" spaniels prior to 1900 or the breed's place of origin in the county of Norfolk in England.

Sir Thomas Boughey, who helped establish the modern breed, had Springers with a pedigree traceable to a bitch that whelped in 1812. One of her descendants was Field Trials Champion Velox Powder, bred in 1903, which won 20 field trial stakes. Sir Thomas's family retained an interest in the breed until the 1930s and many of today's field trials champions are descendants of his strain. The English Springer Spaniel Club was formed in the UK in 1921, but the breed had found fame as a "bird dog" in America long before.

Character and care

The English Springer Spaniel is an intelligent, loyal and popular gundog, which also makes a reliable housepet and is good with children. The breed needs plenty of exercise, a daily brushing and regular checks to ensure that mud does not become lodged in its paws or its ears. The Springer may not be a good choice for the houseproud because it tends to have a good shake when it comes indoors out of the rain!

Spaniels bred to flush game were often known as "springers" because in effect they sprang from cover. The English Springer Spaniel was for a time called the Norfolk Spaniel, reflecting its county of origin.

Outstanding in the field, the English Springer is also an attractive family pet.

KEY CHARACTERISTICS
• **CLASS** Gundog. **Recognized** AKC, ANKC, CKC, FCI, KC(GB), KUSA.
• **SIZE** Height at shoulders: dogs 51cm (20in), bitches 48.5cm (19in). Weight: 22–25kg (49–55lb).
• **COAT** Close, straight and weather-resistant; never coarse.
• **COLOUR** Liver and white, black and white, either of these with tan markings.
• **OTHER FEATURES** Medium-length skull; medium-sized eyes; long, wide ears; strong body; tail set low, and never carried above the level of the back.

WELSH SPRINGER SPANIEL

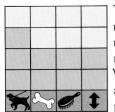

The Welsh Springer Spaniel, or its forerunner, is mentioned in the earliest records of the Laws of Wales, dating back to about AD1300. It is also possible that these red and white spaniels are a cross between the English Springer and the Clumber. Certainly, the breed has the Brittany in its ancestry, being similar both in its marked ability as a gundog and in conformation, although the Welsh Springer is higher in the leg and lighter boned. In the UK it was exhibited as a Welsh Cocker prior to 1902, when it was recognized by the Kennel Club. Over the last 20 years it has been exported to North America and other parts of the world.

Character and care

This loyal and hard-working gundog is somewhere between the Merry Cocker and the English Springer Spaniel in size. It is a good swimmer, has an excellent nose, and combines the role of family dog and sportsman's companion provided the need for exercise is met. It needs brushing daily, and regular checks to make sure that mud does not become lodged in its paws or ears.

KEY CHARACTERISTICS
● **CLASS** Gundog. **Recognized** AKC, ANKC, CKC, FCI, KC(GB), KUSA.
● **SIZE** Height at withers: dogs 45–48cm (18–19in), bitches 42.5–45cm (17–18in). Weight: 15.8–20.2kg (35–45lb).
● **COAT** Straight and flat, silky in texture; some feathering on chest, underside of body and legs.
● **COLOUR** Rich red and white only.
● **OTHER FEATURES** Slightly domed head; medium-sized, hazel or dark eyes; ears set moderately low; strong, muscular body; tail well set on and low.

With a more tapered head and higher-set ears, the Welsh Springer Spaniel is smaller than the English Springer.

The rich red and white coat of the Welsh Springer distinguishes it from other spaniels. The breed is popular in the field and in the show ring.

FIELD SPANIEL

Little known outside Britain, the Field Spaniel shares its origins with the Cocker Spaniel, although the two types became separate breeds in 1892.

This resulted in a better proportioned standard type evolving, which is breeding true and producing some very nice specimens. Despite this, the Field Spaniel is still rarely seen in its country of origin outside the show ring. It is recognized in the United States, but very few specimens are registered there.

Character and care

The Field Spaniel has an equable temperament and makes a good household pet and gundog. Like other spaniels, it thrives on plenty of exercise, and needs to be brushed and combed every day, taking care that its coat does not become matted.

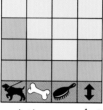

The Field Spaniel has the same origin as the Cocker Spaniel, being, in effect, a larger version of it, and early litters sometimes contained both. Then, in 1892, the varieties went their separate ways. While the Cocker was improved greatly, the Field Spaniel was bred to produce an exaggeratedly long body and short legs, and its popularity and numbers declined sharply.

In 1948 the Field Spaniel Society was reformed in Britain and considerable work was undertaken by dedicated enthusiasts.

KEY CHARACTERISTICS
• **CLASS** Gundog. **Recognized** AKC, ANKC, CKC, FCI, KC(GB), KUSA.
• **SIZE** Height at withers: dogs about 45–47cm (18in), bitches about 42.5cm (17in). Weight: 15.7–25kg (35–55lb).
• **COAT** Long, flat and glossy, without curls; silky in texture.
• **COLOUR** Black, liver or roan with tan markings; clear black, white or liver and white unacceptable.
• **OTHER FEATURES** Head conveys impression of high breeding, character and nobility; eyes wide open; moderately long and wide ears; deep chest; tail set low and characteristically docked.

At one time bred for extreme characteristics, the Field Spaniel has been rehabilitated by enthusiasts over the past half century.

IRISH WATER SPANIEL

The tallest of the spaniels, the Irish Water Spaniel comes into its element in the wetlands, often diving beneath the surface to retrieve injured waterfowl.

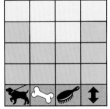

Documentary evidence for water dogs and water spaniels traces back to AD17, and some form of water spaniels has been known in Ireland for more than a millennium. Writing about 80 years ago, the canine historian Hugh Dalziel suggested that the Irish Water Spaniel was the forerunner of all modern spaniels. However, the contemporary view is that this breed developed through crosses with Poodles and Curly-coated Retrievers which, from its appearance, would seem very likely. Prior to 1859, there were two separate strains of the breed in Ireland, one in the north and one in the south. It would seem that the southern strain, which resembled the Standard Poodle, formed the basis of the modern breed.

Character and care
The tallest of the spaniels, the Irish Water Spaniel is a brave, loving and intelligent animal. It excels in retrieving wildfowl, has a fine nose, and will work and quarter as a spaniel. Maintaining this breed's coat of curls and thick undercoat is not such a chore as might be expected. However, it does need to be groomed at least once a week using a steel comb. Some stripping of unwanted hair is necessary, as is trimming around the feet.

KEY CHARACTERISTICS
• **CLASS** Gundog. **Recognized** AKC, ANKC, CKC, FCI, KC(GB), KUSA.
• **SIZE** Height: dogs 53–60cm (21–24in), bitches 51–58cm (20–23in). Weight: dogs 25–29.5kg (55–65lb), bitches 20.2–26kg (45–58lb).
• **COAT** Dense, tight ringlets on neck, body and top part of tail; longer, curling hair on legs and topknot; face, rear of tail and back of legs below hocks smooth.
• **COLOUR** Rich, dark liver.
• **OTHER FEATURES** Good-sized, high-domed head; small, almond-shaped eyes; long, oval-shaped ears; long, arching neck; deep chest; short tail.

Tight curls and a knowing look are part of the appeal of the Irish Water Spaniel.

SUSSEX SPANIEL

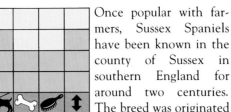

Once popular with farmers, Sussex Spaniels have been known in the county of Sussex in southern England for around two centuries. The breed was originated by a Mr Fuller of Rosehill, Sussex, in 1795. It was first exhibited at Crystal Palace, London, in 1862. Later a bigger strain, known as the Harvieston, was developed. This owed something to the Clumber Spaniel and the Bloodhound, and to this day some Sussex Spaniels have a hound look about them.

The breed has always been relatively rare and credit must go to the British breeder Mrs Freer for keeping it going during the two World Wars. In the early to mid 1950s, more Clumber blood was added, which resulted in improved bone and temperament.

The Sussex is used mainly for partridge and pheasant, being too small to take a hare. It works in thick cover, giving tongue as it works so that its handler knows where it is.

There is more than a hint of hound about the Sussex, now one of the rarest of spaniel breeds.

Character and care

The Sussex is a working spaniel with an excellent nose, which makes an ideal country dog. It tends to attach itself to one person, and is loyal and easy to train. It requires a daily brush and comb and, as with all spaniels, care must be taken that mud does not become caked in its ears and feet.

KEY CHARACTERISTICS
• **CLASS** Gundog. **Recognized** AKC, ANKC, CKC, FCI, KC(GB), KUSA.
• **SIZE** Height at withers: 32.5–40cm (13–16in). Weight: 15.7–23kg (35–50lb).
• **COAT** Abundant and flat, without a tendency to curl; ample weather-resistant undercoat.
• **COLOUR** Rich golden liver shading to golden at tips of hairs, gold predominating; dark liver or puce is undesirable.
• **OTHER FEATURES** Wide head, slightly rounded between the ears; fairly large, hazel-coloured eyes with a soft expression; fairly large, thick ears; deep, well-developed chest; tail set on low and never carried above level of back.

POINTER

Developed in Britain, the Pointer is a descendant of pointing dogs which began appearing all over Europe in the mid-17th century.

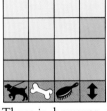

Like the setters, the Pointer is famed for its classic stance, pointing with nose and tail in the direction of game. It is thought by many to have originated in Spain. There is, however, a school of thought that it may be of English origin, developed through crossings of Foxhound, Bloodhound and Greyhound. Also, in the opinion of William Arkwright, who spent a lifetime researching the history of the breed, the Pointer originated in the East and found its way to Italy before arriving in Spain.

William Arkwright, from Sutton Scarsdale near Chesterfield in England, compiled *Arkwright on Pointers* during the period 1890–1919. This work is still regarded as the bible on the breed. In the United Kingdom, the Pointer was accepted by the then Setter and Pointer Club in 1937, and reassessed and confirmed by the Pointer Club as recently as 1970. It is popular internationally and recognized throughout the world.

Character and care

The Pointer is a popular show dog, and admirably combines the roles of sportsman's companion and family pet. It is an affection-ate, obedient dog, which is easy to train, good with children and needs only regular brushing to keep its coat in good condition. It does, however, need plenty of exercise and so is not ideally suited to town life.

KEY CHARACTERISTICS
• **CLASS** Gundog. **Recognized** AKC, ANKC, CKC, FCI, KC(GB), KUSA.
• **SIZE** Height at withers: dogs 62.5–70cm (25–28in), bitches 57.5–65cm (23–26in). Weight: dogs 25–33.7cm (55–75lb), bitches 20.2–29.5kg (45–65lb).
• **COAT** Short, dense and smooth.
• **COLOUR** Lemon and white, orange and white, liver and white, black and white; self (pure) colours and tricolours also correct.
• **OTHER FEATURES** Medium-width head with pronounced stop; dark, round, intense eyes; ears set on level with eyes; thin, sloping shoulders; deep chest; tail thicker at root, tapering to a point.

ENGLISH SETTER

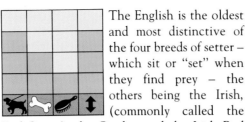

A distinctive feature of the English Setter is the curving feathered tail.

The English is the oldest and most distinctive of the four breeds of setter – which sit or "set" when they find prey – the others being the Irish, (commonly called the Red Setter), the Gordon and the Irish Red and White.

The English Setter has been known since the 14th century, but the name most closely associated with the breed is that of Edward Laverack (1815–77) whose setter pedigrees trace back to about 1860. The breed was registered by the British Kennel Club in 1873. Laverack wrote that "this breed is but a Spaniel improved", and undoubtedly it does derive from spaniels. It was Laverack, too, who, through interbreeding, developed the strain upon which the present-day English Setter breed standard was founded.

Another breeder, Mr R. L. Purcell Llewellin, helped establish the English Setter in America. Mr Llewellin bought several of Mr Laverack's best dogs and crossed them with new blood in the north of England. He introduced a Mr Slatter and Sir Vincent Corbet's strain, which thereafter became known as the Duke–Kate–Rhoebes strain. His Setters found fame in the United States and Canada, where they proved unsurpassed in field trials and firmly established the breed line in North America.

Character and care
Strikingly beautiful, loyal and affectionate, the English Setter is a breed that admirably combines the role of family pet and sportsman's dog. It is good with children, can live as one of the family or be kennelled out of doors, and needs only daily brushing with a stiff brush and the use of a steel comb. Straggly hairs must be removed before exhibition. Like most gundogs, the English Setter requires a good amount of exercise and is not ideally suited to town life, though many do seem to survive in an urban setting.

GORDON SETTER

The heaviest of the setters, the Gordon is Scotland's only native gundog.

Arguably the most elegant of the group, the English Setter was developed mainly to hunt in open country.

The Gordon, formerly the Gordon Castle Setter, owes its existence to Alexander, Fourth Duke of Richmond and Gordon, who bred Scotland's only gundog in the late 1770s. He aimed to produce a larger, heavier setter by introducing Bloodhound and, it is widely thought, collie blood. Gordons are not so fast or stylish as other setters.

Gordons were exhibited at the world's first dog show, held at Newcastle Town Hall, England, on the 28 June, 1859. The setter prize was won by "Dandy", a Gordon which was owned by the pointer judge! Around this time, the breed was introduced into the United States, where there are now more members registered than in Britain.

Character and care

The Gordon is a tireless worker, able to withstand the heat of grouse shooting in August better than other setters and able to work without water for longer. It will combine the role of gundog admirably with that of a family pet and it is a better watchdog than other setters. The Gordon needs plenty of space and lots of exercise, and is not best suited to town life.

IRISH SETTER

The Irish Setter, the most popular and perhaps most light-hearted of the setter group, took on its solid red appearance in the 19th century.

The Irish Red Setter (or Big Red) was developed through the crossing of Irish Water Spaniels, the Spanish Pointer and both the English and Gordon Setters. This resulted in a beautiful, exuberant, pointer-like dog, which is notable for its classic pointing stance.

The person most closely associated with the modern breed is Edward Laverack (1815–77), who spent a lifetime perfecting the Irish (and the English) Setter. Although it originated in Ireland, the breed came into its own in Victorian England, where its speed and energy, developed for the conditions found in Ireland, made it ideally suited to work as a gundog in large open expanses of countryside.

Character and care

While undoubtedly having hunting ability, this breed is widely sought after as a popular and loving family pet. It is good with children and other pets, and has a particular affinity with horses. The Irish Setter has boundless energy and, therefore, needs plenty of exercise, as well as a daily brushing. It will adapt to a suburban home, but is far better suited to country life where it has plenty of freedom. It is, incidentally, far too good natured to be used as a guard dog.

KEY CHARACTERISTICS
• **CLASS** Gundog. **Recognized** AKC, ANKC, CKC, FCI, KC(GB), KUSA.
• **SIZE** Height: 63.5–68.5cm (25–27in). Weight: 27.2–31.7kg (60–70lb).
• **COAT** Short and fine on head, fronts of legs and tips of ears; moderately long, free and as straight as possible on rest of body; good feathering.
• **COLOUR** Rich chestnut with no trace of black; white markings on chest, throat, chin or toes, or small star on forehead or narrow streak or blaze on nose or face permissible.
• **OTHER FEATURES** Long, lean head; dark hazel to dark brown eyes; moderate-sized ears; chest as deep as possible, rather narrow in front; tail moderate in length in relation to size of body.

IRISH RED AND WHITE SETTER

At one time almost eclipsed by the stylish solid Red Setter, the Irish Red and White Setter has enjoyed a revival over the last half century.

The Irish Red and White Setter evolved from spaniels, probably red and white spaniels, that were brought to Ireland from France and crossed with pointers, and by the 18th century, Red and White Setters were being bred to type. Then setter fanciers began to prefer the Red Setter and by the end of the 19th century the Red and White all but disappeared. Since the 1940s the breed has undergone a revival in Ireland. Red and Whites are recognized by the Kennel Club in Britain, have their own breed standard, and have been recognized by the FCI.

Fortunately the breed has recently begun to make its mark on the show scene.

Character and care

The Irish Red and White Setter is a happy, good natured and affectionate dog, which admirably combines the role of sportsman's dog and family pet. It needs space and plenty of exercise, and requires daily brushing.

KEY CHARACTERISTICS

- **CLASS** Gundog.
  Recognized ANKC, FCI, KC(GB), KUSA.

- **SIZE** Height: 59–67cm (23½–27in).
  Weight: 18.1–31.7kg (40–70lb).

- **COAT** Flat, straight and finely textured with good feathering.

- **COLOUR** Clearly particoloured with pearl white base and solid red patches; mottling and flecking, but not roaning, permitted around face and feet, and up foreleg to elbow and up hind leg as far as hock.

- **OTHER FEATURES** Head broad in proportion to body; hazel or dark brown eyes; ears set level with eyes; body strong and muscular; tail strong at root and tapering to fine point.

Particoloured with red patches on a solid white base, the breed is allowed some mottling on the face and paws.

BOURBONNAIS SETTER

The Bourbonnais Setter, little known outside its native France, is distinguished by its abundant freckles and rudimentary tail.

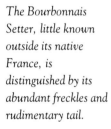

The Bourbonnais Setter or Braque du Bourbonnais is associated with the area of central France after which it is named. However, it seems to derive from the Pyrenees, where a number of other French gundogs also originated. The ancestors of these dogs gradually spread out to other regions, and crossings with local dogs produced varieties which took the name of their new home.

The Bourbonnais is often described as the short-tailed setter because it is almost always born without a tail. It has a striking Dalmatian-like coat pattern on a distinctly thickset body.

Character and care

The Bourbonnais is a good-natured sporting and family dog, which is easy to train. Like most gundogs, it requires a fair amount of exercise, and needs a brush and rub down every few days.

KEY CHARACTERISTICS
• **CLASS** Gundog. **Recognized** FCI.
• **SIZE** Average height: 53cm (21in). Weight: 18.2–25.9kg (40–57lb).
• **COAT** Short.
• **COLOUR** White and light brown, giving a colour that has been described as "like dregs of wine"; fawn without large markings, but having small spots fused into the white, distributed uniformly over the body.
• **OTHER FEATURES** Very long head with arched skull and slight stop; large, dark amber eyes, not sunken; long ears reaching to throat; broad, slightly convex back; tail very short and set low.

SAINT-GERMAIN SETTER

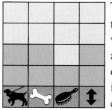

The Saint-Germain Setter is also known as the Saint-Germain Pointer, the Compiègne Setter or, more commonly, the Braque Saint-Germain. This attractive gundog bears a strong resemblance to the English Pointer and has a similar tail carriage, although it is not so heavily boned. It is said to have derived from the crossing of an English Pointer "Miss", owned by King Charles X of France (reigned 1824–30), and a French Setter or Braque at the beginning of the 19th century. According to De La Rue in *Les Chiens d'Arrêt Francais et Anglais*, "Miss produced seven puppies and four of these were given to the Compiègne forest wardens; the latter transferred to Saint-Germain, and took their dogs with them. Their elegance was pleasing to the hunters of Paris."

Character and care

This strong hunting dog, with less refinement and sense of smell than the English Pointer, may be used against large game, and also hunts pheasant and rabbit. It has a good gallop. It is an affectionate dog and is gentle and intelligent, but can be stubborn. It needs a brush and rub down every few days, and requires plenty of exercise.

KEY CHARACTERISTICS
● **CLASS** Gundog. **Recognized** FCI.
● **SIZE** Height: dogs 51–63.5cm (20–25in), bitches 53–58cm (21–23in). Weight: 18.1–25.6kg (40–57lb).
● **COAT** Short and soft.
● **COLOUR** White with orange markings.
● **OTHER FEATURES** Fairly broad head; large, well-set, golden-brown eyes; ears set on level with eyes; short, straight back; loins strong, short and slightly arched; tail undocked.

A refined and stylish dog, the Saint Germain Setter is said to have derived from a 19th century mating between an English Pointer and a French Setter.

PUDELPOINTER

The Pudelpointer is the result of a cross between various pointer breeds and the old Barbet (now extinct) or the Poodle. It is a good all-purpose gundog with a hard, rough, thick coat, enabling it to cope with difficult terrain and cold water. In build it resembles a heavy pointer rather than a Poodle, and has a short, straight back, large round eyes and what has been described as a "bird of prey" expression. Unfortunately, it is becoming rare in Europe as a distinct breed, but some Pudelpointers are now owned by hunters in the USA and Canada.

Character and care

The Pudelpointer is an intelligent, good natured dog, which is eager to learn and possesses great stamina.

KEY CHARACTERISTICS
● **CLASS** Gundog. **Recognized** CKC, FCI.
● **SIZE** Height at withers: over 61cm (24in). Weight: 25–31.7kg (55–70lb).
● **COAT** Short, hard and coarse.
● **COLOUR** Light to chestnut brown.
● **OTHER FEATURES** Medium-length head; long eyebrows and slight beard; round, lively eyes; ears flat and hanging tight to side of head; chest deep but in proportion to rest of body; tail starts high, thick at root and grows thinner towards tip.

BRITTANY

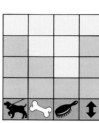

The Brittany, formerly known as the Brittany Spaniel, is the only spaniel in the world that points to game. It is a fine woodcock dog and will also retrieve wildfowl. Believed to have originated in Spain or the Argoat forests of Brittany, it has also been suggested that the Brittany may be the progeny of an English Red and White Setter dog and a Breton bitch. English sportsmen liked to shoot woodcock in Brittany and took their dogs with them, presumably before the quarantine laws which now exist.

The breed was first exhibited in Paris in 1900 and was officially recognized in France in 1905. The standard was prepared in 1907 and altered in 1908.

Character and care

The Brittany has an excellent nose and needs gentle handling. It is a relative newcomer to Britain, but has done well in field trials in the United States. It requires daily brushing and plenty of exercise.

KEY CHARACTERISTICS
• **CLASS** Gundog. **Recognized** AKC, ANKC, CKC, FCI, KC(GB), KUSA.
• **SIZE** Height at shoulders: 44–51cm (17½–20½in). Weight: 13.6–18.1kg (30–40lb).
• **COAT** Body coat flat and dense, never curly; a little feathering on legs.
• **COLOUR** Orange and white or liver and white in clear or roan patterns, or tricolour (also black and white in UK).
• **OTHER FEATURES** Rounded, medium-length head; expressive eyes; drop ears; deep chest reaching to the level of the elbows; tail naturally short or usually docked to 10cm (4in), with a small twist of hair on the end, carried level with back.

Really a small setter, the Brittany is a keen hunting dog, single minded in the field.

The Brittany's well defined stop and tapering muzzle resemble the features of the setter.

DUPUY SETTER

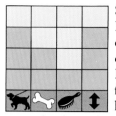

Some sources say that the Dupuy Setter or Pointer or Braque Dupuy owes its existence to a Monsieur Pierre Dupuy, a hunter from Poitou, who mated his white and chestnut setter bitch, Leda, with a dog of unknown breed named Mylord. Others claim that it came about through a setter and greyhound cross. The writer gives most credence to the belief that the Dupuy is an ancient French setter, a few examples of which survived the French Revolution (1789–99) due to the dedication of a game warden at the Anneu d'Argensois who was named Dupuy.

Character and care

A good-sized gundog, the Dupuy is of noble bearing. The expression in its eyes is said to be both gentle and dreamy. It is suitable for any kind of hunting, but is not too keen on water. The Dupuy is fast, keen and obedient. It needs plenty of exercise, and should be groomed every day or two with a bristle or pin brush and given a rub down to make its coat shine. The tail is not docked.

KEY CHARACTERISTICS

- **CLASS** Gundog. **Recognized** FCI.

- **SIZE** Height: dogs 67.5–68.5cm (26½–27in), bitches 65–66cm (25½–26in); males generally leaner than females.

- **COAT** Short and smooth.

- **COLOUR** White and dark brown; the white should be a good white with more or less broad markings or a brown saddle, with or without flecking or streaking.

- **OTHER FEATURES** Fine, long head, narrow and lean; golden or brown eyes, well open and having very little stop; very small neck; small, narrow ears; deep chest, well let down; tail set on neither too high nor too low.

FRENCH SPANIEL

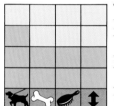

The French Spaniel or Épagneul Français has been written of as "the mainspring of all other breeds of long-haired pointers, commonly called spaniels". The descendant of dogs imported into France from England in the 14th century, it bears a resemblance to the English Springer and Cavalier King Charles Spaniel. Its ancestors, like those of all French and English spaniels, are widely believed to have originated in Spain. Little known today outside France, the French Spaniel is well muscled with a strong head and a long, soft, slightly wavy coat.

Character and care

The French Spaniel is a willing gundog, with considerable stamina. It has an intelligent expression and is good natured. It makes a good family pet provided that it is given plenty of exercise. It is best suited to a country home. It needs grooming daily with a bristle brush or slicker brush and comb.

KEY CHARACTERISTICS

- **CLASS** Gundog. **Recognized** CKC, FCI.

- **SIZE** Average height at shoulders: dogs 56–61cm (22–24in), bitches 53.5–58.5cm (21–23in). Weight: 19.9–25kg (44–55lb).

- **COAT** Long and supple, with some feathering.

- **COLOUR** White with chestnut markings only, tan not permissible.

- **OTHER FEATURES** Strong, fairly long head, not clumsy; medium-sized, dark amber eyes; long ears framing the head; deep, fairly broad chest; tail set on rather low, in many dogs slightly long, carried horizontally and obliquely with slight S-curve, undocked.

GERMAN POINTER

Slower to catch on with the show fraternity, the Wire-haired Pointer differs from its Short-haired relative mainly in its bristly coat.

The German Short-haired Pointer (Deutscher Kurzhaariger Vorstehhund or Kurzhaar) is of Spanish origin, probably derived through crossing the Spanish Pointer with a scenthound, thereby producing a versatile gundog that would both point and trail. English Foxhound blood is also believed to have been added.

Developed some 100 years ago, it was entered in the stud book of the American Kennel Club in 1930. A similar club was set up in Britain in 1951, and since then field trials for the breed have been held there.

The German Wire-haired Pointer (Deutscher Drahthaariger Vorstehhund or Drahthaar) is very similar to the German Short-haired Pointer, except in coat, and obviously had a hand in its make-up, as did the Wire-haired Pointing Griffon and the Stichelhaar, as well as the Airedale Terrier.

Although popular in its homeland, the German Wire-haired took longer than the Short-haired to become established overseas. It was recognized by the American Kennel Club in 1959 and it is still more widespread in the USA than in Britain.

Although pointers had been known in Germany for centuries, the Short-haired did not begin to emerge as a distinct breed until about a century ago.

Character and care

Both varieties are powerful, strong and versatile hunting dogs. They are equally at home on land or in the water, and excellent at working wildfowl and most game. The forest, in water, and for hunting bigger game, especially if the quarry is dangerous. The German Short-haired also makes a good household pet, provided that it receives enough exercise. It is easy to train, usually enough exercise. It is easy to train, usually good with children and does not require a lot of grooming. The Wire-haired, although it can adapt to the role of household pet, has had certain aggressive qualities bred into it, and is best kept purely as a hunting dog.

KEY CHARACTERISTICS
• **CLASS** Gundog. **Recognized** AKC, ANKC, CKC, FCI, KC(GB), KUSA.
• **SIZE** *Short-haired* Height at withers: dogs 58–64cm (23–25in), bitches 53–59cm (21–23in). Weight: dogs 25–31.7kg (55–70lb), bitches 20.2–27.2kg (45–60lb). *Wire-haired* Height at shoulders: dogs 60–67cm (24–25in), bitches 56–62cm (22–24in). Weight: dogs 25–34kg (55–75lb), bitches 20.5–29kg (45–64lb).
• **COAT** *Short-haired* Short and flat, coarse to the touch. *Wire-haired* Thick and harsh, no longer than 3.8cm (1½in) long, with dense undercoat.
• **COLOUR** *Short-haired* Solid liver, liver and white spotted, liver and white spotted and ticked; liver and white ticked; the same variations with black instead of liver; not tricoloured. *Wire-haired* Liver and white, solid liver, also black and white in UK; solid black and tricolour highly undesirable.
• **OTHER FEATURES** *Short-haired* Broad, clean-cut head, with slightly moulded crown; medium-sized eyes; broad ears set on high; chest should appear deep rather than wide, but in proportion to body; tail starts high and thick, growing gradually thinner towards tip. *Wire-haired* Broad head balanced in proportion to body; slightly rounded crown; medium-sized, oval eyes; ears medium-sized in relation to head; chest should appear deep rather than wide but not out of proportion to rest of body; tail starts high and thick, growing gradually thinner towards tip.

FRENCH SETTER

This breed is known in its native France as the Braque Français. The word "Braque" comes from the French *braquer* (to aim) and is used for dogs that point or "set" themselves in the direction of game. The breed is, therefore, called in English either the French Setter or the French Pointer.

The French Setter appears to have originated in the Pyrenees area of Spain and thereafter to have spread throughout Europe. The catalogue of a championship dog show held in Paris described this breed as "the oldest breed of pointer in the world, it has been the origin of nearly all the continental fled, hardy hunting dog, with a powerful nose even in hot and dry weather."

There is a smaller variety of this gundog called the French Pointer.

There is a smaller variety of this gundog called the French Pointer.

Character and care

The French Setter of today is a noble, powerful animal, with a docked tail, a good nose and fine working abilities. It makes a gentle pet as well as gundog, being good natured and getting on well with children and other animals. However, in common with other gundogs, it thrives on a considerable amount of exercise. It needs grooming to make the coat shine.

KEY CHARACTERISTICS
• **CLASS** Gundog. **Recognized** FCI.
• **SIZE** Height at withers: about 61cm (24in). Weight: about 27kg (60lb).
• **COAT** Smooth and rather thick.
• **COLOUR** White and tan with tan or cinnamon flecking; roans and red speckled examples also popular.
• **OTHER FEATURES** Head not too heavy; eyes well open and well set in sockets, affectionate, pensive expression; average-length ears; chest broad when viewed from the front, deep when viewed in profile; tail characteristically docked.

GERMAN SPANIEL

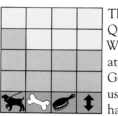

The German Spaniel, Quail Dog or Deutscher Wachtelhund was created in the 1890s in Germany. Its breeders used a variety of long-haired European hunting dogs, including waterdogs, and the resultant dog bears a marked resemblance to the English Springer Spaniel and the German Long-haired Pointer, although it is not so long in the leg. The old German hunting dog, the Stöber, may also have given the breed its keen scenting ability.

The Wachtelhund's long coat protects it in thick forests, where it flushes and retrieves quail and other feathered game and is also used to hunt fox and hare. This enthusiastic worker and fine swimmer is valued by German foresters and hunters, but is little known outside its country of origin.

Character and care

This good all-round gundog has a hardy constitution and reliable temperament. It makes an excellent hunting companion but Germans say that it should "only be in sportsmen's hands". It requires a lot of exercise, daily brushing and regular checks to make sure that mud has not become embedded in its ears or paws.

KEY CHARACTERISTICS
• **CLASS** Gundog. **Recognized** FCI.
• **SIZE** Height: dogs 39.5–49.5cm (15½–19½in), bitches 39.5–44.5cm (15½–17½in). Weight: 19.8–29.7kg (44–66lb).
• **COAT** Strong, glossy and slightly wavy.
• **COLOUR** Roan or brown.
• **OTHER FEATURES** Head clean with slightly rounded crown; expressive eyes, any shade of brown; ears set on high with broad bases; body longer than high; tail set on high, well feathered, and not raised much.

LARGE AND SMALL MÜNSTERLÄNDERS

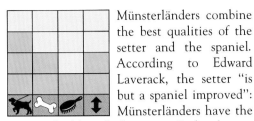

Münsterländers combine the best qualities of the setter and the spaniel. According to Edward Laverack, the setter "is but a spaniel improved": Münsterländers have the setter's build and the spaniel's head.

While officially recorded as one of the newest pointing and retrieving gundog breeds, the Large Münsterländer has been well established in its native Germany as an all-purpose gundog since the beginning of the 18th century. Then it was regarded as a German Long-haired Pointer, but in the early days of the German Kennel Club it was decided that only brown and white German Long-haired Pointers would be eligible for registration and pups of other colours were given away. The "odd-coloured" puppies fell into the hands of farmers whose aim was to perpetuate the best working qualities, irrespective of colour. Thus, the farmers were able to build up and save an interesting and attractive variety of gundog, known today as the Large Münsterländer.

The Small Münsterländer is a more recent breed, derived by crossing the Brittany with the German Long-haired Pointer in the early 20th century.

Character and care

The Münsterländers are loyal, affectionate and trustworthy dogs, which admirably fulfil the roles of sportsmen's companions and family pets. They are energetic and so need plenty of exercise, and a daily brushing.

The Large Münsterländer is an all-purpose pointing/retrieving dog, but also makes an excellent family pet.

KEY CHARACTERISTICS
• **CLASS** Gundog. **Recognized** *Large* ANKC, FCI, KC(GB), KUSA. *Small* FCI, KC(GB).
• **SIZE** *Large* Height: dogs about 61cm (24in), bitches about 58–59cm (23in). Weight: dogs 25–29kg (55–65lb), bitches about 25kg (55lb). *Small* Height: 47.5–55cm (19–22in). Average weight: 15kg (33lb).
• **COAT** Moderately long and dense, with feathering.
• **COLOUR** *Large* Head solid black, white blaze, strip or star allowed; body white or blue roan with black patches, flecks, ticks, or a combination of these. *Small* Liver and white with ticking.
• **OTHER FEATURES** Head well proportioned in relation to body and slightly elongated; medium-sized, intelligent eyes; broad, high-set ears; strong back; tail well set on in line with back.

WEIMARANER

The Weimaraner or "Silver Ghost" bears a striking resemblance to a painting by Van Dyck (*circa* 1631). However, it is said to have been purpose-bred as a gundog in the 1800s by the Grand Duke Karl August of Weimar (the capital of the former state of Thuringia in central Germany), after which the breed is named. Breeds which are likely to have played a part in its make-up include the Saint Hubert or other French hounds, Short-haired Pointers, Spanish Pointers, Bloodhounds and the German Schweisshunds. The result is a fine gundog, which was originally used against big game and, in more recent times, has worked as a police dog.

The Weimaraner made an impact in the United States and Canada after the Second World War. It did not reach the United Kingdom until the 1950s, but it has since become very popular there.

Character and care

The Weimaraner is good natured and distinctive looking, with a metallic silver-grey coat and amber or blue-grey eyes. It excels in obedience and agility, and makes a fine pet provided that it has an outlet for its keen intelligence. It is best housed indoors rather than in a kennel and requires little grooming.

KEY CHARACTERISTICS
● **CLASS** Gundog. **Recognized** AKC, ANKC, CKC, FCI, KC(GB), KUSA.
● **SIZE** Height at withers: dogs 61–69cm (24–27in), bitches 56–64cm (22–25in). Weight: 31.7–38kg (70–85lb).
● **COAT** Short, smooth and sleek.
● **COLOUR** Preferably silver grey; shades of mouse or roe grey permissible.
● **OTHER FEATURES** Head moderately long and aristocratic; medium-sized eyes; long ears; deep chest and moderately long body; tail characteristically docked.

PORTUGUESE SETTER

The Portuguese Setter or Pointer (Perdiguerio Português) probably traces back to the Segugio hounds and the Assyrian Mastiff. The Portuguese Setter has been known since the 14th century and, with the Spanish Pointer, may have been the ancestor of other pointer-type breeds. Originally used as a bird dog (*perdiguerio* means partridge), this is a good all-round gundog with an excellent nose. It is popular with hunters in Portugal but little known outside that country.

Character and care

This prodigious hunter is speedy, attentive, skilful and intelligent. Its aim in life is to please its master and it will retrieve game with the utmost joy. It is also very affectionate, and often fills the role of house dog as well as hunting companion in its native land. It should be given a brush and rub-down every few days.

KEY CHARACTERISTICS
● **CLASS** Gundog. **Recognized** FCI.
● **SIZE** Height: dogs 52–61cm (20½–24in), bitches 48–56cm (19–22in).
● **COAT** Short, strong and dense.
● **COLOUR** Yellow or brown, with or without plain markings.
● **OTHER FEATURES** Head in good proportion to body; eyes full, symmetrical and large; ears medium length and width; body deep and broad, indicative of ample heart and lung room; tail characteristically docked at third joint, if not, should not reach further than hocks, preferably shorter.

The Weimaraner, a favourite at the 19th century Court of Weimar, developed into a versatile utility dog, working for the police as well as in the field.

STABYHOUN

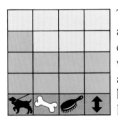

The Stabyhoun originated in the Friesland area of the Netherlands, where it was bred as an all-purpose gundog. It is known to have existed at least since 1800 but was not recognized by the Dutch Kennel Club until 1942. This first-class retriever and pointer is an extremely popular dog in its native land, but is little known outside the Netherlands. In appearance it is somewhere between a setter and a spaniel, and is said to produce a formidable rat-catcher when crossed with the Wetterhoun.

Character and care
Although it is a good versatile sporting dog, the Stabyhoun is now kept mainly as a family pet and has adapted well to this role. It is good with children, easy to train, affectionate, and requires only regular brushing to keep its coat in good condition. It requires a lot of exercise.

KEY CHARACTERISTICS

- **CLASS** Gundog.
  Recognized FCI.

- **SIZE** Maximum height: dogs 49.5cm (19in), bitches somewhat smaller. Weight: 14.8–19.9kg (33–44lb).

- **COAT** Long and sleek, but short on head; bushy feathering on tail.

- **COLOUR** White with black, blue, liver or orange markings.

- **OTHER FEATURES** Lean head narrowing to a black nose; brown eyes; folded, "trowel-shaped" ears; long tail, set on low and hanging straight.

WIRE-HAIRED POINTING GRIFFON

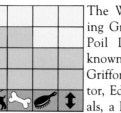

The Wire-haired Pointing Griffon or Griffon à Poil Dur is commonly known as the Korthals Griffon after its originator, Edward Karel Korthals, a Dutchman and dedicated dog-fancier. It was Korthals' desire to produce a gundog that could be used against all game over a variety of terrain. He used various types of griffon, setter and water spaniel, including the French Setter (Braque) and Barbet. Korthals succeeded in producing a versatile gundog of extreme endurance and with a good sense of smell. Unfortunately it is now comparatively rare.

Although listed as a French breed, the Wire-haired Pointing Griffon was developed by a Dutchman from French and German stock.

Character and care
The Wire-haired Pointing Griffon boasts all the fine qualities of its ancestors – strength, good nature, docility, intelligence and fine working ability. It is favoured by the one-dog huntsman, and it can be kennelled out of doors or live in the house as a member of the family. It requires plenty of exercise. Its coat should not be groomed too vigorously, and it needs some trimming.

KEY CHARACTERISTICS
• **CLASS** Gundog. **Recognized** AKC, CKC, FCI.
• **SIZE** Height: dogs 56–60cm (22–24in), bitches 51–56cm (20–22in). Weight: 22.7–27.2kg (50–60lb).
• **COAT** Coarse and hard.
• **COLOUR** Steel grey with chestnut markings; white and chestnut; white.
• **OTHER FEATURES** Large, long head; large eyes, with mild but lively expression; pendant ears; slightly arched neck; muscular tail, customarily docked and carried horizontally.

HUNGARIAN COARSE-HAIRED VIZSLA

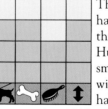

The Hungarian Coarse-haired Vizsla or Setter is the result of crossing the Hungarian Vizsla (a smooth-haired setter) with the German Wire-haired Pointer or Drahthaar in the 1930s. The Hungarian Vizsla probably descended from the Weimaraner (see page 136) and Transylvanian pointing dogs. The product of the cross is a keen-looking, medium-sized hound of regal bearing, with a tough coat, strong bone and considerable powers of endurance.

Character and care
The Hungarian Coarse-haired Vizsla has good scenting ability, and is a hardy all-round gundog. It is good natured and easy to train. It needs plenty of exercise, and should be given a brush and rub down every few days.

KEY CHARACTERISTICS
• **CLASS** Gundog. **Recognized** FCI, KC(GB).
• **SIZE** Height at withers: dogs 57.5–64cm (22½–25½in), bitches 53.5–59.5cm (21–23½).
• **COAT** Short and hard, bearded; hair slightly longer on ears, but fine.
• **COLOUR** Dark yellow.
• **OTHER FEATURES** Lean, noble head; eyes neither protruding nor deep set; ears set on at medium length; back straight, short and very muscular; medium-thick tail set on rather low, should be docked to two thirds of its natural length.

HUNGARIAN VIZSLA

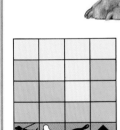

The Hungarian Vizsla or Magyar Vizsla is the national hunting dog of Hungary. This smooth-haired setter was bred on the central Hungarian plain (Puszta), the habitat of a wide variety of game. The Vizsla was developed as an extremely versatile dog, able to hunt, track, point and retrieve hare, ducks, geese and other prey. It is likely that the German Weimaraner, to which it bears a strong resemblance, and Transylvanian pointing dogs played a part in its early development. However, Magyar noblemen took immense care not to introduce new blood that might prove in any way detrimental to the ability of this breed.

It was not until after the Second World War, when many sportsmen had to leave Hungary and took their dogs with them, that the Vizsla became widely known. The breed was recognized by the American Kennel Club in 1960 and now there are also some splendid Vizsla kennels in the United Kingdom.

Character and care

The Vizsla is a versatile, easily trained gundog which also makes a first-class pet and is good with children. It needs plenty of exercise and its coat should be brushed regularly.

KEY CHARACTERISTICS
● **CLASS** Gundog. **Recognized** AKC, ANKC, CKC, FCI, KC(GB), KUSA.
● **SIZE** Height at withers: dogs 57–64cm (22½–25in), bitches 53–60cm (21–23½in). Weight: 20–30kg (48½–66lb).
● **COAT** Short, dense and straight.
● **COLOUR** Russet gold; small white marks on chest and feet acceptable.
● **OTHER FEATURES** Lean head; ears moderately low set; short, level, well-muscled back; tail moderately thick.

Bred for the temperature extremes of the central Hungarian plain, the Vizsla is an all weather sportsman.

KOOIKERHONDJE

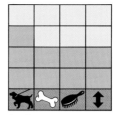

The Kooikerhondje is an old breed, familiar from paintings of 17th century Dutch masters such as Vermeer.

This breed is also known as the Kooiker Dog or Duck-decoy Dog. Its Dutch name means "dog belonging to the Kooiker", the person in charge of the duck decoy. It is a fairly old breed, native to the Netherlands, whose job was to draw ducks out of their cover by walking in and out of low reed fences by the banks of a dyke that was covered with netting. When the ducks investigated, the dyke was closed. Since the Second World War, efforts have been made to improve its breeding, and it has recently been introduced into the United Kingdom.

Character and care
The Kooikerhondje is an intelligent, affectionate dog, which is lively but not over-excitable. A good companion dog, it is a handy size for a household pet. It needs plenty of exercise and daily brushing.

ITALIAN SPINONE

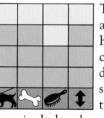

The Italian Spinone is an ancient gundog breed. However, it has only recently become a contender in the international show ring and in field trials. Opinions vary, even in Italy, about the dog's origin, as to whether it is of setter descent – climatic conditions alone accounting for its thick coat – or a relative of the coarse-haired Italian Segugio or, indeed, a Griffon cross.

Other authorities believe that this powerful, versatile hunter originated in the French region of Bresse, later finding its way to Piedmont in Italy, and that its evolution is attributable not only to the French Griffon, but also to German Pointers, the Porcelaine, the now extinct Barbet and the Korthals Griffon. Or the Spinone may be the result of a mating between a Coarse-haired Setter and a white mastiff.

Character and care
Affectionate, agreeable and of loyal temperament, the Italian Spinone has a soft mouth and will both point and retrieve. It needs plenty of vigorous exercise, is a fine swimmer and is best suited to country life.

KEY CHARACTERISTICS
• **CLASS** Gundog. **Recognized** AKC, ANKC, CKC, FCI, KC(GB), KUSA.
• **SIZE** Height at shoulders: dogs 58.75–68.75cm (23½–27½in), bitches 57.5–63.75cm (23–25½in). Weight: dogs 31.75–37kg (70–82lb), bitches 28.2–32.02kg (62–71lb).
• **COAT** Rough, thick, fairly wiry.
• **COLOUR** White, white with orange markings, solid white peppered orange, white with brown markings, white speckled with brown (brown roan), with or without brown markings.
• **OTHER FEATURES** Expressive eyes; ears triangular; body length equal to height at withers; tail thick at base, carried horizontally.

A newcomer to the international show ring, the Spinone is still hunted throughout the Piedmont.

ITALIAN SETTER

The Italian Setter (or Pointer) or Bracco Italiano has a most attractive hound-like appearance with pendulous ears and a kindly expression. It is thought to be one of the oldest of the setters having certainly been well established in the 18th century. The breed was probably derived through crossings with the Italian Segugio and the now-extinct Assyrian Mastiff. In its country of origin, the Italian Setter is divided into two varieties according to colour – the white and orange, and the chestnut roan. The white and orange is believed to have originated in Piedmont and is usually thought of as the original. The roan, which is attributed to Lombardy, is considered by some fanciers to trace back to crosses between imported setters and the old Saint Hubert Hound. However, there is no recognized difference in conformation between the two varieties.

Character and care
The Italian Setter is a good natured, intelligent gundog, and is docile yet powerful. It combines the role of gundog and family companion. It needs plenty of exercise, and a brush and rub down every day or two.

KEY CHARACTERISTICS
● **CLASS** Gundog. **Recognized** FCI, KC(GB).
● **SIZE** Height: 54.5–62cm (21½–26½in) but varies considerably. Weight: 25–40kg (55–88lb).
● **COAT** Short and fine.
● **COLOUR** Generally orange and white, or chestnut roan.
● **OTHER FEATURES** Long, angular head with pronounced, arched eyebrows; yellow or ochre eyes; well-developed, pendant ears; prominent withers; back almost straight as far as 11th vertebra; tail characteristically docked to 15–25cm (6–10in).

HOUNDS

THE PHARAOH HOUND

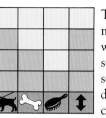

In typical pose, the Pharaoh Hound recalls the Egyptian dog-god Anubis, whose task it was to guide the souls of the newly departed into the after-life.

The Pharaoh Hound is a medium-sized sight breed which will also hunt by scent. It has been described as the oldest domesticated dog in recorded history because it so closely resembles the likenesses of dogs carved on the tomb walls of the pharaohs and on ancient Egyptian artefacts dating back to at least 2000BC. In 1935, archaeologists working in the great cemetery west of the Pyramid of Cheops, at Giza, found an inscription recording that such a dog, named Abuwtiyuw, had been buried with all the ritual ceremony of a great man of Egypt by order of the kings of Upper and Lower Egypt.

It is thought that these hounds were taken to Malta and Gozo by the Phoenicians. First imported into the UK in the 1920s, the breed was re-established in Britain in 1968 when eight examples were imported from Gozo and Malta, and it was soon recognized. It was introduced into North America in the late 1960s and was subsequently recognized.

Character and care

The affectionate and intelligent Pharaoh Hound has a happy, confident personality, likes children and makes a good family pet. Its coat needs little attention but the breed does require plenty of exercise and is not suited to cramped conditions.

KEY CHARACTERISTICS

- **CLASS** Hound.
  Recognized AKC, ANKC, CKC, FCI, KC(GB).

- **SIZE** Height at withers: dogs 55–62.5cm (22–25in), bitches 52.5–60.5cm (21–24in).

- **COAT** Short and glossy.

- **COLOUR** Tan or rich tan with white markings; white tip on tail strongly desirable; white star on chest, white on toes and slim white blaze on centre line of face permissible; flecking or white other than above undesirable.

- **OTHER FEATURES** Long, lean, well-chiselled head; eyes amber, blending with coat; medium-sized ears set high; lithe body with almost straight top line; tail medium set, fairly thick at base and tapering towards tip, reaching just below point of hock in repose.

Large, erect ears designed to radiate heat betray the Pharaoh Hound's desert origins.

SICILIAN HOUND

Bred in Sicily for 3000 years, the Sicilian Hound is a close relative of the Pharaoh Hound.

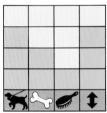

The Sicilian Hound is also known as the Cirneco dell'Etna after the volcano, Mount Etna, on the Italian island of Sicily. It is thought to have been brought from Egypt to Sicily over 3000 years ago by the Phoenicians. They are reputed to have carried on a most profitable trade in greyhounds and other sighthounds, which they acquired in Africa and Asia and unloaded in Aegean and Mediterranean mainland ports and islands, including Sicily. This ancient breed of sighthound is smaller than the obviously related Pharaoh and Ibizan Hounds. The length of its muzzle is approximately that of its skull, its eyes are oval and deep set, and its coat is short and fine. It is a mysterious, wise-looking hound which is said by some to have supernatural powers as well as serving the more practical purpose of hunting wild rabbit, hare and other game on the slopes of Mount Etna.

Character and care

The Sicilian is a quiet hunter with an excellent nose, even though it is primarily a sighthound. It will adapt to the role of a companion. Its coat needs little attention. Its ethereal looks belie a strong constitution.

KEY CHARACTERISTICS
● **CLASS** Hound. **Recognized** FCI.
● **SIZE** Height at shoulders: dogs 45.5–51cm (18–20in), bitches 43–45.5cm (17–18in). Weight: dogs about 12–13.5kg (26–30lb), bitches 10–12kg (22–26lb).
● **COAT** Harsh to the touch.
● **COLOUR** Any shade of fawn, small white markings acceptable; solid white, or white with orange markings.
● **OTHER FEATURES** Long head with oval-shaped skull; triangular ears with stiff, straight points, carried erect; body as long as it is high; fairly long tail set on low, without brush or long hair.

IBIZAN HOUND

The Ibizan Hound, seen above in wire-haired form, is descended from the same stock of Middle Eastern prick-eared dogs as the Pharaoh and Sicilian Hounds.

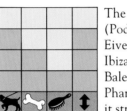

The Ibizan Hound (Podenco Ibicenco, Ca Eivessenc) is native to Ibiza, one of the Spanish Balearic Isles. Like the Pharaoh Hound, which it strongly resembles, it is descended from hunting dogs kept by the ancient Egyptians. In the 9th century BC, Egypt was invaded by the Romans, and the neighbouring Carthaginians and Phoenicians were driven out to the island of Ibiza, where they lived for about a century. However, the hounds they took with them remained on Ibiza for the next 3000 years, still retaining the colours depicted on Egyptian drawings of their ancestors. The breed was also used for hunting in southern Spain and France. The Ibizan Hound comes in three varieties: smooth-, coarse- and long-haired.

Character and care

This noble-looking animal has a kindly nature, is good with children, rarely fights and makes a fine gundog or housepet. It is extremely sensitive and has acute hearing, so must never be shouted at, but responds well to kind treatment. Like all hounds it needs a lot of exercise. Its coat is easy to maintain, needing only a daily brushing.

SPANISH GREYHOUND

The Spanish Greyhound or Galgo Español is an ancient breed, whose ancestors are believed to have been brought by the Phoenicians many centuries BC. Favoured by the Spanish nobility, it is used mainly for coursing. It is smaller and slightly sturdier than the English Greyhound. There is also an Anglo-Spanish variety produced by crosses to the English Greyhound for use on the race-track. The Anglo-Spanish is closer in appearance to the English Greyhound but has darker eyes and a longer tail.

Character and care

Like all greyhounds, the Spanish is a gentle dog and, once de-trained, makes a very good pet, provided that care is taken around livestock. Greyhounds kept for coursing are accustomed to being kennelled in fairly confined spaces and a pet greyhound quickly adapts to the confines of an average-sized home. Regular exercise is more important than speed or distance travelled, and regular brushing is also required.

KEY CHARACTERISTICS
• **CLASS** Hound. **Recognized** FCI.
• **SIZE** Height: dogs 65–70cm (25½–27½in), bitches slightly smaller. Weight: 27.2–29.7kg (60–66lb).
• **COAT** Close, shiny and short.
• **COLOUR** Tawny with black mask, or black usually streaked with light undercoat; white muzzle, belly and feet.
• **OTHER FEATURES** Long, narrow head; dark, bright, vivacious eyes; rose-type ears falling down back; very long, slightly sabred tail carried low.

KEY CHARACTERISTICS

- **CLASS** Hound.
  Recognized AKC, ANKC, CKC, FCI, KC(GB), KUSA.

- **SIZE** Height at withers: dogs 59–69cm (23½–27½in), bitches 56–65cm (22½–26in). Weight: dogs about 22.7kg (50lb), bitches about 20.2kg (45lb).

- **COAT** Smooth or rough; always hard, close and dense.

- **COLOUR** Solid white, chestnut or lion, or any combination of these.

- **OTHER FEATURES** Long, fine head; flat skull with prominent occipital bone; clear amber, expressive eyes; large, thin, stiff, highly mobile ears; level back; long thin tail set on low.

A fast, silent hunter, the Ibizan is extremely agile, and can jump up to 2.5m (8ft) in height from a standstill.

PORTUGUESE PODENGO

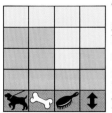

The Podengo or Portuguese Hound is known, but rarely seen, outside its native Portugal, but it is popular there, particularly in the north. It is kept as a companion, and as a hunter of rabbit, hare and deer.

The breed is descended from a number of ancient sighthounds, and over the years three size varieties have been developed to suit different terrains and prey. The Large (Grande) chases larger, fleet quarry over flat ground, the Medium (Medio) is used over rougher terrain, while the Small (Pequeño) can go down burrows to flush out rabbits. The Small Podengo looks rather like a big Chihuahua, indeed, the Chihuahua was originally a larger dog with the same large prick ears. The Medium closely resembles the Ibizan Hound.

Character and care
The Podengo is an attractive, good-natured hunter, which also makes a fine guard and a lively companion. All three varieties need plenty of exercise and daily brushing.

KEY CHARACTERISTICS

- **CLASS** Hound.
  Recognized FCI.

- **SIZE** Height: *Small* 20.5–30.5cm (8–12in); *Medium* 50–56cm (20–22in); *Large* 56–58.5cm (22–27in).

- **COAT** Long and harsh; short and silky.

- **COLOUR** Predominantly fawn or yellow, with or without white markings.

- **OTHER FEATURES** Sharp nose; large ears set high and carried erect, open at front; tail carried like a sickle; moderately long, muscular body.

BASENJI

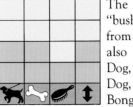

The Basenji (meaning "bush thing") comes from central Africa and is also called the Zande Dog, Belgian Congo Dog, Congo Bush Dog, Bongo Terrier, Congo Terrier and Nyam Nyam Terrier. Its likeness is depicted on the tombs of the pharaohs and its very expression seems to hint at inner wisdom and antiquity. Used as a hunting dog in its native land, the Basenji is famed for the fact that it does not bark, instead giving a kind of yodel.

European explorers came upon the breed in the mid-19th century in the Congo and southern Sudan and the first Basenjis reached Britain in 1895. They were exhibited at Crufts as Congo Terriers and evoked considerable interest. Unfortunately, they succumbed to distemper before any breeding programme could be attempted, and further imports in the 1920s and 1930s also perished. Then, in 1941, two African-bred pups imported into Massachusetts survived, and the Basenji Club of America was established in 1942. Later, Miss Veronica Tudor Williams pioneered the breed in the United Kingdom.

The Basenji, descended from the earliest Pariah dogs of African prehistory, is today best known as the dog with no bark.

Character and care

The Basenji is playful, extremely loving, dislikes wet weather and needs a reasonable amount of exercise. It washes itself like a cat and has no doggie smell, so a daily rub-down with a hound glove will suffice. In common with certain other breeds, the bitch comes into season only once a year. Pups may be destructive if unchecked. Some good friends who took in a misplaced Basenji frequently complained about the damage their young dog had done. That period soon passed, however, and 15 years later the family were inconsolable at Benji the Basenji's passing.

KEY CHARACTERISTICS
• **CLASS** Hound. **Recognized** AKC, ANKC, CKC, FCI, KC(GB), KUSA.
• **SIZE** Height at withers: dogs about 43cm (17in), bitches 40cm (16in). Weight: dogs about 10.8kg (24lb), bitches 9.9kg (22lb).
• **COAT** Short, sleek, close and very fine.
• **COLOUR** Black, red, or black and tan; all should have white on chest, on feet and tail tips; white blaze, collar and legs optional; black and tan with tan melon pips and black, tan and white mask.
• **OTHER FEATURES** Dark, almond-shaped eyes: small, pointed ears, erect and slightly rounded; well balanced body with short, level back; tail set on high, curling tightly over spine and lying close to thigh, with a single or double curve.

Though Basenjis may vary in colour, the white "shirt front" is a standard feature.

BLACK AND TAN COONHOUND

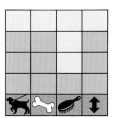

The (American) Black and Tan Coonhound is one of a number of varieties of coonhound recognized by America's United Kennel Club, the others including the Redbone (see below) and Treeing Walker (see page 249). All were purpose bred to hunt raccoon and opossum, and will chase their quarry up a tree and hold it there for the hunters. The energetic Black and Tan also has the endurance needed to trail larger game such as stags and bears.

The Black and Tan is a descendant of the extinct Talbot Hound and various Bloodhound crosses to which the blood of the American Virginia Foxhound has been added. It bears a close resemblance to the Bloodhound and has similar, long pendulous ears, but lacks the skin folds. Although a frequent contender in field trials, it is rarely seen in the show ring except at special coonhound shows.

Character and care
This friendly, intelligent dog is able to cope with both extremes of climate and difficult terrain. It is a hard worker and obedient to its master. A secure, high fence is needed to keep it in, and it is usually kennelled out of doors. Its ears need regular checking as they need to be kept clean.

KEY CHARACTERISTICS
• **CLASS** Hound. **Recognized** AKC, CKC, FCI.
• **SIZE** Height at shoulders: dogs 63.5–68.5cm (25–27in), bitches 58.5–63.5cm (23–25in). Weight: dogs 27–36.5kg (60–80lb), bitches 25–34kg (55–75lb).
• **COAT** Short and dense.
• **COLOUR** Black and tan only.
• **OTHER FEATURES** Finely modelled head; round, chestnut-coloured eyes; long, pendant ears; well-proportioned body; strong tail carried freely.

REDBONE COONHOUND

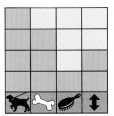

This is one of six varieties of Coonhound recognized by the United Kennel Club of America (UKC), the others being the Black and Tan, English, Bluetick, Treeing Walker and Plott. All are mainly descended from foxhounds. However, other hounds played a part in their development and, in common with the Black and Tan, the Redbone resembles more closely the English Bloodhound than a foxhound.

As their name suggests, the coonhounds were bred to hunt the raccoon, a quarry that is prevalent throughout the United States except for Alaska and Hawaii, and is also found in Canadian forests. Since the raccoon is nocturnal, it is hunted at night. The Redbone has excellent scenting and hunting abilities. It also adapts well to working in a variety of terrains. As well as being popular in the US, the Redbone is also now found in Central and South America and Japan.

Character and care
The Redbone Coonhound is an efficient and handsome working dog, which is faithful to its owner and generally good natured. It requires plenty of exercise and grooming with a hound glove.

KEY CHARACTERISTICS
• **CLASS** Hound. **Recognized**
• **SIZE** Height: 63.5–68.5cm (25–27in), bitches 58.5–63.5cm (23–25in).
• **COAT** Dense, short and harsh.
• **COLOUR** Red, sometimes with small white marks on chest and feet.
• **OTHER FEATURES** Eyes hazel to dark brown; ears set low and well back; strong tail with base slightly below level of back line.

BLOODHOUND

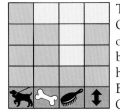

The world's finest tracker, the Bloodhound can follow a cold trail after hours or even days have passed.

Long, drooping ears, wrinkles and dewlaps give the Bloodhound an expression of inconsolable sadness.

The Bloodhound or Chien de Saint Hubert is one of the oldest hound breeds. It is believed to have been brought to Britain by William the Conqueror in 1066, and the description of it written by the dog historian, Doctor Caius, in 1553 differs little from that of the dog we know today.

It is generally believed that the earliest ancestors of the Bloodhound were dogs bred in Assyria, in Mesopotamia, around 2000–1000BC. Some of these were probably taken to the Mediterranean region by Phoenician traders, and from there spread north through Europe. A concentration of hounds developed in Brittany in the 7th and 8th centuries, from which emerged the Saint Hubert, thought to be the direct ancestor of the Bloodhound.

The Bloodhound has the keenest sense of smell of any domestic animal. Able to follow a days-old scent, it has been used to track down lost people as well as game and, having found its quarry, this gentle animal does not kill it. To help develop its skills, owners join a Bloodhound Club and participate in what is known as "Hunting the Clean Boot". Pups learn early on how to "follow a line", beginning by playing simple games of hide and seek with their owners. There are Bloodhound clubs in many countries.

Character and care

Good with children and exceedingly affectionate, the Bloodhound makes an ideal companion for those who have the room to accommodate it, the energy to exercise it, and neighbours who do not object to its baying. It can be kept in an average-sized home provided that it has adequate exercise, but is best suited to a rural environment. It should be groomed daily with a hound glove.

KEY CHARACTERISTICS
• **CLASS** Hound. **Recognized** AKC, ANKC, CKC, FCI, KC(GB), KUSA.
• **SIZE** Height: dogs 63–67.5cm (25–27in), bitches 58–63cm (23–25in). Weight: dogs 40.5–48.6kg (90–110lb), bitches 36.3–45kg (80–100lb).
• **COAT** Smooth, short and weatherproof.
• **COLOUR** Black and tan, liver (red) and tan, or red.
• **OTHER FEATURES** Head narrow in proportion to length, and long in proportion to body; medium-sized eyes; thin, soft ears set very low; well-sprung ribs; tail (stern) long, thick and tapering to a point.

OTTERHOUND

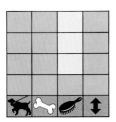

The big, strongly built British Otterhound is believed to trace back to the Griffon Vendéen and the now extinct rough-coated Griffon de Bresse. According to the Otterhound Club, these hounds were imported into Britain in significant numbers before 1870. Shortly afterwards, the Comte le Couteuix de Canteleu sent his entire pack of Griffons to a Mr Richard Carnaby Forster who gave them to his stepdaughter, Lady Mary Hamilton. In 1906, the Hamilton Otterhounds were sold individually to masters of Otterhounds.

The Otterhound has keen scenting abilities almost on a par with the Bloodhound. The dogs, which are fine swimmers, would swim upriver, following the otter's "wash" (trail of bubbles). When otter hunting was outlawed in the United Kingdom in the late 1970s, the Master of the Kendal and District Otterhounds in the Lake District set up the Otterhound Club to ensure its survival. In 1981, a breed standard was approved by the British Kennel Club and since then, the attractive Otterhound has become a popular contender in the show ring on both sides of the Atlantic.

Character and care

The Otterhound makes an amiable though stubborn pet, which can be somewhat destructive within the household, if undisciplined. Like other thick-coated breeds it can be kennelled outdoors, if the owner wishes, though many Otterhounds do live indoors. It needs a considerable amount of exercise and its rough coat should be groomed once a week, and bathed as necessary.

The Otterhound is a shaggy breed with a majestic head framed by long, pendulous ears.

KEY CHARACTERISTICS
• **CLASS** Hound. **Recognized** AKC, ANKC, CKC, FCI, KC(GB), KUSA.
• **SIZE** Height: dogs 60–67.5cm (24–27in), bitches 57.5–65cm (23–26in). Weight: dogs 33.7–51.7kg (75–115lb), bitches 29.5–45kg (65–100lb).
• **COAT** Long (4.8cm/1½–3in), dense, rough and harsh, but not wiry.
• **COLOUR** All hound colours permissible.
• **OTHER FEATURES** Clean, very imposing head; intelligent eyes; long, pendulous ears – a unique feature of the breed – set on level with corner of eyes; deep chest with fairly deep, well-sprung rib-cage; tail (stern) set on high, carried up when alert or moving.

Said to possess scenting abilities almost on a par with those of the Bloodhound, the Otterhound is increasingly rare now that otter are a protected species.

ITALIAN SEGUGIO

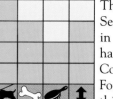

The Italian Segugio or Segugio Italiano comes in two coat types, Short-haired (a Pelo Raso) and Coarse-haired (a Pelo Forte). The origins of this ancient Italian hunting dog trace back to the coursing dogs of ancient Egypt and it still has something of the Greyhound in its appearance. As well as having keen eyesight, it is blessed with an exceptional sense of smell, and was used against a wide variety of game. Today it is used mainly to hunt hare. The Segugio will remain bravely within firing distance once it has found its quarry.

Character and care

It can cope with most types of terrain, and is a natural hunter, but it should be trained in its working role during its early months. It is generally good natured, if a little strong willed, and can be kept as a companion dog. It needs plenty of exercise, but its coat needs little attention apart from regular brushing.

Fixed in type at least since the Renaissance, the Italian Segugio stands midway between the sight- and scent hounds.

RHODESIAN RIDGEBACK

Before Europeans began to settle in southern Africa, the local Khoikhoi people were accompanied on their hunting expeditions by a dog with the distinctive ridge of hair growing in the reverse direction along its back. During the 16th and 17th centuries, Dutch, German and Huguenot immigrants to southern Africa brought as guards and hunters their own working dogs including Pointers, Mastiffs, Greyhounds and Bulldogs. These crossed with the Ridgeback, gradually producing an animal with the best qualities of the imported and local dogs.

The Rhodesian Ridgeback was named after the country of Rhodesia (now Zimbabwe), where it was highly valued by the settlers. It was also known once as the Lion Dog because it was used in packs to hunt lions and other big game, as well as to guard property. The standard was drawn up by the South African Kennel Club in 1922 and has altered little since. It attracts good entries in shows in North America and Britain and behaves well in the ring.

Character and care

This attractive animal is obedient, good with children and will guard its owners with its life. It has a gentle temperament but can move with great speed when it spies a rabbit or some other prey. It needs plenty of exercise and daily grooming with a hound glove.

Ancestors of the modern Ridgeback came originally from South Africa – the product of European dogs crossed with Hottentot hounds.

KEY CHARACTERISTICS
● **CLASS** Hound. **Recognized** AKC, ANKC, CKC, FCI, KC(GB), KUSA.
● **SIZE** Height at withers: dogs 63–67cm (25–26½in), bitches 61–66cm (24–26in). Weight: 29.5–33.7kg (65–75lb).
● **COAT** Short, dense, sleek and glossy.
● **COLOUR** Light wheaten to red wheaten.
● **OTHER FEATURES** Flat skull, broad between ears; round eyes, set moderately well apart; ears set rather high; chest very deep but not too wide; tail strong at root and tapering towards tip.

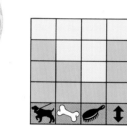

The Segugio's long muzzle is slightly convex, with very little stop and no excess skin. The ears are long and narrow.

KEY CHARACTERISTICS

- **CLASS** Hound.
  Recognized FCI, KC(GB).

- **SIZE** Height: dogs 53–58.5cm (21–23in), bitches 48–56cm (19–22in). Weight: 17.7–28kg (39–62lb).

- **COAT** Dense, glossy and smooth; or coarse on head, ears, body, legs and tail.

- **COLOUR** Various shades of red, fawn or black and tan.

- **OTHER FEATURES** Large, luminous eyes; ears flat, should hang and be flat for almost their entire length; length of body from the shoulder to the buttock should equal the height at the withers; tail set on high in line with croup.

Bred as a guard dog by European settlers, the Rhodesian Ridgeback also developed the speed, stamina and courage to hunt lion.

TAHLTAN BEAR DOG

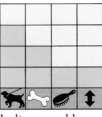

This Canadian breed, native to mountainous areas of north-west Canada, is named after the Tahltan Indians, who used it for hunting bear, lynx and porcupine. The Indians would carry the dogs on their backs in sacks to preserve their strength until the quarry was sighted. Then the dogs would be released and would hold the quarry at bay, circling it, nipping its ankles and barking like a fox, until the hunters went in for the kill.

The Tahltan Bear Dog's courage and ferocity are belied by its appealing looks. It is an attractive, fox-like little dog with enormous ears, an alert expression and, most unusually, a tail which is some 12.5–20.5cm (5–8in) long, and carried erect and thick from tip to stern. The breed was recognized by the Canadian Kennel Club in 1941 but, sadly, has not adapted to living outside its native environment and is now almost extinct. Its decline has been aggravated by breeding difficulties. The Tahltan Bear Dog only mates once a year, has a maximum of four pups and the dam will kill her offspring if she is in any way disturbed.

Character and care

A lively, fearless hunter, powerful for its size, the Tahltan Bear Dog is said to have shared a tent with its human family and to have been gentle and affectionate with them. Its coat requires regular brushing.

KEY CHARACTERISTICS

- **CLASS** Hound.
  Recognized CKC.

- **SIZE** Height: 30.5–40.5cm (12–16in). Weight: about 6.8kg (15lb).

- **COAT** Thick and long, with a soft undercoat.

- **COLOUR** Black, black and white, greyish blue or white.

- **OTHER FEATURES** Fox-like head; dark, medium-sized eyes; erect, bat-like ears; flexible body; wiry tail, very thick from root to tip, carried vertically.

ANGLO-FRENCH HOUNDS

The Middle-sized Anglo-French White and Orange Hound, more delicate than the larger variety, was produced by crossings with the Harrier, Poitevin and Porcelaine.

Great Anglo-French Hounds like this pack of Tricolours are hunting dogs and are almost never seen in the show ring. They have heavier bodies and smaller ears than the Medium-sized and Small varieties.

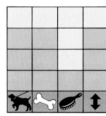

As its name suggests, the Anglo-French or Anglo-Français de Moyen Venerie came about through crossings between French medium-sized hounds and an English hound, the Harrier. At one time, the dogs were named after the breeds that had produced them, such as Harrier-Poitevin and Harrier-Porcelaine. In addition, as the experts George Johnston and Maria Ericson have recorded,

the word Bâtard (meaning crossbred hounds) was often used as a prefix, as in, for example, the Bâtard-Anglo-Gascon-Saintongeois. In 1957, the Anglo-French was given its current title and categorized by colour as Anglo-French White and Black, Anglo-French White and Orange, and Anglo-French Tricolour. The latter is one of the most popular hounds in France and all are used to hunt deer, wild boar and other quarry.

Like the Anglo-French, the Great Anglo-French or Grande Anglo-Français was pro-

duced by crossing French and English hounds. In the case of this larger breed the English blood introduced was that of the English Foxhound. At one time the dogs tended to be identified by the crossing, for instance, the Anglo-French-Poitevin and Anglo-Gascon-Saintongeois. Then, in 1957, the breed was given its current name and categorized by colour as the Great Anglo-French Tricolour, Great Anglo-French White and Black, and Great Anglo-French White and Orange.

It is usually kept in packs, and used to hunt large and small game. The Small Anglo-French or Anglo-Français de Petite Venerie is the result of crossings between the Beagle or Beagle Harrier and short-haired, medium-sized French hounds. Except for size, it is similar in appearance to its larger relatives, the Anglo-French and the Great Anglo-French. The Small has fine attributes and is used for hunting rabbit, pheasant and other small game. However, it has never become popular. It is recognized by the FCI, but there is still too much variation for it to achieve a breed standard.

Character and care
The Anglo-French are, in the main, robust and good natured hounds. They are usually kept as one of a pack, looked after by professional hunt staff.

KEY CHARACTERISTICS
• **CLASS** Hound. **Recognized** FCI.
• **SIZE** *Anglo-French* Height: about 50cm (20in). Weight: 22–25kg (49–55lb). *Great Anglo-French* Height at withers: 61–68.5cm (24–27in). Weight: 29.7–31.9kg (66–71lb). *Small Anglo-French* Height: 48–56cm (19–22in).
• **COAT** Short and smooth.
• **COLOUR** *Anglo-French* Tricolour – black, white and orange; white and black; white and orange. *Great Anglo-French* As for Anglo-French. *Small Anglo-French* Usually tricolour – black, white and orange; may have black saddle covering upper torso and back.
• **OTHER FEATURES** *Anglo-French* Head moderate in size in relation to body; dark eyes; pendulous ears; tail carried low. *Great Anglo-French* Kindly eyes; large, hound-like ears; large, big-boned body; tail carried low. *Small Anglo-French* As for Anglo-French.

BILLY

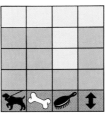

The Billy was devised by Monsieur Hublot du Rivault on his estate in Poitou, south-west France, for the express purpose of hunting wild boar and deer. His pack of dogs, formed in 1877, were known as the Chiens de Haut Poitou. He commenced selective breeding in 1888, using the wolf-hunter, the Poitevin, the Céris, a hunter of both wolf and hare, and the Montembœuf a large, noble hound that would follow only those animals selected as quarry. He called the new breed Billy after a town of that name.

Character and care
The Billy is a tall, intelligent dog, with exceptional hunting and scenting abilities and a melodious voice. It is known to be somewhat argumentative with its fellows. It is usually kept in a pack.

KEY CHARACTERISTICS
• **CLASS** Hound. **Recognized** FCI.
• **SIZE** Height at shoulder: dogs 61–66cm (24–26in), bitches 58.5–63.5cm (23–25in). Weight: 25–29.7kg (55–66lb).
• **COAT** Short and hard to the touch.
• **COLOUR** White or "café au lait"; white with orange or lemon blanket or mottling.
• **OTHER FEATURES** Large, dark, expressive eyes; rather flat ears, set high for a French hound; very deep narrow chest; long, straight tail, sometimes lightly feathered.

With its long legs and streamlined body, the Billy is swift in pursuit of prey across open ground and through thick woodland.

FRENCH HOUNDS

There are three varieties of French Hounds (Chiens Français): the French Tricolour (Chien Français Tricolore), the French White and Black (Chien Français Blanc et Noir) and the French White and Orange (Chien Français Blanc et Orange). Like the Anglo-French (see pages 154–5) they are the result of matings between French and English hounds, particularly the English Foxhound and the Harrier. Until 1957 they were known by a wide variety of names. Then an inventory was made of all hound packs in France and those of French type were given the title French Hounds.

Of the three varieties the White and Black is the most popular and widely represented, being a strong and fast hunter of roe and other deer. The French White and Orange, which was produced by an English Foxhound and Poitevin or Billy cross, is very similar to the Tricolour except in colour.

The Tricolour is a fairly muscular, sophisticated-looking hound of medium build. Its cheeks are more substantial than those of the Poitevin and its stop is more accentuated.

Character and care

These hounds are quiet, affectionate and obedient. However, they are bred only for hunting. They are kept in packs, kennelled out of doors, and looked after by professional hunt staff.

Packs of large hunting dogs have been kept on the great estates of France for centuries. Many varieties have become extinct, but the Tricolour, Orange and White and Red and White have survived.

KEY CHARACTERISTICS

- **CLASS** Hounds. **Recognized** FCI.

- **SIZE** *Tricolour* and *White and Orange* Height: dogs 62–72.5cm (24½–28½in); bitches 62–68.5cm(24½–27in). Weight: 27.2kg (60lb). *White and Black* Height: dogs 65–71cm (25½–28in); bitches 62–68.5cm (24½–27in). Weight: 27.9kg (62lb).

- **COAT** *Tricolour* Smooth and rather fine. *White and Orange* Short and smooth. *White and Black* Smooth, strong and close.

- **COLOUR** *Tricolour* White, black and tan with extensive saddle. *White and Orange.* White and orange *White and black* White and black; extended black saddle or markings; some blue mottling permissible; tan mottling permissible only on legs.

- **OTHER FEATURES** *Tricolour* and *White and Orange* Head not too large; large brown eyes; wide ears; deep chest descending to level of elbows; rather long tail, carried elegantly, hound-fashion. *White and Black* Large, rather long head; dark, intelligent, confident eyes; ears set on above the line of the eyes; chest deep rather than wide; rather long tail, strong at the base and carried elegantly.

POITEVIN

An outbreak of rabies in 1842 nearly wiped out the Poitevin, but, happily, this stylish scenthound has been revived.

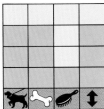

The Poitevin was developed in the late 1600s in the Poitou, south-west France, where wolves existed in large numbers. In 1692, the Marquis François de Larrye of Poitou obtained a dozen Foxhounds from the kennels of the Dauphin of France and crossed these with his own Céris dogs. This produced hounds that were unsurpassed as wolf hunters, possessing great speed, courage and scenting ability. Sadly, most were destroyed during the French Revolution (1789–99) but a few were saved by loyal supporters. Despite crossings thereafter, the Poitevin's original qualities survived and were enhanced by an infusion of English Foxhound blood. The Poitevin now closely resembles the English Foxhound, although it differs in colour and its ears are longer and more slender.

Character and care

The Poitevin is a large, distinguished hound, which is swift and intelligent, but timid and reserved. It is usually happiest when kept as a member of a pack, and looked after by professional hunt staff.

KEY CHARACTERISTICS
● **CLASS** Hound. **Recognized** FCI.
● **SIZE** Height at shoulders: 61–71cm (24–28in). Weight: around 30kg (66lb).
● **COAT** Short and glossy.
● **COLOUR** Tricolour with black saddle; tricolour with large black patches; sometimes orange and white or badger-pied.
● **OTHER FEATURES** Head long but not exaggerated; large, brown, expressive eyes; medium-width ears; very deep chest; back well muscled and very well coupled; medium-length, fine, smooth tail.

GRIFFONS VENDÉEN, GRAND AND BASSET

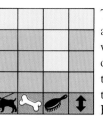

The bewhiskered face and floppy ears give the Grand Griffon Vendéen a disarming expression.

The Griffons Vendéen are French sporting dogs which occur in a number of varieties, including the Grand, the Briquet, the Basset and the Petit Basset. The Grand Griffon Vendéen is the largest and is reputed to be the oldest, of the varieties. It is thought to be a descendant of a white Saint Hubert Hound crossed with a tawny and white Italian bitch, and the resultant dogs were known as the King's White Dogs. The introduction of Nivernais Griffon and setter blood is said to have added stamina and endurance. The Basset Griffon Vendéen, descended from the Grand, is now comparatively rare. It is short legged but otherwise rather similar to the Grand. It has been bred by the Desamy family in the Vendée for more than a century. The Grand was initially used to hunt wolves and, when this role became obsolete, proved itself an agile wild boar hunter. The Grand, Basset and other varieties are also used against hare and rabbit.

Character and care

The Griffons Vendéen are extremely attractive, intelligent dogs which make good family pets as well as hunters. They are independent and love to wander, so all escape routes should be sealed. They require a considerable amount of exercise, and the Grand needs regular grooming with brush and comb to prevent its coat from matting.

KEY CHARACTERISTICS
● **CLASS** Hound. **Recognized** *Grand, Basset* and *Petit Basset* AKC, ANKC, CKC, FCI, KC(GB), KUSA. *Briquet* FCI.
● **SIZE** *Grand* Height at shoulders: 61–66cm (24–26in). Weight: 30–35kg (66–77lb). *Basset* Height at shoulders: 38–43cm (15–17in). Weight: 18–20kg (40–44lb). *Petit Basset* Height at shoulders: 34–38cm (13½–15in). Weight: 11.3–15.7kg (25–35lb). *Briquet* Height at shoulders: 51–56cm (20–22in). Weight: 15.7–23.8kg (35–53lb).
● **COAT** Rough, long and harsh to the touch – never silky or woolly – with a thick undercoat.
● **COLOUR** Solid fawn or hare; white with red, fawn, grey or black markings; bicolour or tricolour.
● **OTHER FEATURES** *Grand, Basset* and *Briquet* Domed head; large, dark eyes, without white, and with a kindly expression; narrow, supple ears; long, wide back; tail set on high, and strong at the base. *Petit Basset* Head medium length and not too wide; large, dark eyes; narrow, fine, supple ears; deep chest with a prominent sternum; medium-length tail, set on high and strong at base.

The sturdy body and thick coat of the Grand Griffon Vendéen equip it to work in all weathers over rough terrain.

PETIT BASSET GRIFFON VENDÉEN

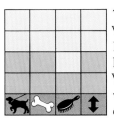

The Petit Basset Griffon Vendéen is a short-legged, rough-coated hound, developed in the Vendée district of south-west France. It was bred down from the Grand Griffon Vendéen, a larger variety originally used in France for wolf hunting and now used against wild boar.

The Petit Basset Griffon Vendéen has been described by Monsieur P. Doubigne, an expert on this breed, as a miniature Basset reduced proportionately in size while retaining all its qualities – a passion for hunting, fearlessness in the densest coverts, activity and vigour. It is now used for hunting hare and rabbit, but can also manage larger game.

It is very popular in France, particularly in its native Vendée region. It is becoming popular in the UK show ring, and is also recognized in the USA.

Character and care
This most attractive animal makes a good family pet provided that it receives plenty of exercise. It needs little grooming and considers humans its friends.

Unlike its larger relatives, the Petit Basset Griffon Vendéen works well in thick undergrowth. It is also strong enough to pursue sizeable prey.

BRIQUET GRIFFON VENDÉEN

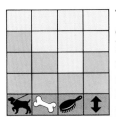

The Briquet Griffon Vendéen is a medium-sized hound from the Vendée region of France. The modern breed was established around 1910. It is popular in Europe both as a tracker and gundog, and is used for hare coursing, like the Grand and Basset Griffon Vendéen, being a smaller version of the former. Strong, fast and agile, this hound is kept in many small packs, or used on its own as a single hunter, in its native France. It is popular in France, but is little known elsewhere.

Character and care
It is courageous and good natured, but difficult to handle. It is usually kept as a member of a pack and looked after by professional hunt staff. It needs a considerable amount of exercise, and regular grooming with brush and comb to prevent its coat from matting.

BEAGLE HARRIER

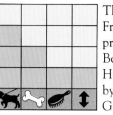

The Beagle Harrier is a French breed which was produced by crossing the Beagle and the larger Harrier. It was developed by the Frenchman, Baron Gérard, whose intention was to produce a hound with the stature of the Harrier and the scenting and hunting ability of the Beagle. Solidly built but graceful, the breed was designed to hunt deer, fox and hare, and has the stamina to run for hours without tiring. It is still used in France today but is not seen outside that country. Like its forebears, it is a typical English hound.

Character and care
The Beagle Harrier is courageous, lively, intelligent and good natured. Like the Beagle, it is affectionate but is much better suited to the role of hunter than as a pet and prefers to live as a member of a pack. It should be groomed with a hound glove.

The vivacious Beagle Harrier is a graceful, compact hunting dog bred expressly to work in small packs.

KEY CHARACTERISTICS
• **CLASS** Hound. **Recognized** FCI.
• **SIZE** Average height at shoulders: 43–48cm (17–19in). Average weight: 20kg.
• **COAT** Short, thick and rather flat.
• **COLOUR** Most colours are acceptable, but it usually occurs in grey or tricolour.
• **OTHER FEATURES** A typical hound with a somewhat regal appearance and flat, high-set ears; deep chest with slightly curved ribs; legs long and muscular; tail carried "sabre" fashion.

HANOVER HOUND

The Hanover Hound or Hannoverischer Schweisshund is a descendant of heavy German tracking dogs, which were closely related to the Saint Hubert Hound and performed similar tasks to the Bloodhound in England and the Saint Hubert Hound in France. From the 5th century, this ancestor was made leader of the pack and sent ahead to rouse game because of its keen scenting ability. It would also follow a cold trail and track down wounded animals.

In about 1800, near Hanover, hunters crossed the ancient German hound with the lighter Harz Hound (Harzerbracke) to produce a faster tracking dog. The Hanover inherited its Bloodhound ancestors' keen nose, its sad expression and characteristic skinfolds.

Character and care

Highly valued by gamekeepers and wardens in Germany, the Hanover Hound is a calm, trustworthy dog, devoted to its owners. It requires a lot of exercise and a rub down with a hound glove from time to time.

KEY CHARACTERISTICS
• **CLASS** Hound. **Recognized** FCI.
• **SIZE** Height: dogs 51–60cm (20–24in), bitches somewhat less. Weight: 37.8–44.5kg (84–99lb).
• **COAT** Dense, abundant, smooth and glossy.
• **COLOUR** Grey-brown with a dark brown mask on the cheeks, lips and around the eyes and ears; brown-red, yellow-red, yellow-ochre, dark yellow or speckled brown.
• **OTHER FEATURES** Long, strong head; forehead slightly wrinkled; clear, expressive eyes; very broad ears, rather more than medium length, set on high, and with rounded tips; long back; loins broad and slightly arched; slanting croup; belly only slightly drawn up; tail long, and straight at the root.

NIVERNAIS GRIFFON

The Nivernais Griffon or Griffon Nivernais is descended from the Saint Louis Grey Dog. Packs of these shaggy hounds were used for hunting wolves and wild boar in central France; but as larger prey diminished in number, various crosses, including one to a Foxhound named Archer, produced a hound used mainly for smaller prey. It was called the Griffon-Vendéen-Nivernais, but towards the end of the last century the word Vendéen was omitted. At that time the Nivernais was in danger of extinction, but survived due to the efforts of a small band of enthusiasts, and was officially recognized in 1925.

Character and care

This large, thickset and rather mournful-looking shaggy dog is built for endurance rather than speed. It is brave, affectionate and companionable. Its long coat needs regular grooming with brush and comb, and it requires a lot of exercise.

KEY CHARACTERISTICS
• **CLASS** Hound. **Recognized** FCI.
• **SIZE** Height at shoulders: dogs 53.5–58.5cm (21–23in), bitches proportionately less. Weight: 22.7–25kg (50–55lb).
• **COAT** Long, unkempt and shaggy.
• **COLOUR** Preferably wolf grey or slate grey; can also be black, with or without tan markings, or fawn.
• **OTHER FEATURES** Head fleshless and light without being small, skull almost flat; eyes preferably dark; supple ears set on slightly above the line of the eye; deep chest; tail well set on and carried "sabre" fashion.

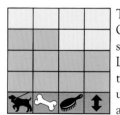

PORCELAINE

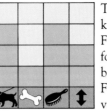

The Porcelaine is also known as the Chien de Franche-Comté after a former French region bordering Switzerland. Following the French Revolution (1789–99) examples of the Porcelaine were found at the Franco-Swiss border, leading to confusion over whether it is of French or Swiss origin. However, the breed is recognized as French, and is thought to descend from the English Harrier and ancient French hounds. The breed has been recorded in France since 1845, and in Switzerland since 1880, when the first hunting packs were established.

Bred to hunt hare and roe deer, the Porcelaine has a glossy white coat like fine porcelain. As befits one of the most popular hounds of France, it looks every inch purebred and has dark eyes, a medium-length tail and thin, well-curled ears.

Character and care
The Porcelaine is an energetic and fierce hunter, but gentle at home and easy to handle. It needs a lot of exercise, but its coat requires only an occasional sponge over, for example before a show.

The modern Porcelaine is smaller than the original breed of that name which flourished in the 18th century.

KEY CHARACTERISTICS
• **CLASS** Hound. **Recognized** FCI.
• **SIZE** Height at withers: dogs 56–58.5cm (22–23in), bitches 53.5–56cm (21–22in). Weight: 25–27.9kg (55–62lb).
• **COAT** Sparse and fine, particularly in summer, giving appearance of porcelain.
• **COLOUR** White with round, orange spots, particularly on ears.
• **OTHER FEATURES** Head rather long and finely sculpted; dark, slightly hooded eyes with sweet expression; fine, well-folded ears; deep, medium-width chest; well-attached tail.

ARTOIS HOUND

The Artois Hound or Chien d'Artois is more commonly known in its native France as the Briquet, which appears to mean "small braque". The original Briquet hounds were large and ponderous, and were replaced in the hunting field by the shorter-legged Basset Artésien Normand. The Artois of today results from the crossing of a hound with a braque and it differs from the Basset Artésien Normand only in the matter of its flatter ears and narrower head.

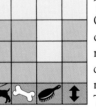

Character and care
With its sweet and melancholy expression, the intelligent and courageous Artois Hound is now mainly used for hunting hare. It is usually kept only in packs, kennelled out of doors and looked after by the hunt staff.

KEY CHARACTERISTICS
• **CLASS** Hound. **Recognized** FCI.
• **SIZE** Height at shoulders: 53–59cm (20¾–23¼in). Weight: 18.1–23.8kg (40–53lb).
• **COAT** Short and smooth.
• **COLOUR** Tricolour – white, black and deep fawn – mantle pattern or light patches; head generally fawn or charcoal grey.
• **OTHER FEATURES** Small, short head; medium-length ears that turn inwards; wide chest; sturdy body.

HAMILTONSTÖVARE

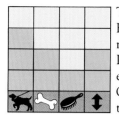

The Hamiltonstövare or Hamilton Hound is named after Count Adolf Patrick Hamilton, founder of the Swedish Kennel Club, who standardized the breed about a century ago. This medium-sized hound, used to flush game in the forests of Sweden, resulted from cross-breedings between the English Foxhound, the Holstein Hound, the Hanoverian Haidbracke, Hanover and Kurland Beagles (now extinct). The Hamiltonstövare is currently the most popular hunting hound in its native land and has achieved international publicity over the past 20 years, becoming a popular contender in the show ring.

Character and care

This smart, affectionate and intelligent dog makes a good companion which may be kept in the home, provided that it receives plenty of exercise. It is easily trained and needs daily grooming using a hound glove.

KEY CHARACTERISTICS

- **CLASS** Hound.
  Recognized ANKC, FCI, KC(GB), KUSA.

- **SIZE** Height: dogs 50–60cm (19½–23½in), bitches 46–57cm (18–22½in). Weight: 22.7–27.2kg (50–60lb).

- **COAT** Strongly weather-resistant upper coat lying close to body; short, close, soft undercoat.

- **COLOUR** Black, brown and white – upper side of neck, back, sides of trunk and upper side of tail, black; head, legs, side of neck, trunk and tail, brown; blaze on upper muzzle, underside of neck, breast, tip of tail and feet, white; mixing of black and brown undesirable, as is predominance of any one of the three colours.

- **OTHER FEATURES** Fine long head, flat; expressive, clear amber eyes; large, thin, stiff ears; level back; long, thin, low-set tail.

The Hamilton was developed by the founder of the Swedish Kennel Club, a hound connoisseur, using English and German stock.

SWISS, BERNESE AND LUCERNESE HOUNDS

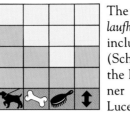

The scenthounds or *laufhunde* of Switzerland include the Swiss Hound (Schweizer Laufhund), the Bernese Hound (Berner Laufhund) and the Lucernese Hound (Luzerner Laufhund). The similar and closely related Jura Hounds (Bruno de Jura and Saint Hubert Jura) are described on page 165. There are also short-legged versions of all these hounds, produced by crossing the Dachshund with some of the full-size versions, to produce specialized hunters for certain types of terrain. They are used to hunt deer and fox.

The ancestors of the *laufhunde* trace back to pre-Christian times when hunting dogs of similar type were brought to southern Europe by the Greeks and Phoenicians, and spread to Switzerland when it was under Roman rule. By the Middle Ages, they had developed into dogs very similar to the *laufhund* of today as shown by 12th-century illustrations that adorn the cathedral in Zurich. The modern Swiss, Bernese and Lucernese Hounds are very similar in abilities, character and in appearance, except for colour of coat. They have keen noses, great powers of endurance and will work over any terrain. They make excellent tracking dogs and are used to hunt a variety of game, including hare, fox and deer.

Character and care

The *laufhunde* are calm companions but have strong hunting instincts and are powerfully built, and so are not suitable as household pets. They need a lot of exercise, and should be groomed with a hound glove, and a slicker for the rough-coated varieties.

KEY CHARACTERISTICS
● **CLASS** Hound. **Recognized** FCI.
● **SIZE** Minimum height: 44.5cm (17½in), generally 45.4–56cm (18–22in). *Short-legged varieties* 30–37.5cm (12–15in).
● **COAT** *Swiss* Rough and wiry, with a thick undercoat. *Bernese* As for the Swiss. *Lucernese* Short and very dense.
● **COLOUR** *Swiss* White with orange markings. *Bernese* Tricolour – white, black, strong tan markings. *Lucernese* White with grey or blue speckling and broad dark or black markings.
● **OTHER FEATURES** Clean, refined head; long muzzle; mouth with scissor bite; eyes as dark as possible; very long ears; long, sloping shoulders; good-length back, tail not too long, carried horizontally. *Short-legged varieties* Medium-sized head; mouth with scissor-bite; fairly large eyes with tight lids; ears long enough to reach tip of nose; body of good hound type, proportionately built; medium-length tail, set neither too low nor too high.

Living near the French border, the Swiss Hounds are closely related to Orange and White French Hounds.

JURA HOUNDS

The Jura Hounds, named after the mountain range, are closer to the older pure Celtic hounds; they have no white in their coat.

There are two varieties of Jura Hound, the Bruno (Bruno de Jura, Bruno Jura Laufhund) and the Saint Hubert (Saint Hubert Jura Laufhund). Both are native to the Jura mountains area in western Switzerland and have a similar origin to the other Swiss hounds (see page 164), which they resemble. However, they are closer in appearance than the other Swiss hounds to the Saint Hubert Bloodhound, particularly the Saint Hubert Jura which has a heavier head, larger ears and more pronounced folds of skin on the chin and neck than the Bruno. There are also short-legged versions of the Jura Hounds.

Strong, enthusiastic hunters, the Jura Hounds are used mainly against hare. They have a good nose, a strong, clear voice, and can cope with any type of terrain.

Character and care

Like the other Swiss Hounds, the Bruno and Saint Hubert varieties of Jura Hounds are gentle, affectionate dogs which make excellent hunting companions, but have strong hunting instincts and are not really suited to life as a household pet. They need plenty of exercise and grooming with a hound glove.

KEY CHARACTERISTICS
• **CLASS** Hound. **Recognized** FCI.
• **SIZE** Minimum height: 44.5cm (17½in), generally 45.5–56cm (18–22in).
• **COAT** Short.
• **COLOUR** Yellowish or reddish brown, with or without large black saddle; black with tan markings over eyes, on cheeks and on underparts of body; may have white mark on chest.
• **OTHER FEATURES** Heavy, domed head; eyelids not close fitting; large, very long ears, set on low and well back; moderate-length tail.

BASSET HOUND

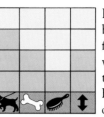

With its Bloodhound expression and short legs, the Basset is among the few hound breeds to have become popular household pets.

In common with members of the Greyhound family, Basset-type dogs were depicted on the tombs of the ancient Egyptians and so have obviously existed for a long time. However, the Basset Hound is fairly recent, having been developed in Britain from the late 1800s. It was bred from the French Basset Artésien Normand crossed with the Bloodhound to produce a slow but sure dog, which was used in tracking rabbits and hare. The Basset Artésien Normand first reached Britain in 1866 when the Comte de Tournow sent a pair, later named Basset and Belle, to Lord Galway. In 1872 a litter produced by them was acquired by Lord Onslow, who increased his pack with further imports from France. It is from this stock that the best British Basset Hounds are descended.

Character and care

The Basset Hound is now mainly kept as a companion, pet and show dog. It is a lovable animal, which gets on well with children, but needs lots of exercise. Sweet-voiced and a superb tracker, it also has a propensity to wander, and fencing is essential if you own a Basset. The breed requires daily grooming with a hound glove and, in the writer's opinion, is unsuited to a hot climate. One of the saddest sights I have ever seen was a Basset Hound in such an environment.

KEY CHARACTERISTICS
• **CLASS** Hound. **Recognized** AKC, ANKC, CKC, FCI, KC(GB), KUSA.
• **SIZE** Height at withers: 33–35cm (13–14in). Weight: 18.1–27.2kg (40–60lb).
• **COAT** Hard, smooth, short and dense.
• **COLOUR** Generally black, white and tan (tricolour) or lemon and white (bicolour), but any recognized hound colour acceptable.
• **OTHER FEATURES** Head domed, with some stop and occipital bone prominent; lozenge-shaped eyes; ears set low; body long, and deep throughout length; tail (stern) well set on.

The Basset was bred to work close to the ground, hunting in thick cover.

BEAGLE

The Beagle, smallest of the hounds, was smaller still in Elizabethan times, when it often travelled in its owner's pocket.

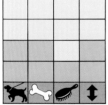

This small hound has existed in Britain at least since the reign of King Henry VIII (1509–47). His daughter Elizabeth I of England (1533–1603) kept numerous Beagles, some of which were so small they could be put in one's pocket and so became known as Pocket Beagles (now extinct).

The breed is often known as the "singing Beagle" but is not noisy indoors, reserving its voice for the chase. In Britain it is adept at hunting hare and wild rabbit, and it has been used against wild pig and deer in Scandinavia, and the cottontail rabbit in the United States. In the latter country and in Canada it works as a gundog both seeking out and retrieving. It is also a favourite companion and was the most popular dog in the United States in 1954.

Character and care

This affectionate, determined and healthy dog is usually long-lived and good with children. It makes a fine show dog, and is a good choice of family pet for those who do not demand exemplary behaviour. It is not renowned for obedience and, in common with other hounds, will take advantage of an open gate, possibly ending up some distance away. Its short, weatherproof coat requires little or no attention, and the Beagle needs only average exercise when kept as a pet.

KEY CHARACTERISTICS
• **CLASS** Hound. **Recognized** AKC, ANKC, CKC, FCI, KC(GB), KUSA.
• **SIZE** Height: USA two varieties: under 33cm (13in), and 33–37.5cm (13–15in); UK at withers: 33–40cm (13–16in).
• **COAT** Short, dense and weatherproof.
• **COLOUR** Any recognized hound colour other than liver; tip of stern, white.
• **OTHER FEATURES** Head fairly long and powerful without being coarse; dark brown or hazel eyes; long ears with pointed tips; top-line straight and level; moderately long, sturdy tail.

With its lively intelligence and easy going nature, the Beagle is as happy in the family home as in the hunt.

ARIÉGEOIS

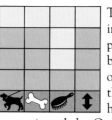

The Ariégeois originated in the Ariège, a French province on the Spanish border. It is the result of a crossing between the native medium-sized hounds, the Gascon Saintongeois and the Gascony Blue. While not a very fast hound, it does have considerable stamina and a keen nose, and this intelligent, eager worker has hunted hare throughout this century. A breed standard was drawn up by the Gaston Phoebus Club, which was formed in 1908 with the aim of encouraging the selective breeding of both the Ariégeois and the French Setter (Braque).

A superb scenthound, the Ariégeois combines the fine head and long ears of the Gascon-Saintongeois and the endurance of the Blue Gascony.

Character and care
The Ariégeois is a finely built hound with a calm disposition and friendly expression, and is altogether a most pleasant animal. Like all hounds, it requires a lot of exercise. Its short coat requires little attention.

KEY CHARACTERISTICS
● **CLASS** Hound. **Recognized** FCI.
● **SIZE** Height at shoulders: dogs 56–61cm (22–24in), bitches 53.5–58.5cm (21–23in). Weight: about 29.7kg (66lb).
● **COAT** Fine and close.
● **COLOUR** Usually white with black markings and small tan spots over eyes; black puppies occasionally occur; rich tan should not be encouraged.
● **OTHER FEATURES** Long, light, narrow head with no wrinkle or dew lap; dark eyes well open and with a sweet expression; fine supple ears; back generally level and well supported; tail well attached and carried "sabre" fashion.

HARRIER

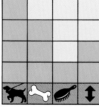

The name of this ancient English breed comes from a Norman word meaning "all-round hunting dog" and its ancestors may have arrived on British shores with the invading Norman armies of William the Conqueror in 1066. The first Harrier pack, established in England in 1260, was descended from the old Talbot and Saint Hubert Hounds, possibly crossed with a basset-type hound.

The Harrier is a very fast hound with considerable powers of endurance, a short, smooth coat, drop ears and a lengthy tail. Packs were mainly used to hunt hare and the Master of the Pack would selectively breed those dogs best suited to the local terrain. The Harrier is usually kept in packs. It is now rare, even in the UK, and is not recognized by the British Kennel Club.

Character and care
The Harrier is usually gentle and good natured. It should be groomed occasionally.

KEY CHARACTERISTICS
● **CLASS** Hound. **Recognized** AKC, ANKC, CKC, FCI.
● **SIZE** Height: 47.5–52.5cm (19–21in). Weight: 21.6–27.2kg (48–60lb).
● **COAT** Short and hard.
● **COLOUR** Usually black, tan and white, but all hound colours acceptable.
● **OTHER FEATURES** Head fairly long and shallow in the muzzle and stop; small, oval eyes; V-shaped, pendant ears; deep body; medium length tail carried somewhat high.

GREAT GASCONY BLUE

The Great Gascony Blue (Grand Bleu de Gascogne) is famed for its ability to pick up a "cold" scent. It descends from the scenting dogs of pre-Roman times and the ancient Saint Hubert Hound. Developed by the Count of Foix, Gaston Phoebus, in the 14th century, it became a favourite of the French King Henry IV (1553–1610) who kept a pack. Even though this aristocratic animal is taller and lighter than many other it is very strong and is possessed of great stamina and a strong melodious voice. It excelled at hunting wolves, which it pursued to extinction.

French explorers probably brought the Great Gascony Blue to North America in the 17th century, and, in 1785, General Lafayette gave a small pack to George Washington, who also bred them. They were crossed with other American hounds to produce a breed with improved tracking ability and stamina.

Character and care

The Great Gascony Blue has a calm and friendly temperament. However, it requires a great deal of exercise and is not a suitable housepet. It should be groomed regularly and the long ears checked frequently.

KEY CHARACTERISTICS
• **CLASS** Hound. **Recognized** AKC, FCI, KC(GB).
• **SIZE** Height: dogs 63.5–70cm (25–28in), bitches 60–65cm (23½–25½in). Weight: 34.2–36kg (71–77lb).
• **COAT** Short, smooth, weather resistant and somewhat coarse.
• **COLOUR** White with black patches and extensive black ticking to give appearance of blue dog; tan markings on head.
• **OTHER FEATURES** Large, elongated head; ears set low, elongated and folded; chest deep and slightly rounded; legs long and muscular; tail well set on, slight upward curl.

The large head and melancholy expression of the Great Gascony Blue give it a distinguished appearance.

The Great Gascony Blue is a classic French scenting dog, long legged and with a square body, capable of hunting over great distances.

TAWNY BRITTANY BASSET

The Tawny Brittany Basset or, as it is more commonly known, the Basset Fauve de Bretagne, originated in Brittany, north-west France. It was developed from the Basset Griffon Vendéen and other short-legged bassets to track over moorland and other rough terrain, where it is fast and active. A pack of these first-rate fox hunters was maintained by Francis I of France (1515–47), but by the mid 1800s the type had become all

The Basset's wheaten colour and rough coat come directly from its taller ancestor, the Tawny Brittany Griffon.

Swift for its size, the Brittany Basset was developed to track over rough country, after small game.

but extinct, possibly due to their somewhat headstrong temperament despite undoubted courage. Resembling a large, rough-haired dachshund in appearance, this hound has large, pendulous ears, a rough close coat and is described as being "dumpy overall".

It has been granted an interim breed standard by the British Kennel Club in the past seven years and is gradually gaining impetus in the British show ring.

Character and care

This short-legged, wire-coated hound has courage and a good nose. It requires a generous amount of exercise but its rough coat needs little attention.

KEY CHARACTERISTICS
• **CLASS** Hound. **Recognized** AKC, FCI, KC(GB), KUSA.
• **SIZE** Height: 33–43cm (13–17in).
• **COAT** Harsh and close.
• **COLOUR** Golden, wheaten or fawn; white spot on neck or chest permissible.
• **OTHER FEATURES** Moderate-length skull; dark, alert eyes; thin ears set on at eye level; chest quite wide and well let down; tail thick at root and tapering towards the tip.

DACHSBRACKES

There are three varieties with this name – the Dachsbracke, Westphalian Dachsbracke and the Erz Mountains Dachsbracke. The Dachsbracke is native to the Austrian Alps, the Westphalian to western Germany, and the Erz Mountains variety originated in the Erz mountains of Bohemia. All are short-legged versions of longer-legged local hounds or brackes that were crossed to Dachshunds. Heavier and longer in the leg than the Dachshunds, the Dachsbrackes are used to hunt hare, fox and other game in the mountains, tracking and locating their quarry by scent. The Dachsbracke and Erz Mountain variety are similar in size but differ in colour, while the Westphalian Dachsbracke is smaller.

Character and care

The Dachsbrackes are all splendid small hounds of considerable endurance and hunting ability. They are good natured and make fine family pets despite their propensity to dig the garden and their somewhat loud bark. They need plenty of exercise and should be groomed with a hound glove.

KEY CHARACTERISTICS
• **CLASS** Hound. **Recognized** ANKC, CKC, FCI, KC(GB), KUSA.
• **SIZE** Height at shoulders: *Dachsbracke and Erz Mountains Dachsbracke* 33–43cm (13–17in). *Westphalian Dachsbracke* 30.5–35.5cm (12–14in).
• **COAT** Short and dense with little undercoat.
• **COLOUR** *Dachsbracke* Black with tan markings; shades of tan or white with tan markings. *Westphalian Dachsbracke* Reddish fawn with white markings or tricolour. *Erz Mountains Dachsbracke* Red or black and tan.
• **OTHER FEATURES** Long narrow head; dark, medium-sized, almond-shaped eyes; broad, medium-length ears with rounded tips; back fairly long; tail set on relatively high and carried horizontally.

DACHSHUND

The oldest of the Dachshund varieties, the Smooth-haired is a favourite in Britain and the United States.

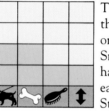

There are six varieties of the Dachshund (Teckel or Badger Hound): Smooth-haired, Long-haired and Wire-haired, each occurring as both Standard and Miniature.

The Dachshund derives from the oldest breeds of German hunting dogs, such as the Bibarhund, and is known to have existed as long ago as the 16th century. It was bred to go to ground, as most owners who garden know to their cost! It has been said that the English inability to translate the Dachshund's name caused the dog to be placed in the hound group rather than with the terriers, and it has remained there ever since.

The British Queen Victoria was the first person to own a Dachshund in England, in 1839. The following year, when she married the German Prince Albert, he brought over more Dachshunds to Britain and the breed gained in popularity there. Dachshunds were exhibited in Britain in 1866 and given breed status in 1873. The English Dachshund Club was formed in 1881, the first club of its kind in the world. The Dachshund Club of America was formed in 1895.

Originally there was only one variety, the Smooth-haired Dachshund, whose wrinkled paws are a characteristic now rarely seen. The Wire-haired was produced through the introduction of Dandie Dinmont and other terrier blood, while the Long-haired was formed by introducing the German Stöber, a gundog, to a Smooth-haired Dachshund and Spaniel cross.

KEY CHARACTERISTICS
• **CLASS** Hound. **Recognized** AKC, ANKC, CKC, FCI, KC(GB), KUSA.
• **SIZE** Weight: *Standard* USA 7.2–14.4kg (16–32lb); UK 9–12kg (20–26lb). *Miniature* USA under 5kg (11lb); UK about 4.5kg (10lb).
• **COAT** *Smooth-haired* Dense, short and smooth. *Long-haired* Soft and straight, and only slightly wavy. *Wire-haired* Short, straight and harsh, with a long undercoat.
• **COLOUR** All colours but white permissible; small patch on chest permitted but not desirable; dappled dogs may include white but should be evenly marked all over.
• **OTHER FEATURES** Long head, conical in appearance when seen from above; medium-sized eyes; ears set high; body long and full muscled; tail continues along line of spine but is slightly curved.

The Wire-haired Dachshund results from cross-mating with various terrier breeds.

Cross-breeding between the Smooth-haired and gundog types yielded the Long-haired Dachshund.

Character and care

Sporty and devoted, the Dachshund makes an excellent family pet and a good watchdog, with a surprisingly loud bark for its size. It can walk fairly long distances provided that these are worked up to from an early age. The Short-haired is easy to groom, requiring only daily attention with a hound glove and soft cloth. The Wire-haired and Long-haired should be brushed with a stiff bristled brush and also combed.

Warning The Dachshund is prone to disc trouble so care must be taken to prevent it jumping on, or from, heights.

SLOUGHI

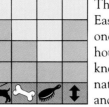

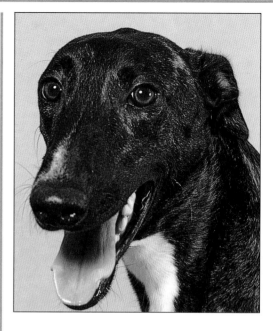

The Sloughi, Slughi or Eastern Greyhound, is one of the rarest sight-hounds in the West. It is known by the Arabs in its native lands as El Hor and is the only dog they recognize apart from the Saluki. Like the Saluki, which it resembles, the Sloughi has keen eyesight, is capable of immense speed and is a hunter of gazelle. Its success at this task is said to be helped by its sandy colour which makes it difficult for gazelle to detect the dog against the desert sands until danger is upon them.

Character and care

The Sloughi is a gentle, healthy, intelligent dog, which makes a first-class pet provided that it has plenty of space in which to exercise and is not allowed to roam near livestock. It requires only a daily grooming with a soft brush and a hound glove.

The Greyhound has been prized for thousands of years as a dog of war, a keen sight- and scent-hound, a racing dog and companion.

KEY CHARACTERISTICS
● **CLASS** Hound. **Recognized** ANKC, FCI, KC(GB), KUSA.
● **SIZE** Height: 60–70cm (23½–27½in). Weight: 20.2–27.2kg (45–60lb).
● **COAT** Tough and fine.
● **COLOUR** Sable or fawn in all shades with or without black mask; white, brindle or black with tan points; brindle pattern or fawn pattern on head, feet and sometimes breast. Dark with a white patch on chest, undesirable; parti-colours not permissible; solid black or white undesirable.
● **OTHER FEATURES** Head fairly strong without being heavy; large, dark eyes, set well into orbit; triangular ears, not too large, with rounded tips; chest not too broad; tail fine and well set on.

GREYHOUND

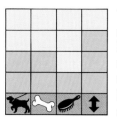

The Greyhound is arguably the purest breed on Earth, appearing to have changed little from dogs depicted on the tombs of Egyptian pharaohs. It also has the distinction of a mention in the Holy Bible in the Book of Solomon. It is likely that the Greyhound found its way to Afghanistan, where its coat thickened to contend with the colder climate, and was then brought by Celts to Britain. The breed became a favourite with the nobility there, and in 11th- and 14th-century England, only persons of royal or noble blood were permitted to own one.

Possessing keen eyesight and capable of great speed, this sighthound was highly valued as a courser and, more recently, as a competitor on the racing track. Greyhounds are still widely used as racing dogs, and now appear with regularity in the show ring.

Character and care
The Greyhound does have a propensity to chase anything that moves, but is also a gentle, faithful animal, which is good with children. Even the ex-racer, once retrained, makes a fine and often long-lived companion. It needs a daily brush and average but regular exercise on hard ground, and takes up relatively little space, having a liking for its own special corner.

Reputedly the fastest dog on earth, the Greyhound has fanciers dating back to the Egyptian Fourth Dynasty.

KEY CHARACTERISTICS
• **CLASS** Hound. **Recognized** AKC, ANKC, CKC, FCI, KC(GB), KUSA.
• **SIZE** Height: dogs 71–76cm (28–30in), bitches 68–71cm (27–28in). Weight: dogs 29.5–31.7kg (65–70lb), bitches 27.2–29.5kg (60–65lb).
• **COAT** Fine and close.
• **COLOUR** Black, white, red, blue, fawn, fallow brindle, or any of these colours broken with white.
• **OTHER FEATURES** Long, moderately broad head; bright, intelligent eyes; small, close-shaped ears; long, elegant neck; deep, capacious chest; long tail set on rather low.

ENGLISH FOXHOUND

The English Foxhound is a descendant of the heavier Saint Hubert Hounds and another extinct hound, the Talbot. The Saint Hubert Hounds got their name from the Bishop of Liège, later Saint Hubert, the patron saint of hunters, and were brought to England by the invading Normans in the 11th century.

The Foxhound's prime function is to hunt foxes alongside mounted huntsmen. It can work for several hours without a break in various types of terrain.

Character and care

In Britain, the strong, lively and noisy English Foxhounds are never kept as pets but are the property of individual hunting packs. They cannot be bought in Britain by individuals and, unlike the American Foxhound, are not exhibited other than at special hound shows. It is, however, sometimes possible for hunt supporters to walk a Foxhound pup, and accustom it to various road hazards, before returning it to its pack.

KEY CHARACTERISTICS
• **CLASS** Hound. **Recognized** AKC, ANKC, CKC, FCI, KC(GB).
• **SIZE** Height: dogs 55–62.5cm (22–25in), bitches 50.5–60cm (21–24in). Weight: 29.5–31.7kg (65–70lb).
• **COAT** Short and hard.
• **COLOUR** Tricolour – black, white and tan – or bicolour with a white background.
• **OTHER FEATURES** Head not heavy, and with pronounced brow; ears set on low and hanging close to head; muscular, level back; straight legs; tail (stern) well set on and carried gaily.

The English Foxhound has a deep girth and long back which allow it to run well over varied terrains.

AMERICAN FOXHOUND

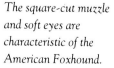

Since its arrival in the New World, the American Foxhound has produced many strains to work in diverse conditions. The AKC Foxhound resembles its English progenitor, but with a lighter body and longer legs.

The American Foxhound is a descendant of English Foxhounds taken to Maryland, United States, by Robert Brooke in 1650. These were later crossed with other British and French hounds to obtain dogs well suited to hunting the red fox. George Washington is also known to have imported Foxhounds from England in around 1770 and to have received a gift of some French hounds in 1785. A pack from Ireland was introduced in 1830. The Gloucester Fox-hunting Club (founded in 1808) and the Baltimore Club obtained the best type of English Foxhounds and used them as foundation stock. While the English Foxhound is never kept within a family or exhibited except in special hound shows, the rangier American Foxhound is a popular show dog as well as a highly valued hunting dog.

Character and care

The American Foxhound is good natured, but can become less attentive and more wilful as it grows older. It needs a large amount of exercise. It is not groomed in the manner of a pet dog, and needs only an occasional sponge over before a hound show.

KEY CHARACTERISTICS
• **CLASS** Hound. **Recognized** AKC, CKC, FCI, KC(GB).
• **SIZE** Height: dogs 55–62.5cm (22–25in), bitches 52.5–60cm (21–24in).
• **COAT** Hard and close.
• **COLOUR** All colours acceptable.
• **OTHER FEATURES** Large skull; large, broad, pendant, wide-set ears, flat to head; streamlined body; sabre-shaped tail.

The square-cut muzzle and soft eyes are characteristic of the American Foxhound.

WHIPPET

The Whippet looks like a Greyhound in miniature, and the Greyhound un-doubtedly played a part in its make-up. It is uncertain whether the Pharaoh Hound, as seems likely, or some other imported hound or terrier, was the other half of the cross. The Whippet was bred expressly as a racing dog, and is the fastest breed in the world. It has been timed at 8.4 seconds over a standard 137m (150yd) straight course (58.76km/h, 36.52mph). Known as the "poor man's racehorse", it became the sporting pet of miners in the north of England, where Whippet racing is still very popular. It has spread to other countries as well. Originally, the dogs raced after live rabbits but now artificial lures are used instead.

The Whippet was recognized by the Kennel Club in Britain in 1902, having been exhibited in 1897 at Crufts Dog Show in London. It is also popular in the United States, where a slightly larger dog is preferred.

Character and care

The Whippet is a gentle dog, which is good with children and makes a fine pet and show dog, and a splendid watchdog. While it can adapt to domestic life, this powerful runner needs plenty of exercise. Its short coat requires little other than a brush and rub-down, but it does mean that the dog is better housed indoors year round rather than kennelled outside.

KEY CHARACTERISTICS
• **CLASS** Hound. **Recognized** AKC, ANKC, CKC, FCI, KC(GB), KUSA.
• **SIZE** Height: dogs 47–51cm (18½–20in), bitches 44–47cm (17½–18½in). Weight: about 12.5kg (28lb).
• **COAT** Short, fine and close.
• **COLOUR** Any colour or mixture of colours.
• **OTHER FEATURES** Long, lean head; bright, oval-shaped eyes with a very alert expression; rose-shaped ears; very deep chest with plenty of heart-room; long, tapering tail with no feathering.

Developed in Britain as the poor man's racehorse, the Whippet was taken to America by emigrant Lancashire textile workers.

HUNGARIAN GREYHOUND

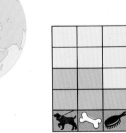

The Hungarian Grey-hound or Magyar Agár has a history traceable at least to the 9th century, when likenesses of it were depicted on tomb-stones in its native Hun-gary. Its ancestors were Asiatic sighthounds that arrived in Hungary with the Magyars, probably crossed with local hounds.

A dog of great speed and beauty, the Agár is used to course hare and to catch and kill both fox and hare in its native land. In the 19th century crosses were made to the English Greyhound to produce faster dogs, and by the Second World War it is estimated that this blood was present in all but a handful of Agárs. Since then, breeders in Hungary have been working to revive the original type.

Character and care

Like most Greyhounds, the Hungarian is gentle and affectionate by nature and makes a calm, devoted housepet, once it has been re-trained and provided that it is kept away from livestock. It requires little grooming and needs regular rather than extensive exercise.

Note: This dog has a fine coat, feels the cold and must be provided with a coat when it is taken out of doors in winter.

KEY CHARACTERISTICS

- **CLASS** Hound.
  Recognized FCI.

- **SIZE** Weight: dogs 27–32kg (60–70lb),
  bitches 22.5–27kg (50–60lb).

- **COAT** Short, smooth and fine.

- **COLOUR** Black, Isabella, grey, brindle,
  ash, piebald, often white.

- **OTHER FEATURES** Head broad
  between the ears; brown, medium-sized
  eyes with a lively expression; ears broad
  and set well back, the upper third folded
  forward; broad back; long, thin tail with
  a hook-like curve at the tip, carried low.

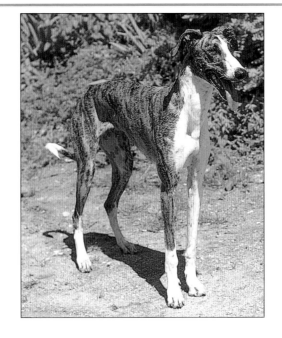

*Smaller than its
English cousin, the
Hungarian Greyhound
was used for hunting
and coursing on the
Central European
steppe.*

179

DEERHOUND

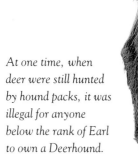

At one time, when deer were still hunted by hound packs, it was illegal for anyone below the rank of Earl to own a Deerhound.

Immortalized in the paintings of Landseer, the Deerhound is almost as evocative of the Highlands as the red deer it used to hunt.

The Scottish Deerhound is the emblem of the Kennel Club in Scotland. It also features largely in the writings of the novelist, Sir Walter Scott (1771–1832), who referred to his bitch, Maida, as "the most perfect creature of heaven", and was a favourite subject of the British painter, Edwin Landseer (1802–73).

One of the most ancient of British breeds, the Deerhound may have arrived in Scotland with Phoenician traders about 3000 years ago, and thereafter developed its thick weather-resistant coat to combat the colder climate. Very similar hounds were certainly in existence there in the early centuries AD. The breed became a favourite of chieftains in the Scottish Highlands, hunting with them by day and gracing their baronial halls by night. Then, with the advent of breech-loading rifles, the dog's use as a hunter came to an end. The Deerhound does, however, still have a staunch band of devotees.

Character and care

Today, the Deerhound is used for coursing, draws good entries at dog shows, and makes a faithful and devoted pet for the energetic. Although gentle in the home, the breed needs careful training around livestock, for it can kill when its hunting instincts are roused. With its shaggy coat it is no hardship for this breed to be kennelled out of doors – in fact, it does not like intense heat. It needs lots of exercise but the minimum of grooming – just the removal of stray hairs for showing.

KEY CHARACTERISTICS
● **CLASS** Hound. **Recognized** AKC, ANKC, CKC, FCI, KC(GB), KUSA.
● **SIZE** Height: dogs 76–80cm (30–32in), bitches at least 71cm (28in). Weight: dogs 38–48.6kg (85–110lb), bitches 33.7–42.7kg (75–95lb).
● **COAT** Shaggy but not overcoated.
● **COLOUR** Dark blue grey and lighter greys; brindles and yellows; sandy red or red fawn with black points.
● **OTHER FEATURES** Head broadest at ears, tapering slightly towards eyes; dark eyes; ears set on high, folded back in repose; body and general formation that of a Greyhound, with larger size and bone; long tail, thick at root.

IRISH WOLFHOUND

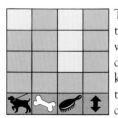

The Irish Wolfhound is the tallest dog in the world, and the national dog of Ireland. Bred to kill wolves, it is thought to be descended from dogs brought by the Celts as they spread across Europe from Greece, which they invaded in about 279BC, to Ireland. The Irish Wolfhound became highly prized and many were exported to Europe, including a brace presented to the king of Spain in the 16th century. In 1652 Oliver Cromwell (1599–1658) forbade their future export on the grounds that they were far too valuable in keeping down wolves.

By 1800, the last wolf in Britain and Ireland had been killed, and the Wolfhound was redundant and in danger of extinction. Then, in 1885, Captain George Graham, a Scot serving in the British army, commenced a 23-year breeding programme which restored the breed to its former glory.

Character and care

The Irish Wolfhound is a breed that many people would choose to own if only their lifestyle and house size enabled them to. However, the Wolfhound does not require more exercise than average-sized breeds and, although it can be kennelled out of doors, it has a calm temperament, and many of these giants have a place by the fireside. The breed is popular in the show ring and, since it is exhibited in what is deemed a "natural state", brushing and the removal of straggly hairs are all the preparation that is required.

KEY CHARACTERISTICS
● **CLASS** Hound. **Recognized** AKC, ANKC, CKC, FCI, KC(GB), KUSA.
● **SIZE** Minimum height: dogs 80cm (32in), bitches 75cm (30in); 80–85cm (32–34in) to be aimed for. Minimum weight: dogs 54.5kg (120lb), bitches 48kg (105lb).
● **COAT** Rough and harsh.
● **COLOUR** Grey, steel grey, brindle, red, black, pure white, fawn or wheaten.
● **OTHER FEATURES** Long head carried high; dark eyes; small, rose-shaped ears; very deep chest; long, slightly curved tail.

More than two centuries after the last wolf disappeared from Britain and Ireland, the Irish Wolfhound remains a coveted breed. It is the tallest dog in the world.

SALUKI

The Saluki, graceful hound of the desert.

The Saluki, like the Sloughi, is an ancient breed whose likeness appears on the tombs of Egyptian pharaohs. It takes its name from the ancient city of Saluk in the Yemen, or possibly from the town of Seleukia in the ancient Hellenic empire in Syria. It is also known as the Gazelle Hound, the Arab Gazelle Hound, the Eastern Greyhound and the Persian Greyhound.

The Saluki is esteemed by the Arabs, including the nomadic Bedouin, who prize it for its ability to keep pace with fleet-footed Arab horses and, paired with a falcon, to hunt gazelle. Elsewhere in the world it is kept as a companion and show dog.

In 1895, an Englishwoman, Lady Florence Amherst, was given two Saluki puppies, and was so impressed by the breed that she imported others and did her best to popularize it. Despite this the Saluki was not recognized by the Kennel Club in Britain until 1923. The breed was recognized in the US in 1927.

Character and care

This elegant, if somewhat aloof, breed is loyal, affectionate and trustworthy, and is now sought after both as a pet and show dog. It requires plenty of exercise, and care should be taken in the countryside that its hunting instincts are kept under control. The Saluki's coat should be groomed daily, using a soft brush and a hound glove.

KEY CHARACTERISTICS
• **CLASS** Hound. **Recognized** AKC, ANKC, CKC, FCI, KC(GB), KUSA.
• **SIZE** Height: dogs 58.4–71cm (23–28in), bitches smaller.
• **COAT** Smooth, silky in texture.
• **COLOUR** White, cream, fawn, golden red, grizzle, silver grizzle, deer grizzle, tricolour (white, black and tan) and variations of these colours.
• **OTHER FEATURES** Long, narrow head; eyes dark to hazel; long, mobile ears, not set too low; fairly broad back; strong hip bones set wide apart; tail set on low from long, gently sloping pelvis.

Once much prized among the desert tribes, the Saluki is popular today as a show dog and pet.

BORZOI

Another of the world's great hounds is the Borzoi, bred to run down wolves for Russian noblemen.

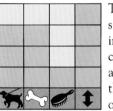

The noble Borzoi or Russian Wolfhound was used in Russia from the 17th century for wolf hunting and coursing, a sport of the tsars and noblemen of imperial Russia. The Borzoi tracked the wolf, when it was beaten from cover, but did not kill it. The dog's task was to grab the wolf by the neck and throw it, whereupon it would be finished off with a blow from a dagger.

Originally there were various strains of Borzoi, including the Sudanese Borzoi, the Turkoman Borzoi and the Borzoi Tartar. However, it was a strain developed in Russia which formed the basis of the present breed standard, the others having become extinct. The Borzoi reached Britain in the mid-1800s and went from there to America in 1889. Then in 1903, Mr Joseph B Thomas started importing the Borzoi into the United States direct from Russia, his source being the Grand Duke Nicholas Romanoff. The Revolution in 1917 brought breeding to a halt.

Until fairly recently, information about the Borzoi in its native land was sketchy. Now, breeders in Russia appear anxious to cooperate in exporting their stock, there is a Borzoi database in Moscow, and information can be obtained from the Russian Cyndromic Association "Dromos" (Borzoi section).

Character and care

The Borzoi has made its mark in Europe and America as an elegant, intelligent and faithful, albeit somewhat aloof, pet and a reasonably popular show dog. It is not ideally suited to being a child's pet as it does not take kindly to teasing. It requires a considerable amount of space and exercise, and care must be taken that it does not, true to its hunting instincts, worry livestock. Its coat needs surprisingly little attention.

KEY CHARACTERISTICS
● **CLASS** Hound. **Recognized** AKC, ANKC, CKC, FCI, KC(GB), KUSA.
● **SIZE** Minimum height at withers: dogs 74cm (29in), bitches 68cm (27in). Weight: dogs 33.7–65kg (75–105lb), bitches about 6.8–9kg (15–20lb) less.
● **COAT** Silky, flat, and wavy or rather curly; never woolly.
● **COLOUR** Any colour acceptable.
● **OTHER FEATURES** Long, lean head, in proportion to overall size; dark eyes with intelligent, alert expression; small ears, pointed and delicate; chest deep and narrow; long tail, rather low set.

The Borzoi has a long, tapering head, slightly convex and with almost no stop.

ELKHOUND

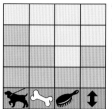

The Grey Norwegian Elkhound has probably existed in its native Scandinavia for millennia. Archaeologists have discovered bones of similar dogs dating back to 5000–4000BC. Its task was to seek an elk and hold it at bay until its master moved in for the kill.

The breed was first exhibited in 1877, when the Norwegian Hunters' Association began holding shows. In 1923, the British Elkhound Club was formed and the breed was officially recognized by the British Kennel Club. The Norwegian Elkhound Association of America was recognized by the American Kennel Club in about 1930. There is also a Miniature Elkhound, although no breed standard is yet available for it. There is also a Black Elkhound, but it is little known outside its native Norway.

The Elkhound – one time hunter, herder and sled dog.

AFGHAN HOUND

The Afghan – a fearless hunter turned elegant status symbol.

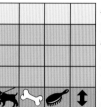

As its aloof oriental expression suggests, the Afghan Hound is an ancient breed, said by legend to have been one of the animals taken aboard Noah's Ark at the time of the flood! This member of the Greyhound family, possibly related to the Saluki, has certainly existed for centuries. Its ancestors somehow found their way from their original home Persia (Iran) to Afghanistan, where the breed undoubtedly developed its long, shaggy coat to withstand the harsh climatic conditions. Its speed and stamina meant that, in its native land, it was used to hunt leopards, wolves and jackals. It is only in the West that it has become a status symbol.

The first Afghan Hound breed club was formed in Britain in 1926 and, in that same year, the breed was officially recognized by the American Kennel Club. It has since become one of the most popular show dogs and, in recent years, has also been utilized in the growing sport of Afghan racing.

Character and care

Although somewhat wilful in youth, the Elkhound is generally a good natured household pet, which has no doggie odour and is reliable with children. It requires daily brushing and combing and plenty of exercise.

KEY CHARACTERISTICS
● **CLASS** Hound. **Recognized** AKC, ANKC, CKC, FCI, KC(GB), KUSA.
● **SIZE** Height at shoulders: dogs about 52cm (20½in), bitches about 49cm (19½in). Weight: dogs about 23kg (50lb), bitches about 20kg (43lb).
● **COAT** Close, abundant and weather-resistant; outer coat coarse and straight, undercoat soft and woolly.
● **COLOUR** Various shades of grey with black tips to hairs on outer coat; lighter on chest, stomach, legs, underside of tail, buttocks and in a harness mark.
● **OTHER FEATURES** Wedge-shaped head; slightly oval eyes; ears set high; powerful body; strong tail, set on high.

Character and care

The Afghan is an elegant, beautiful and affectionate dog, which is generally good natured but does not tolerate teasing. It is intelligent, somewhat aloof and requires plenty of exercise. The coat should be groomed with an air-cushioned brush and will soon become matted if it is not given sufficient and regular attention.

KEY CHARACTERISTICS
● **CLASS** Hound. **Recognized** AKC, ANKC, CKC, FCI, KC(GB), KUSA.
● **SIZE** Height: dogs about 68cm (27in), bitches about 63cm (25in). Weight: dogs about 27.2kg (60lb), bitches about 22.7kg (50lb).
● **COAT** Long and fine.
● **COLOUR** All colours acceptable.
● **OTHER FEATURES** Head long and not too narrow; eyes preferably dark, but golden, not debarred; ears set low and well back; moderate-length, level back; tail not too short.

JÄMTHUND

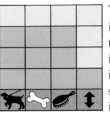

The Jämthund or Swedish Elkhound, named after the area of Jämtland in Sweden, is popular in its native land but is seldom seen elsewhere. It is closely related to the Norwegian Elkhound, which is considerably better known internationally. The Jämthund has existed in northern Scandinavia for many years, having been developed by keen Swedish huntsmen who wanted an improved local variety of Elkhound. It was recognized as a breed distinct from the Norwegian Elkhound in 1946.

This powerful spitz is similar in appearance to the Norwegian Elkhound, but is about 10cm (4in) taller and has light facial markings. Like its Norwegian relative, the Jämthund was bred to hunt large game, including elk, bear and wolf, and is now used against a variety of quarry. Opinions differ on whether it is actually a better elk hunter than the Norwegian.

Character and care

The Jämthund is assertive and intelligent, but is friendly and good with children. It requires plenty of exercise and daily grooming with a bristle brush and comb.

KEY CHARACTERISTICS
● **CLASS** Hound. **Recognized** FCI.
● **SIZE** Height: dogs 58.5–63.5cm (23–25in), bitches 53.5–58.5cm (21–23in).
● **COAT** Harsh and dense, with a short, soft undercoat.
● **COLOUR** Grey with lighter grey or cream markings on muzzle, cheeks, throat and underside of body.
● **OTHER FEATURES** Long, narrow head; small, dark, lively eyes; erect, pointed ears; deep chest; tail tightly rolled on the back.

TERRIERS

BULL TERRIER

Some people consider this breed the picture of ugliness, while others, like myself, have only admiration for the Bull Terrier, which is described somewhat poetically in its standard as "the gladiator of the canine race".

Like the Staffordshire Bull Terrier, the Bull Terrier began life as a fighting dog and was the result of crossing an Old English Bulldog with a terrier. The first Bull Terriers were said to have closely resembled the Staffordshire but then Dalmatian and possibly other blood was introduced. Much work on the breed's refinement was done by James Hinks of Birmingham, England, in the 19th century. He selected for white colour and Bull Terriers were invariably white, until after the Second World War, when coloureds appeared.

Character and care
If you admire the Bull breeds, you will adore the Bull Terrier. Despite its fierce appearance and strength, it makes a faithful and devoted pet. The bitch, in particular, is utterly reliable with children. However, this breed is too strong for other than the able bodied to handle, and needs careful training. Its short, flat coat is easy to look after.

Unique among dog breeds, the Bull Terrier's head shape is set off by naturally erect ears. The eyes are small and triangular.

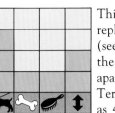

KEY CHARACTERISTICS
● **CLASS** Terrier. **Recognized** AKC, ANKC, CKC, FCI, KC(GB), KUSA.
● **SIZE** Height: 52.5–55cm (21–22in). Weight: 23.5–27.9kg (52–62lb).
● **COAT** Short and flat.
● **COLOUR** For white, pure white coat; for coloureds, brindle preferred; black, red, fawn and tricolour acceptable.
● **OTHER FEATURES** Long, straight head, and deep right to end of muzzle; eyes appear narrow; small, thin ears set close together; short tail, set on low and carried horizontally.

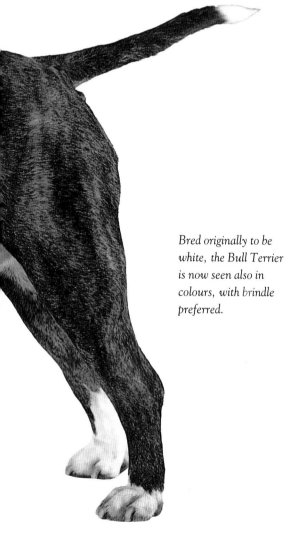

Bred originally to be white, the Bull Terrier is now seen also in colours, with brindle preferred.

MINIATURE BULL TERRIER

This dog is a smaller replica of the Bull Terrier (see page 188) and shares the same breed standard apart from height. Bull Terriers weighing as little as 4.5kg (10lb) were recorded early in the breed's history, but it was not until 1939 that the Miniature was given a separate breed register by the Kennel Club in Britain. It has never been very popular and few specimens are seen in the show ring.

Character and care

This loving and companionable little dog has the same characteristics as its larger relative, making an excellent pet and being generally good with children. It requires daily brushing and plenty of exercise.

KEY CHARACTERISTICS
● **CLASS** Terrier. **Recognized** AKC, ANKC, CKC, FCI, KC(GB), KUSA.
● **SIZE** Height at shoulders: 25–35.5cm (10–14in). Weight: 4.5–18.1kg (10–40lb).
● **COAT** Short, flat, with a fine gloss.
● **COLOUR** Pure white, black, brindle, red, fawn and tricolour acceptable.
● **OTHER FEATURES** Eyes appear narrow, obliquely placed and triangular in shape; thin ears set close together; very muscular, long, arched neck, tapering from shoulders to head, free from loose skin; short tail, set on low and carried horizontally.

The Miniature Bull Terrier was bred to help out its larger relative when ratting.

189

STAFFORDSHIRE BULL TERRIER

The Staffordshire Bull Terrier should not be confused with the American Staffordshire Terrier, or Pit Bull, which has been developed along quite different lines. The lovable Staffordshire or Staffy has a bloody history. It derived from the crossing of an Old English Bulldog and a terrier, most likely the extinct Black and Tan, at a time when bull-baiting and dog fighting were two of the most popular "sports" in Britain. The resultant dogs had the ideal attributes for combat: the strength and tenacity of a bulldog coupled with the agility and quick wits of a terrier. When bull-baiting and, thereafter, dog fighting were outlawed in Britain, the Staffy was developed along gentler lines as a companion dog. It was recognized by the British Kennel Club as a pure variety in 1935, and by the American Kennel Club in 1974.

Heavily built of almost solid muscle, the Staffordshire Bull Terrier still resembles its bulldog/terrier ancestors.

Since bull-baiting and dog fighting became illegal, the "Staffy" has gained widespread popularity as a family pet.

Character and care

The Staffy is one of the most popular pets and show dogs. It makes a fine household dog as well as guard, being an affectionate and game companion which adores children. However, it is not averse to having a scrap with its fellows, usually emerging the victor, and so it is sensible to keep it on the leash while out walking. This totally reliable, smooth-coated dog is easy to look after, requiring little other than regular brushing.

KEY CHARACTERISTICS
• **CLASS** Terrier. **Recognized** AKC, ANKC, CKC, FCI, KC(GB), KUSA.
• **SIZE** Height at shoulders: 35.5–40.5cm (14–16in). Weight: dogs 12.7–17.2kg (28–38lb), bitches 10.9–15.4kg (24–34lb).
• **COAT** Smooth, short and dense.
• **COLOUR** Red, fawn, white, black or blue, or any one of these colours with white; any shade of brindle, or any shade of brindle with white.
• **OTHER FEATURES** Short, deep through, broad skull; eyes preferably dark, but may bear some relation to the coat colour; rose or half-pricked ears; close-coupled body; medium-length tail.

AIREDALE TERRIER

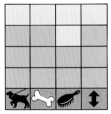

The Airedale is the king of the terriers, being the largest member of the terrier group. Originally known as the Waterside Terrier and sometimes also as the Bingley Terrier, the Airedale was named after the Valley of Aire in Yorkshire, England. It was the progeny of a working terrier probably crossed with the Otterhound. The breed was first classified separately for show purposes in 1879, but did not really come into its own as a show dog until the 1930s. Airedales were introduced into the United States by 1910.

An expert ratter and duck-catcher, the Airedale can also be trained to the gun and is a splendid guard. It has therefore undertaken a multitude of tasks ranging from service in both the British and Russian armies to acting as messenger and collector of money for the Red Cross and as a railway police patrol dog. It seems to have lost its niche as a guard since the emergence of the German Shepherd Dog.

Character and care
The multi-purpose Airedale is a good choice for the terrier devotee who wants a bigger dog. As a family pet, it is good with children,

extremely loyal and, despite its size, seems to adapt well to fairly cramped conditions – provided that it has plenty of exercise. It will, however, need to be hand stripped twice a year, if it is the intention to exhibit.

KEY CHARACTERISTICS
• **CLASS** Terrier. **Recognized** AKC, ANKC, CKC, FCI, KC(GB), KUSA.
• **SIZE** Height: dogs about 58–61cm (23–24in), bitches 56–59cm (22–23in). Weight: about 19.9kg (44lb).
• **COAT** Hard, dense and wiry.
• **COLOUR** Body-saddle, top of neck and top surface of tail, black or grizzle; all other parts tan; ears often a darker tan, and shading may occur round neck and side of skull; a few white hairs between forelegs is acceptable.
• **OTHER FEATURES** Long, flat skull; small, dark eyes; V-shaped ears; deep chest; short, strong, straight, level back; tails set on high and carried gaily, customarily docked.

The Airedale, the largest of the terrier group, has a distinguished record in the police, military and rescue services.

Half-drop ears, small dark eyes and a beard combine to give the Airedale its benign look.

BEDLINGTON TERRIER

The Bedlington may look like a lamb, but its past record ranges from poaching to pit fighting.

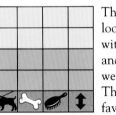

The Bedlington Terrier looks like a shorn lamb with its distinctive thick and linty coat standing well out from the skin. This breed was once a favourite with poachers and is still known by some as the Gypsy Dog. It is believed that the Greyhound or Whippet played a part in its ancestry and possibly also the Dandie Dinmont Terrier. The Bedlington probably originated in Northumberland, England, and the first of its kind is thought to have been a dog known as Old Flint, owned by Squire Trevelyan.

The dog, which whelped in 1782, is said to have had descendants traceable until 1873. Then the British Kennel Club was formed, making record-keeping more reliable.

A strain of similar terriers, known as Rothbury Terriers, existed in the Rothbury Forest of Northumberland in the 18th century. In 1820, Mr J. Howe came to the village of Bedlington in that county with a bitch Phoebe, which was given to Joseph Ainsley. Ainsley mated Phoebe to a dog called Old Piper producing Young Piper, the first dog to bear the new name of Bedlington Terrier. The breed was first exhibited in the United Kingdom during the 1860s and the British Bedlington Terrier Club was formed in 1875. It is moderately popular in the US and UK.

Character and care

The Bedlington is a true terrier: lovable, full of fun, and a terror when its temper is provoked. It is, however, easy to train and usually adores children. It does not need a great deal of space, enjoys average exercise and, while its coat needs regular trimming, a good grooming every day using a stiff brush will normally keep it tidy.

KEY CHARACTERISTICS
● **CLASS** Terrier. **Recognized** AKC, ANKC, CKC, FCI, KC(GB). KUSA.
● **SIZE** Height at withers: dogs 40.5–44cm (16–17½in), bitches 37.5–41cm (15–16½in). Weight: 8.2–10.5kg (18–22lb).
● **COAT** Thick and linty.
● **COLOUR** Blue, liver or sandy, with or without tan; darker pigment to be encouraged; blues, and blue and tans must have black noses; livers and sandies must have brown noses.
● **OTHER FEATURES** Narrow skull; small, bright, deep-set eyes; moderate-sized, filbert-shaped ears; muscular body; moderate-length tail, thick at root and tapering to a point.

FOX TERRIER (SMOOTH AND WIRE)

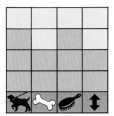

The Smooth Fox Terrier started life as a stable dog, its job being to hunt vermin. It probably descends from terriers in the English counties of Cheshire and Shropshire with some Beagle blood added. The Wire, which is a great rabbiter, originated in the coal-mining areas of Durham and Derbyshire in England, and in Wales. As their names imply, they will also go in pursuit of the fox.

For many years, the Smooth and Wire Fox Terriers were bred together, regardless of coat. All the great Wires resulted from the mating of a Smooth Fox Terrier called Jock with a bitch of unknown antecedents, but definitely wire-haired, called Trap. The Smooth was given its own register in 1876, three years after the British Kennel Club was founded, but the conformation of the two breeds still remains the same.

Both varieties of Fox Terrier were much sought after in Britain in the 1930s. Sadly, they are now seen less frequently. The Wire is more popular than its smooth-coated relative, which is rarely seen outside the show ring.

Character and care

The Fox Terriers are affectionate, and trainable, and make the ideal small child's companion for rabbiting. The Smooth needs daily grooming with a stiff brush, and trimming and chalking before a show. The Wire needs to be hand-stripped three times a year, and to be groomed regularly.

The Wire-haired was probably developed some years before the Smooth, although it was slower to make its début in the show ring.

Today fairly rare, the Smooth differs from its wiry relative only in the texture of its coat.

KEY CHARACTERISTICS
• **CLASS** Terrier. **Recognized** AKC, ANKC, CKC, FCI, KC(GB), KUSA.
• **SIZE** Maximum height at withers: dogs 39cm (15½in), bitches slightly less. Weight: 7.2–8.2kg (16–18lb).
• **COAT** *Smooth* Straight, flat and smooth. *Wire* Dense and very wiry.
• **COLOUR** *Smooth* All white; white with tan or black markings, white should predominate; brindle, red or liver markings highly undesirable. *Wire* White should predominate with black or tan markings; brindle, red, liver or slate-blue markings undesirable.
• **OTHER FEATURES** *Smooth* Flat, moderately narrow skull; dark, small eyes, rather deep set; small, V-shaped ears dropping forward close to cheek; chest deep, not broad; tail customarily docked. *Wire* Topline of skull almost flat; dark eyes, full of fire and intelligence; small, V-shaped ears, of moderate thickness; short, strong, level back; tail customarily docked.

GLEN OF IMAAL TERRIER

A game little dog, the Glen of Imaal Terrier is little known outside its home territory.

Character and care

The Glen of Imaal is nowadays to be found mainly as a family pet and/or working terrier on Irish farms and small holdings. It is affectionate, brave, good with children and very playful. Maintaining its charming, "shaggy dog" appearance requires only a good daily brushing.

KEY CHARACTERISTICS
• **CLASS** Terrier. **Recognized** ANKC, FCI, KC(GB), KUSA.
• **SIZE** Height: about 35.5cm (14in). Weight: about 15.7kg (35lb).
• **COAT** Medium length and harsh textured, with a soft undercoat.
• **COLOUR** Blue, brindle or wheaten, all shades.
• **OTHER FEATURES** Head of good width and fair length with a strong foreface; medium-sized, brown eyes; small ears, rose-shaped or pricked when alert, thrown back in repose; powerful jaws; deep, medium-length body; tail strong at root, well set on and carried gaily, docking optional.

This short-legged terrier derives from the Glen of Imaal in County Wicklow, Ireland, where it has existed for a very long time. It was used to dispel vermin, including fox and badger, and in dog fights. Badger hunting and dog fighting are now illegal, but its other skills continue to be employed.

The Glen of Imaal Terrier received official breed recognition in its own country in 1933. It is now also recognized by the British Kennel Club but remains little known outside its native Ireland.

The Glen still serves as a working terrier on Irish farms.

IRISH TERRIER

Similar in appearance to the Airedale, but smaller, the Irish Terrier is a keen ratter and can also be trained to the gun.

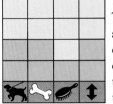

The Irish or Irish Red Terrier is reminiscent of a small Airedale Terrier, except for its fiery coat colour. The Irish claim that this, their national terrier, is a smaller version of the Irish Wolfhound and has been in existence in Ireland for centuries. However, the first official record of it did not occur until 1875, and the breed did not rate a mention in Idstone's *Book of Dogs*, published in 1872. It seems more likely that the Irish Terrier is a descendant of wire-haired Black and Tan Terriers, whose job was to repel vermin and hunt some 200 years ago. One study of the very similar Welsh and Lakeland Terriers adds substance to this suggestion. In the case of the Irish, the blood of a large Wheaten Terrier said to have existed around County Cork may also have been introduced.

Whatever its ancestry, the Irish Terrier varied greatly in size, conformation and colour until 1879. In that year, a specialist breed club was formed in Ireland, standardization began, and the Irish Terrier went on to become a firm favourite internationally.

Character and care

The attractive Irish is an expert ratter and has been trained to the gun with success. It also makes an affectionate pet. Its coat should be stripped two or three times a year, and it should be groomed regularly.

KEY CHARACTERISTICS
● **CLASS** Terrier. **Recognized** AKC, ANKC, CKC, FCI, KC(GB), KUSA.
● **SIZE** Height at shoulders: about 46cm (18in). Weight: 11.3–12.1kg (25–27lb).
● **COAT** Harsh and wiry.
● **COLOUR** Whole-coloured, preferably red, red wheaten, or yellow-red; small amount of white on chest acceptable; white on feet or any black shading highly undesirable.
● **OTHER FEATURES** Long head, flat and narrow between ears; small, dark, unprominent eyes; small, V-shaped ears; deep, muscular tail, customarily docked.

Though the Irish Terrier had been around for centuries, it varied greatly in type until a breed club was formed.

KERRY BLUE TERRIER

Once a mascot for Irish patriots, the Kerry Blue is very game, even tackling otters in deep water.

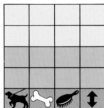

The Kerry Blue Terrier originated in County Kerry, south-western Ireland. An excellent sporting dog and fine swimmer, it was used there to hunt badgers, foxes and otters. Its ancestors are thought to have included the Irish, Bedlington and Bull Terriers. As with the Irish Terrier, there is a school of thought that the Irish Wolfhound also contributed to its make-up. According to a legend, however, the Kerry Blue traces its lineage back to a blue terrier survivor from a shipwreck in Tralee Bay, County Kerry. This dog was so ferocious that it killed every opponent with which it did battle, establishing the right to found its own strain. Whatever its true origin the Kerry Blue is certainly not the breed one would wish to encounter off the lead when exercising one's Peke or Chihuahua.

The breed was first exhibited at Crufts Dog Show in England, and in the United States, in 1922. It was recognized by the British Kennel Club in the same year, and in the United States two years later.

Character and care

Although it began life as a sporting dog, the Kerry Blue is now mainly kept as a pet. It is good with children, while retaining excellent guarding qualities. However, it may display a fierce temper against dogs or other pets when roused and so, if you own a fiery Kerry, you would be wise to insure yourself against other people's veterinary bills. The Kerry is not the easiest dog to prepare for the show ring, requiring knowledgeable trimming. It needs daily grooming with a stiff brush and metal-toothed comb.

KEY CHARACTERISTICS
● **CLASS** Terrier. **Recognized** AKC, ANKC, CKC, FCI, KC(GB), KUSA.
● **SIZE** Height: dogs 45–49cm (18–19½in), bitches 44–47.5cm (17½–19in). Weight: 14.8–18.1kg (33–40lb).
● **COAT** Soft, spiky, plentiful and wavy.
● **COLOUR** Any shade of blue, with or without black points; a small white patch on chest should not be penalized.
● **OTHER FEATURES** Eyes as dark as possible; small to medium-sized, V-shaped ears; short-coupled body with good depth of brisket and well-sprung ribs; tail set on high and carried erect, customarily docked.

LAKELAND TERRIER

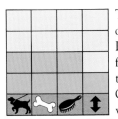

The Lakeland Terrier, originally known as the Patterdale Terrier, comes from the Lake District in the old English county of Cumberland. It was developed with the aim of protecting lambs from foxes. To meet this aim, there were various terrier crossings, and it is thought that the Border, the Bedlington and the Dandie Dinmont Terriers, and probably later the Fox Terrier, all contributed. The result is a practical and courageous working animal, resembling an Airedale Terrier in miniature, which is small enough to follow prey underground.

Although the Lakeland worked with local hunts for years, it did not appear in the show ring until 1912. After the First World War a breed club was formed, and the Lakeland was recognized by the Kennel Club in Britain in 1921. In 1964, a Lakeland Terrier, Champion Stingray of Derryabah, won Best in Show at Crufts Dog Show in London and, a year later, repeated this triumph at the Westminster Dog Show in New York.

Character and care

The Lakeland Terrier has retained its sporting instincts yet makes an excellent handy-sized housepet, being a smart little guard and good with children. However, it is a lively dog, needing a fair amount of exercise. Its coat requires daily brushing and, if it is the intention to exhibit, will have to be stripped three times a year.

KEY CHARACTERISTICS
• **CLASS** Terrier. **Recognized** AKC, ANKC, CKC, FCI, KC(GB), KUSA.
• **SIZE** Maximum height at shoulders: 37cm (14½in). Weight: dogs about 7.7kg (17lb), bitches about 6.8kg (15lb).
• **COAT** Dense and harsh, with weather-resistant undercoat.
• **COLOUR** Black and tan, blue and tan, red, wheaten, red grizzle, liver, blue or black; mahogany or deep tan not typical; small tips of white on feet and chest undesirable but permissible.
• **OTHER FEATURES** Flat skull; refined, dark or hazel eyes; moderately small ears; reasonably narrow chest; tail customarily docked.

Another breed resembling a small-scale Airedale, the Lakeland Terrier hunted foxes across rugged terrain.

MANCHESTER TERRIER

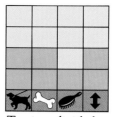

The Manchester Terrier is a professional ratter turned household pet.

The Manchester Terrier and English Toy Terrier (known in the United States as the Toy Manchester Terrier) were once exhibited under the name of Black and Tan Terrier, divided only by weight. Nowadays the two breeds are classified separately.

Although not well documented, the history of the Manchester Terrier suggests that the breed has been long established. Its ancestors were sporting terriers that would demolish rats in a pit for the amusement of spectators in the mid 19th century. This sport was popular among poorer people in areas such as the city of Manchester in northern England. The Manchester Terrier appears to descend from the now extinct White English Terrier, with the addition of Dachshund, Whippet and King Charles Spaniel blood. The Doberman and Italian Greyhound also contributed, both accounting for the Manchester's smooth shiny coat and colouring, and the latter for its slightly arched back.

PARSON JACK RUSSELL TERRIER

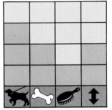

Bred by a hunting parson, the Jack Russell is still in demand as a working terrier and boisterous household pet.

The Parson Jack Russell Terrier was only recognized by the British Kennel Club in January 1990. Until then it was believed that there was far too much variation in the breed's colour, conformation, size and coat texture for it to be granted pure-bred status. The Kennel Club recognized one type of Jack Russell only, the Parson Jack. Although people have got into the habit of calling similar terriers Jack Russells, they are not recognized as such. They are often also referred to as hunt terriers, and are very popular in North America and the UK.

This breed takes its name from a sporting parson, Jack Russell, who lived in the county of Devon, England, in the 1800s. He was a horseman, a terrier judge and one of the early members of the British Kennel Club. Parson Russell developed this strain of terriers from various early types of wire-haired fox terriers to obtain dogs that would run with hounds and bolt the fox from its lair. Their coat may be either rough and broken or smooth.

Character and care
The long-lived Manchester Terrier tends to be a one-person animal and, regardless of its sporting past, is often a pampered pet of old ladies. It also makes an extremely good family pet, and is suited to a town or country existence. The only grooming required is a daily brush and rubdown.

KEY CHARACTERISTICS
• **CLASS** Terrier. **Recognized** AKC, ANKC, CKC, FCI, KC(GB). KUSA.
• **SIZE** Height at shoulders: dogs about 40.5cm (16in), bitches 38cm (15in). Weight: 5.4–9.9kg (12–22lb).
• **COAT** Close, smooth, short and glossy.
• **COLOUR** Jet black and rich tan.
• **OTHER FEATURES** Long, flat, narrow skull; small, dark, sparkling eyes; small, V-shaped ears; chest narrow and deep; short tail, set on where arch of back ends.

Character and care
The Parson Jack Russell is still an extremely good working terrier, and has become enormously popular as a household pet with many people, including the elderly. However, it can be somewhat excitable and is really better suited to being the companion of an active child. It requires little grooming.

KEY CHARACTERISTICS
• **CLASS** Terrier **Recognized** ANKC, FCI, KC(GB), KUSA
• **SIZE** Height at withers: dogs 33–35cm (13–14in), bitches 30–33cm (12–13in).
• **COAT** Smooth, or rough and broken.
• **COLOUR** Entirely white or with tan, lemon or black markings, preferably confined to head and root of tail.
• **OTHER FEATURES** Strong-boned head; almond-shaped eyes; V-shaped ears; strong hindquarters; tail is customarily docked.

GERMAN HUNT TERRIER

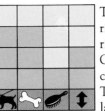

The German Hunt Terrier or Deutscher Jagdterrier was developed in Germany, probably by crossing the English Fox Terrier with the Lakeland Terrier. Careful selection achieved a terrier that would go to earth and retrieve small game from land or water. The German Hunt Terrier is a courageous hunter, which will take on fox and boar as well as small rodents.

Character and care
This hunter and gundog possesses an aggressive temperament and is not a suitable pet. It should be kennelled outdoors, and can be groomed with a hound glove.

KEY CHARACTERISTICS
• **CLASS** Terrier. **Recognized** FCI.
• **SIZE** Maximum height at withers: 40.5cm (16in). Weight: dogs 8.7–9.9kg (19½–22lb), bitches 7.2–8.1kg (16–18lb).
• **COAT** *Smooth* Smooth, harsh, dense and lying flat; *Rough* Harsh and wiry.
• **COLOUR** Predominantly black, greyish black or dark brown with small, even tan markings.
• **OTHER FEATURES** Rather heavy head; small, dark eyes set obliquely; V-shaped ears, folded so that tips fall forward; long back; tail set on high and carried erect, characteristically docked.

Although ideal for its purpose, the German Hunt Terrier is not suitable as a pet.

SOFT-COATED WHEATEN TERRIER

One of the oldest Irish Terriers, the Wheaten did not emerge from the farmyard until fairly recently.

HARLEQUIN PINSCHER

The Harlequin Pinscher or Harlekinpinscher is the newest pinscher breed, having been recognized by the FCI in 1958. It was bred down from the Pinscher, possibly with the addition of other blood. The main difference between the Harlequin and its larger relative is coat colour. It was bred for beauty and companionability rather than for work. It is rarely seen outside Germany.

Character and care

The Harlequin Pinscher is alert and, like all terrier-type dogs, will warn its owner of intruders, but its main purpose is as a companion and pet. It has an excellent temperament. It is lively and needs some exercise, and requires grooming with a brush or hound glove once or twice a week.

KEY CHARACTERISTICS
• **CLASS** Terrier. **Recognized** FCI.
• **SIZE** Height at withers: 30.5–35.5cm (12–14in).
• **COAT** Short, smooth, dense and glossy.
• **COLOUR** Pied on a white or pale-coloured ground; grey dappled with black or dark patches; brindle with or without tan points.
• **OTHER FEATURES** Skull and muzzle proportionate, forming smooth line; eyes not too large, too round or too small; small ears erect, with pointed or forward-hanging tips (cropped); muscular body; tail, characteristically docked.

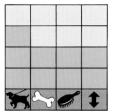

One of the oldest native dog breeds of Ireland, the Soft-coated Wheaten Terrier is believed to be a progenitor of the Irish and Kerry Blue Terriers. It is said that a blue dog swam ashore from a ship wrecked in Tralee Bay, Ireland, around 180 years ago. This dog mated with the native Wheaten and the result of the union was the Kerry Blue Terrier.

The Soft-coated Wheaten was developed as a farm dog to hunt rabbits, rats and other prey. It will work any kind of covert and no respectable Irish farmer would be without one. Recognized by the Irish Kennel Club in 1937 and by the British Kennel Club in 1971, the breed first appeared in the United States at the beginning of the 1970s and was recognized by the American Kennel Club in 1973. It is now making progress in the show ring on both sides of the Atlantic.

Character and care
Despite being bred as a farmyard dog the Soft-coated Wheaten does best when housed indoors as a family pet. It is gentle and devoted, and generally loves children. It revels in plenty of exercise, and the coat should be groomed regularly using a medium-toothed metal comb and a wire brush.

KEY CHARACTERISTICS
• **CLASS** Terrier. **Recognized** AKC, ANKC, CKC, FCI, KC(GB), KUSA.
• **SIZE** Height at withers: dogs 45.5–49.5cm (18–19½in), bitches slightly less. Weight: 15.7–20.2kg (35–45lb).
• **COAT** Soft and silky.
• **COLOUR** A good, clear wheaten, the shade of ripening wheat; white and red equally objectionable; dark shading on ears not untypical.
• **OTHER FEATURES** Head and skull flat and moderately long; clear, bright, dark hazel eyes; V-shaped ears; compact body; tail customarily docked.

With a stocky body and profuse, silky coat, the Wheaten has small ears and a docked tail.

JAPANESE TERRIER

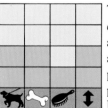

This Japanese breed was developed in the 1700s around the ports of Kobe and Yokohama, using imported British terriers, particularly the Smooth Fox Terrier. These were crossed with local breeds to produce a dog that is lighter throughout and lacks the heavy bone, short, strong body and clean-cut reach of Smooth Fox Terriers. Kept principally as a pet in Japan, it is thought to have gone through so many changes that it is now described as a terrier with some reservation. It is rarely seen outside the country of origin.

Character and care
The Japanese Terrier is a lively pet and so probably retains something of the terrier temperament. Its smooth coat needs little grooming, but it requires regular exercise.

KEY CHARACTERISTICS
• **CLASS** Terrier. **Recognized** FCI.
• **SIZE** Height: 30.5–38cm (12–15in).
• **COAT** Smooth and sparse.
• **COLOUR** Predominantly white with black and tan markings.
• **OTHER FEATURES** Small head; small eyes; small V-shaped ears; muscular body; small tail, customarily docked.

WELSH TERRIER

Of Celtic origin, the Welsh Terrier was used to hunt badger, fox and otter.

Like the Airedale, the Welsh Terrier has half-drop ears and small, deep-set eyes.

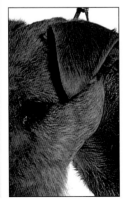

The Welsh Terrier resembles very closely both the Lakeland Terrier and the larger Airedale Terrier. Like another similar terrier, the Irish, the Welsh Terrier is of Celtic origin. Two strains of it were evolved by the Welsh, a Celtic strain using a coarse-haired Black and Tan Terrier and an English strain using an Airedale and a Fox Terrier cross, and appeared as a distinct breed in the late 18th century. The English strain is said to have died out, though, to the writer's way of thinking, both the Airedale and Fox Terrier influences are visibly apparent. In any event, the Celtic strain was presented in 1885 and a Welsh Terrier Club was formed a year later. In 1887, the Kennel Club in Britain awarded the breed championship show status. The first Welsh Terriers reached America in about 1901, and there a smaller dog is preferred. These terriers were originally popular for hunting badger, fox and otter.

Character and care
A fun dog, the Welsh Terrier is energetic, affectionate and good with children. It enjoys plenty of exercise and will need to have its coat stripped at least twice a year, if it is the intention to exhibit. Many owners of pet Welsh Terriers have their dog's coat clipped.

KEY CHARACTERISTICS
• **CLASS** Terrier. **Recognized** AKC, ANKC, CKC, FCI, KC(GB), KUSA.
• **SIZE** Maximum height at shoulders: 39cm (15½in). Weight: 9–9.5kg (20–21lb).
• **COAT** Abundant, wiry, hard and close.
• **COLOUR** Black and tan for preference; also black, grizzle and tan; free from black pencilling on toes; black below hocks most undesirable.
• **OTHER FEATURES** Head flat and moderately wide between ears; small, dark eyes well set in; small, V-shaped ears carried forward; short, well ribbed-up body; long, muscular legs; tail well set on but not carried too gaily, customarily docked.

BORDER TERRIER

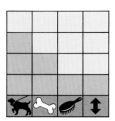

This attractive, tough little dog derives from the Border country, the area around the boundary between England and Scotland, and is probably still seen in its largest numbers there. The Border Terrier was bred in the middle of the 19th century to run with hounds and yet be small enough to bolt the fox from its lair.

Recognized by the British Kennel Club in 1920 the breed has been less spoilt by the dictates of fashion than many others. It has always been a working terrier. When James Davidson wrote in 1800 that he had purchased "twa red devils o' terriers, that has hard wiry coats and would worry any demned thing that crepit", he could have been describing the Border Terrier of today.

Character and care

The smallest of the working terriers, the Border makes a first-class pet. It usually loves all children, is long lived, will literally walk its owners off their feet, and is a good watchdog. It requires little routine grooming, and only a slight tidying up before exhibiting.

KEY CHARACTERISTICS
● **CLASS** Terrier.   **Recognized** AKC, ANKC, CKC, FCI, KC(GB), KUSA.
● **SIZE** Height: about 25cm (10in). Weight: dogs 6–7kg (13–15½lb), bitches 5.1–6.4kg (11½–14lb).
● **COAT** Harsh and dense with close undercoat.
● **COLOUR** Red, wheaten, grizzle and tan, blue and tan.
● **OTHER FEATURES** Dark eyes with keen expression; small, V-shaped ears; deep, narrow, fairly long body; moderately short tail.

The Border, smallest of the working terriers, was sent in to bolt the fox from its lair.

CAIRN TERRIER

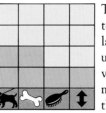

Bright eyes, erect ears and a short muzzle help give the Cairn its attitude of keenness.

This popular Scottish terrier, or one very similar, has been known and used for putting down vermin for 150 years or more. It was named after the cairns (a Scottish word which means a heap or pile of stones), which often harboured vermin. The Cairn Terrier originated in the Western Highlands, where the Skye Terrier is well known. There appears to have been some confusion between the breeds at one time, and the Cairn, predominantly a working breed, used to be known as the Short-haired Skye Terrier.

The oldest known strain of Cairn Terriers is that founded by the late Captain MacLeod of Drynoch in the Isle of Skye. Mr John MacDonald, gamekeeper to the Macleod of Macleod at Dunvegan Castle for more than 40 years, kept this strain alive.

The Cairn Terrier made its first appearance in the show ring in 1909, and is now known and admired the world over. However, like the Border Terrier, it still tends to be seen most in the North of England and in its native Scotland.

Character and care
This intelligent, lively little working terrier is still well able to prove its worth as a dispeller of vermin and is also a popular and affectionate pet. It is hardy and enjoys plenty of exercise though it can adapt to most living situations. The Cairn is an easy dog to show, requiring little grooming other than brushing, combing and removing of excess feathering.

KEY CHARACTERISTICS
• **CLASS** Terrier. **Recognized** AKC, ANKC, CKC, FCI, KC(GB), KUSA.
• **SIZE** Height: 24–30cm (9½–12in). Weight: 5.9–7.5kg (13–16lb).
• **COAT** Profuse, harsh but not coarse, with short, soft, close undercoat; weather resistant.
• **COLOUR** Cream, wheaten, red, grey or nearly black; brindling acceptable in all these colours; not solid black, solid white, nor black and tan; dark points, such as ears and muzzle, very typical.
• **OTHER FEATURES** Small head; eyes set wide apart; small, pointed ears; level back; short, balanced tail, well furnished with hair but not feathery.

DANDIE DINMONT TERRIER

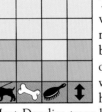

The appealing and devoted little Dandie Dinmont Terrier is generally believed to be a relative of the Skye Terrier. It was originally bred to hunt badgers and foxes. Most Dandies trace back to a pack owned by "Piper" Allan of Northumberland (now Northumbria), England, in the 1700s. His dogs are also credited with helping in the development of the Bedlington Terrier.

James Davidson, a farmer in the Borders (the area around the boundary between England and Scotland), kept a pack of these short-legged, rough-haired terriers, and Sir Walter Scott (1771–1832), the novelist, acquired some of them. Though Scott subsequently denied that there was any connection, his famous novel *Guy Mannering*, published in 1814, includes a character called

One of several terriers originally bred in the Western Highlands, the Cairn was used to clean vermin out of wayside cairns.

An engaging little character, the Dandie Dinmont takes its name from a novel by Sir Walter Scott.

Dandie Dinmont, who is a Borders farmer with a pack of little terriers. Thereafter, the dogs became known as Dandie Dinmont's Terriers, and, in time, as Dandie Dinmonts. They were also known as Pepper and Mustard Terriers after the colours for which Davidson's dogs were renowned.

When the Dandie Dinmont Terrier was first shown at the Birmingham Dog Show in 1867, the judge, Mr W. Smith, refused to award the exhibits a prize, being of the opinion that they were "just a bunch of mongrels". The breed has been vastly improved since then.

Character and care

Now kept mainly as a pet, the Dandie Dinmont makes a most affectionate, playful and intelligent companion, and is in its element as the family's sole pet. It will be happy with as much exercise as its owner is able to provide. This breed is also fairly simple to groom, use of a stiff brush and comb, and the removal of surplus hair, being all that is necessary.

KEY CHARACTERISTICS
● **CLASS** Terrier. **Recognized** AKC, ANKC, CKC, FCI, KC(GB), KUSA.
● **SIZE** Height at shoulders: 20–27.5cm (8–11in). Weight: 8.1–10.8kg (18–24lb).
● **COAT** Soft, linty undercoat and harder topcoat, not wiry and feeling crisp to the hand.
● **COLOUR** Pepper (from bluish black to pale silvery grey) or mustard (from reddish brown to pale fawn).
● **OTHER FEATURES** Strongly made head, large but in proportion to dog's size; rich, dark hazel eyes; pendulum ears; long, strong and flexible body; rather short tail.

NORFOLK TERRIER

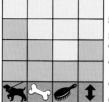

This breed was once classified with, and known as, the Norwich Terrier. The drop-eared Norfolk Terrier and the prick-eared Norwich Terrier originated in the East Anglian area of England and were once very popular with students at Cambridge University. Both little dogs were known as Norwich Terriers from as early as the 1880s. They were probably a mixture of Cairn, Border and Irish Terriers, and their litters contained both the prick-eared and drop-eared varieties.

The only difference between the Norfolk and Norwich Terriers today is still their ears. The writer distinguishes the two breeds by the fact that the ears of the Norfolk are flat like that English county, while those of the Norwich are upright like the spire of Norwich Cathedral. The Norfolk Terrier only gained official recognition as a separate breed from the Kennel Club in Britain in 1964 and, in the United States, it took until 1979 for the varieties to be separated.

Character and care

Despite being among the smallest of the terriers, the Norfolk is described in its breed club standard as being a "demon" for its size. A sociable dog, this hardy, lovable terrier is certainly alert and fearless, but it is good with children, has an equable temperament and makes a fine household pet for those prepared to exercise it. It enjoys a day's rabbiting, and honourable scars are not a drawback in the show ring. It requires daily brushing, and some trimming is all the preparation that is needed for exhibition.

KEY CHARACTERISTICS
● **CLASS** Terrier. **Recognized** AKC, ANKC, CKC, FCI, KC(GB), KUSA.
● **SIZE** Height at withers: about 25.5cm (10in). Weight: 5–5.4kg (11–12lb).
● **COAT** Hard, wiry and straight.
● **COLOUR** All shades of red, wheaten, black and tan, or grizzle; white marks and patches undesirable but permissible.
● **OTHER FEATURES** Broad skull; deep-set, oval-shaped eyes; medium-sized, V-shaped ears, slightly rounded at tip; compact body; tail-docking optional.

The Norfolk Terrier is distinguished by its ears, which drop forward.

NORWICH TERRIER

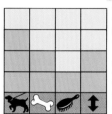

The Norwich is a traditional terrier breed, well suited to hunting small prey in open terrain.

From 1964 in Britain, and from 1979 in the United States, the prick-eared Norwich Terrier has been classified separately from an otherwise identical drop-eared dog now known as the Norfolk Terrier (see page 206). The breed is named after the city of Norwich, which lies in the county of Norfolk in the East Anglian area of eastern England. The Norwich Terrier appears to have originated in East Anglia, and probably includes Cairn, Border and Irish Terrier blood. It was popular with students at Cambridge University, who kept both varieties.

Controversy exists over whether a Colonel Vaughan from Ballybrick in southern Ireland, or a horse dealer named Jodrell Hopkins from the Cambridge area, deserve credit for founding the Norwich Terrier. In the 1860s Colonel Vaughan hunted with a pack of small red terriers, which included many outcrosses and contained terriers with both dropped and pricked ears. There was a tendency to crop the ears of the drop-eared dogs until this practice became illegal. Then the Norwich Terrier Club requested that the breed's standard be amended to include only those terriers with pricked ears. Hopkins's claim lies in his ownership of a bitch, some of whose pups came into the hands of an employee of his, Frank Jones. Jones crossed them with other terriers, including the smaller examples of Irish and Glen of Imaal Terriers. The progeny became known as Trumpington Terriers or Jones Terriers, and a line of Norwich Terriers in existence today claims direct descent from Frank Jones' litters.

Character and care

This hardy and adaptable terrier is usually good with children. It enjoys regular exercise and needs only a daily brushing for its role as housepet and some trimming in preparation for show.

The upright ears of the Norwich Terrier signal its keenness to work.

KEY CHARACTERISTICS
● **CLASS** Terrier. **Recognized** AKC, ANKC, CKC, FCI, KC(GB), KUSA.
● **SIZE** Height at withers: 25.5cm (10in). Weight: 4.5–5.4kg (10–12lb).
● **COAT** Hard, wiry and straight.
● **COLOUR** All shades of red, wheaten, black and tan, or grizzle; white marks and patches undesirable.
● **OTHER FEATURES** Strong, wedge-shaped muzzle; small, dark, oval-shaped eyes; erect ears set well apart on top of skull; short back; docked tail optional.

SCOTTISH TERRIER

A separate breed for more than a century, the "Scottie" has a number of terrier cousins in the Highlands.

Erect ears and prominent eyebrows on a long face give the Scottie a somewhat stern appearance.

The Scottish Terrier or Scottie was once known as the Aberdeen Terrier, after the Scottish city. Like the Cairn, it was bred with the express purpose of dispelling vermin. The Scottie has existed for many centuries and taken many different forms. Indeed, at the end of the 19th century it was exhibited alongside the Skye, Dandie Dinmont and West Highland White Terrier under the classification, Scotch Terriers. Many people still tend to think that the West Highland White and the Scottish Terriers are one and the same breed. In fact, line breeding of the Scottie began in earnest in around 1800. In 1892, the first Scottish Terrier Club was formed in Scotland and a standard was laid down for the breed.

Character and care
The Scottie tends to be a one- or two-person dog, perhaps at its best as the pampered pet of a childless couple. It has a reliable temperament but does not welcome interlopers and has no interest in anyone outside its own human family. It enjoys walks, loves to play ball games, and is thoroughly sporty, home-loving and independent. The Scottie requires daily brushing. Its beard needs gentle brushing and combing, and its coat should be trimmed twice a year.

KEY CHARACTERISTICS
● **CLASS** Terrier. **Recognized** AKC, ANKC, CKC, FCI, KC(GB), KUSA.
● **SIZE** Height at withers: 25.5–28cm (10–11in). Weight: 8.6–10.4kg (19–23lb).
● **COAT** Sharp, dense and wiry, with a short, dense, soft undercoat.
● **COLOUR** Black, wheaten or brindle of any shade.
● **OTHER FEATURES** Head and skull long without being out of proportion to size of dog; almond-shaped eyes; neat, fine-textured ears; well-moulded ribs flattening to deep chest; moderate-length tail giving general balance to dog.

SEALYHAM TERRIER

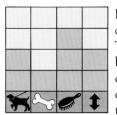

Freeman Lloyd, an authority on the Sealyham Terrier, has traced the breed back to the 15th century, when a family called Tucker is reputed to have imported a small, white, long-backed Flemish terrier into Wales. One of the Tuckers' descendants, the sportsman, Captain Edwardes, wanted dogs that would hunt with hounds and go to ground in the now illegal sport of badger digging. In the 1880s, he developed the Sealyham from various terrier breeds.

The breed took its name from the village of Sealyham near Haverfordwest, Wales, where it was created. The first Sealyham Terrier breed club was formed in 1908 and its founder, Fred Lewis, is said to have done a great deal to perfect the strain. Sealyhams were recognized by the British and American Kennel Clubs in the same year, 1911. Since then, the breed has proved successful in show rings throughout the world. However, the immense rise in popularity of the rather similar West Highland White Terrier over the past decade has resulted in the Sealyham rarely being seen outside the show ring today.

Character and care

The Sealyham makes a fine show dog and family pet. It is good with children, but not averse to a scrap with its fellows. This breed requires regular brushing and must be hand-stripped for the show ring. If intending to exhibit, advice on grooming should be sought from the breeder or some other expert.

KEY CHARACTERISTICS
• **CLASS** Terrier. **Recognized** AKC, ANKC, CKC, FCI, KC(GB), KUSA.
• **SIZE** Maximum height at shoulders: 31cm (12in). Weight: dogs about 9kg (20lb), bitches about 8.2kg (18lb).
• **COAT** Long, hard and wiry, with a weather-resistant undercoat.
• **COLOUR** All white, or white with lemon, brown, blue or badger pied markings on head and ears; much black or heavy ticking undesirable.
• **OTHER FEATURES** Head slightly domed; dark, well-set eyes; medium-sized ears; medium-length body; tail set in line with back and carried erect, customarily docked.

Today quite rare, the Sealyham was named after its place of origin in Pembrokeshire, west Wales.

SKYE TERRIER

The Skye Terrier, which evolved on the island of the same name, used to be known as the Terrier of the Western Islands.

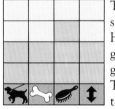

The Skye developed from small dogs kept in the Highlands of Scotland to go to ground after badger, fox, otter and rabbit. The best of these "earth" terriers were said to originate in the Isle of Skye. For a considerable time, the Skye and Cairn Terriers were thought to be one breed, the Cairn being described as a Short-haired Skye. There were also Skyes with drop and pricked ears. These varieties were divided in 1904, and challenge certificates have since been awarded to both drop-eared and prick-eared Skyes. Although the drop-eared variety is still permissible, it is rarely seen in Britain these days, and while it may be more numerous, it is still less common than the prick-eared Skye in the United States.

Probably the most famous Skye Terrier is Greyfriars Bobby, the subject of a romantic tale. In the 1850s, Bobby's master died and was buried in the graveyard of Greyfriars' Church in Edinburgh. Bobby lay on his master's grave for 14 years until his own death, breaking his vigil only to visit the café he had frequented with his late master. A statue to commemorate Bobby's faithfulness still stands, near Greyfriars' Church.

Character and care

The Skye Terrier tends to be suspicious of or uninterested in anyone other than its owner. Its magnificent long coat requires a considerable amount of grooming, particularly as this little dog enjoys country walks.

KEY CHARACTERISTICS
• **CLASS** Terrier. **Recognized** AKC, ANKC, CKC, FCI, KC(GB), KUSA.
• **SIZE** Ideal height at shoulders: dogs 25cm (10in), bitches 24cm (9½in). Weight: about 11.3kg (25lb).
• **COAT** Long, hard, straight, flat and free from curl, with a short, close, soft, woolly undercoat.
• **COLOUR** Black, dark or light grey, fawn or cream, all with black points.
• **OTHER FEATURES** Head and skull long and powerful; brown, preferably dark, eyes; prick or drop ears; long, low body with level back; when tail is hanging, upper part pendulous and lower part thrown back in a curve, when raised looks like extension of the back line.

WEST HIGHLAND WHITE TERRIER

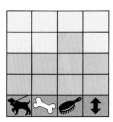

Like other small Scottish terriers, the West Highland White Terrier or Westie was bred to hunt vermin. At one time it was classed along with the Cairn and Skye Terriers as a Small Highland Working Terrier. The Westie has also gone under a number of other names. In the late 1800s, there was a strain of white Scottish Terriers owned by Colonel Malcolm of Poltalloch and known as Poltalloch Terriers. A picture of Colonel Malcolm with his dogs reveals that they were not all that different to the Westie we know today. Dogs of this type were also known as Roseneath Terriers or White Roseneath Terriers, and in a breed supplement published in 1899, they were classified as a sub-variety of the Scottish Terrier.

The first West Highland White Terrier Club was formed in 1905, and the first class for the breed seems to have been held in October 1904 at the Waverley Market in Edinburgh, organized by the Scottish Kennel Club. The Westie was recognized in America and Canada in 1909 and 1911 respectively, but not in Australia until the mid-1960s. Today it is among the most popular of purebred dogs.

Character and care

The Westie is described in its standard as being "possessed of no small amount of self esteem with a varminty appearance". This game and hardy little terrier is easy to train, gets on well with children and is a suitable housepet for people in town as well as in the country. Regular brushing keeps the white coat clean, but stripping and trimming are required for show, and, if it is the intention to exhibit, advice on preparation should be sought from the breeder.

KEY CHARACTERISTICS
● **CLASS** Terrier. **Recognized** AKC, ANKC, CKC, FCI, KC(GB), KUSA.
● **SIZE** Height: dogs about 27.5cm (11in), bitches about 25cm (10in). Weight: 6.8–9.9kg (15–22lb).
● **COAT** Harsh and free from curl, with a short, soft, close furry undercoat.
● **COLOUR** White.
● **OTHER FEATURES** Slightly domed head; eyes set wide apart; small, erect ears, carried firmly; compact body with level back and broad, strong loins; tail 12.5–15cm (5–6in) long.

Undeniably cute with its pricked ears and black button nose, the "Westie" is none the less a game little terrier well able to perform in the field.

In its hunting days, the white-coated Westie was more easily distinguished from game than were other terriers.

CZESKY TERRIER

A stylish newcomer to the terrier group, the Czesky or Bohemian Terrier was bred by a Czech fancier using British stock.

Still less than half a century old, the breed is well established in blue-grey or light brown versions.

The Czesky or Bohemian Terrier is a short-legged terrier, little known outside its native home of the Czech Republic. It was developed in the middle of this century by crossing the Scottish, Sealyham and possibly other terriers. The result is a tough, sturdy dog that will go to ground after quarry, and is an excellent ratter and guard.

Character and care
As well as being a fine working terrier, the Czesky's equable temperament also makes it a good children's companion. It requires plenty of exercise and expert clipping for the show ring, although pet owners could probably get away with the occasional visit to the grooming parlour and a good daily brushing.

KEY CHARACTERISTICS

- **CLASS** Terrier.
  Recognized FCI, KC(GB).

- **SIZE** Height at shoulders: 28–35.5cm (11–14in). Weight: 5.9–9kg (13–20lb).

- **COAT** Fine and silky, with tendency to curl.

- **COLOUR** Blue-grey or brown with light markings.

- **OTHER FEATURES** Long head; deep-set eyes; pendent ears; sturdy body; tail 17.5–20cm (7–8in) long, carried horizontally when terrier is excited.

KROMFOHRLÄNDER

This is a hunting and gundog, and a companion dog, but little known outside its native Germany. It was developed by crossing a Griffon and a terrier. There are three varieties, the rough-coated being far and away the most popular. The others are the long-straight and medium-straight varieties.

It was developed after the Second World War, and was recognized by the German Kennel Club in 1953. Shortly afterwards it was recognized by the FCI.

Character and care
The Kromfohrländer is an intelligent and affectionate companion, and a good guard. It requires plenty of exercise and daily brushing.

KEY CHARACTERISTICS

- **CLASS** Terrier.
  Recognized FCI.

- **SIZE** Height: 38–45.5cm (15–18in). Weight: about 11.8kg (26lb).

- **COAT** Rough and wiry; medium-long and straight; long and straight.

- **COLOUR** White with light to dark brown markings on head and body; head may be brown with white star.

- **OTHER FEATURES** Flat, wedge-shaped skull, little stop; ears set high and U-shaped; tail set high and carried curled to left side of back.

AUSTRALIAN TERRIER

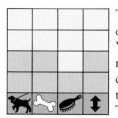

The Australian Terrier is often mistaken for a large Yorkshire Terrier. This is not surprising since it is considered to result from the mating of a Yorkshire Terrier bitch and a dog that resembled a Cairn Terrier. By the time the breed was first exhibited in 1899, it had been in existence for about 20 years and was reputed to be an unsurpassed vermin killer, which could also dispose of a snake.

When the Australian Terrier first arrived in England in 1906, it caused only a ripple of interest. However, it was recognized by the British Kennel Club in 1936 and experienced a boost in popularity when the Duke of Gloucester acquired a breed member following a tour of Australia. The breed was even slower making its mark in the United States, where it was not recognized until 1960.

Character and care

This breed is now proving a popular dog, both in the international show ring and as an alert, hardy and devoted family pet. The Australian needs only a good daily grooming with a bristle brush. Since it has a weather-resistant coat, it may be kennelled out of doors, though most owners do keep them indoors.

KEY CHARACTERISTICS

- **CLASS** Terrier.
  Recognized AKC, ANKC, CKC, FCI, KC(GB), KUSA.

- **SIZE** Height at withers: 25–27.5cm (10–11in). Weight: about 6.3kg (14lb).

- **COAT** Harsh, straight, dense and long, with short, soft undercoat.

- **COLOUR** (A) Blue, steel blue or dark grey-blue with rich tan (not sandy) on face, ears, under body, lower legs and around the vent (puppies excepted); top-knot blue or silver, of a lighter shade than leg colour. (B) Clear sandy or red; smuttiness or dark shadings undesirable; top-knot a lighter shade.

- **OTHER FEATURES** Long head with flat skull and powerful jaw; small eyes; small, erect, pointed ears; body long in proportion to height; tail set on high, customarily docked.

Brought over by settlers, terriers from Scotland and the north of England contributed to the Australian Terrier's make-up.

TOY BREEDS

COTON DE TULEAR

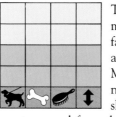

The Coton de Tulear is a member of the bichon family (see page 43). Its ancestors arrived in Madagascar and the nearby islands on trading ships prior to the 17th century, and from these imported dogs arose on Reunion Island, the Coton de Reunion. This dog is now extinct, but its descendants on Madagascar developed through a programme of cross-breeding, including introducing the Maltese. This has produced the breed now known as the Coton de Tulear after the city of Tulear in Madagascar.

The little Coton became known as the "dog of royalty" because it was a favourite of the French nobles who inhabited the islands during colonial times. Indeed, before the 20th century, it was a criminal offence for a commoner to own such a dog, and to this day it is usually only those in the upper strata of Malagasy society who are fortunate enough to own a Tulear. The breed is still comparatively rare although it is gradually becoming established in both Britain and America.

Character and care
The Coton de Tulear is a happy, friendly, intelligent little dog, which is devoted to its owners and likes to be with them. One of its most endearing qualities is its ability to walk on its hind legs. It can adapt to most climates and environments, and requires only daily brushing and average exercise.

KEY CHARACTERISTICS
• **CLASS** Toy. **Recognized** FCI, KC(GB).
• **SIZE** Height: 25.5–30.5cm (10–12in). Weight: 5.5–7kg (12–15lb).
• **COAT** Fluffy, like cotton.
• **COLOUR** White, with or without champagne markings; black and white.
• **OTHER FEATURES** Head carried high; eyes dark and deep-set; tail never docked, carried high and curled gracefully.

AFFENPINSCHER

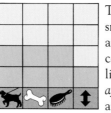

The Affenpinscher is the smallest of the pinschers and schnauzers. Its name comes from its monkey-like face (the German *affen* means "monkeys") and it is also known in its native country as the Zwergaffenpinscher or dwarf pinscher and in France, as the Diabletin Moustache ("the moustached little devil"). It greatly resembles the Griffon Bruxellois, but whether it was the Griffon that contributed to the Affenpinscher or vice versa is debatable. The Affenpinscher was recognized by the American Kennel Club as early as 1938. However, it has made its mark in Britain only within the past 15 years, and was exhibited for the first time at Crufts Dog Show, London, in 1980.

Character and care
This appealing, naturally scruffy-looking toy dog has a keen intelligence and is exceedingly affectionate. It makes a good watchdog and, terrier-like, is not averse to rabbiting. Its thick coat benefits from daily brushing.

KEY CHARACTERISTICS
• **CLASS** Toy. **Recognized** AKC, ANKC, CKC, FCI, KC(GB), KUSA.
• **SIZE** Height: 24–28cm (9½–11in). Weight: 3–4kg (6½–9lb).
• **COAT** Rough and thick.
• **COLOUR** Preferably black, but grey shading permissible.
• **OTHER FEATURES** Slightly undershot jaw; small, high-set ears, preferably erect, but neat drop-ear permissible; round, dark, sparkling eyes; short, straight back; high-set tail, docked in some countries.

BOLOGNESE

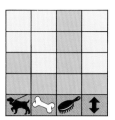

The Bolognese or Bichon Bolognese is a member of the bichon family, all of which are small white dogs from the Mediterranean area. It has been noted that the Bolognese's coat was white and black in the past, but black is now prohibited. The Italians claim that it originated in Bologna and it is recognized as an Italian breed. The Bolognese was a favourite with European royalty centuries ago but is now little seen outside Italy.

Character and care

This companion dog is serious, intelligent, not particularly vivacious, and seeks to please its owner. It requires only a moderate amount of exercise but needs fairly intricate trimming and scissoring for show purposes, and a good daily brush and comb when kept as a pet.

KEY CHARACTERISTICS
• **CLASS** Toy. **Recognized** FCI, KC(GB).
• **SIZE** Height at shoulders: dogs 28–30.5cm (11–12in), bitches 25.5–28cm (10–11in). Weight: 2.5–4.1kg (5½–9lb).
• **COAT** Long, flocked, standing off from body.
• **COLOUR** Pure white without shadings.
• **OTHER FEATURES** Eyes well open, round and large; long, hanging ears set on high; tail well feathered with long, flocked hair, set on at level of croup and carried curved over back.

MALTESE

Much painted and praised, the Maltese is one of the oldest lap dogs, popular with men and women.

In the Maltese a slightly rounded, broad skull is set off by long, silky, snow white fur.

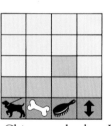

A member of the bichon family, this small, white dog is one of the oldest European breeds. It has existed on the island of Malta for centuries, and also found its way to China and the Philippines via Maltese traders. However, in about AD25, the Greek historian Strabo reported that "There is a town in Sicily called Melita whence are exported many beautiful dogs called Canis Melitei", raising the possibility of Italian origin for the breed.

The Maltese was a favourite in England from Tudor times, and in the reign of Queen Elizabeth I (1558–1603), the early dog historian, Doctor Johannes Caius, wrote, "They are called Meliti, of the Island of Malta . . . they are very small indeed and chiefly sought after for the pleasure and amusement of women who carried them in their arms, their bosoms, and their beds . . .".

The Maltese has been painted by many famous artists, notably Goya, Rubens and Sir Edwin Landseer. It was first exhibited in England in 1864, and a dog named "Leon" was shown in America in 1877 under the title Maltese Lion Dog.

Character and care

The long established Maltese seems to have been overtaken in popularity by other toys, and is now seldom seen outside the show ring. This is unfortunate because it is a happy, healthy, long-lived little dog, which is good with children and makes a lovable pet. It is fairly adaptable as far as exercise is concerned, but requires grooming every day with a bristle brush. Owners are advised to check with the breeder about show preparation.

KEY CHARACTERISTICS
• **CLASS** Toy. **Recognized** AKC, ANKC, CKC, FCI, KC(GB), KUSA.
• **SIZE** Height at withers: not exceeding 25.5cm (10in). Weight: 1.8–2.7kg (4–6lb) not exceeding 3.2kg (7lb).
• **COAT** Long, straight coat, silky texture.
• **COLOUR** White; slight lemon markings on ears permissible.
• **OTHER FEATURES** Slightly rounded, broad skull; well-defined stop; slightly tapered muzzle; long, well-feathered ears; oval eyes; compact body; long, plumed tail carried arched over back.

LÖWCHEN

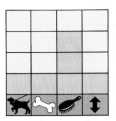

The Löwchen is also known as the Petit Chien Lion (Little Lion Dog) because it was traditionally given a lion clip, similar to that sported by the exhibition poodle. Complete with mane and tufted tail, the Löwchen does look like a lion in miniature.

This breed is a member of the bichon family, and is thought to have originated in the Mediterranean area. It is recognized as a French breed, but has been known in both France and Spain since the late 1500s. The Löwchen is widely believed to be the dog included by the Spanish artist, Francisco de Goya (1746–1828), in a painting of his friend, the Duchess of Alba.

Character and care

The Löwchen is an affectionate, intelligent dog, which is popular in the show ring but rarely seen walking in the park. It enjoys life as a pet given the chance, and is a lively animal, requiring daily brushing. If it is your intention to exhibit your Löwchen, expert advice on clipping should be sought.

KEY CHARACTERISTICS
• **CLASS** Toy. **Recognized** ANKC, FCI, KC(GB), KUSA.
• **SIZE** Height at withers: 25–33cm (10–13in). Weight: 3.6–8.2 kg (8–18 lb).
• **COAT** Moderately long and wavy.
• **COLOUR** Any colour or combination of colours permissible.
• **OTHER FEATURES** Wide, short skull; long pendent ears, well fringed; round, dark eyes with intelligent expression; short, strong body; medium length tail, clipped to resemble a plume.

Established in Spain, France and Germany since the 16th century, the Löwchen, or Little Lion Dog, featured in Goya's portrait of the Duchess of Alba.

BRUSSELS GRIFFON (AND PETIT BRABANCON)

The Brussels Griffon has a terrier-like disposition.

The Brussels Griffon, or Griffon Bruxellois, was first shown at the Brussels Exhibition of 1880. An early example of the breed is depicted in a painting of 1434 by Jan Van Eyck, the Flemish painter. Once kept by hansom cab drivers of 17th-century Brussels to rid their stables of vermin, the Brussels Griffon became a companion breed by virtue of its appealing character.

The smooth-coated Petit Brabançon probably owes its existence to the introduction of pug blood. Other breeds, including the Yorkshire and Irish Terriers, have undoubtedly contributed to the modern griffons. The rough-coated Brussels Griffon and smooth-haired Petit Brabançon are recognized as two distinct breeds in Europe. In America and Britain however, they are exhibited together.

Character and care

This intelligent, cheerful little dog, with its terrier-like disposition, make a fine companion. The Griffon has never suffered from the

YORKSHIRE TERRIER

The popularity of the "Yorkie" is quite disproportionate to its small size.

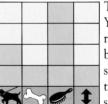

The Yorkshire Terrier or Yorkie is a comparatively recent breed, having been developed in Yorkshire, England, within the last hundred years or so through the crossing of a Skye Terrier and the extinct Black and Tan Terrier, a forerunner of the Manchester Terrier. The Maltese and Dandie Dinmont may also have contributed to its make-up.

It was recognized by the Kennel Club in Britain in 1886. It was introduced into the USA in about 1880 but took some time to become established there. Today, this lively little terrier is one of the most popular toy breeds in the world.

The Yorkie may be seen in so many different sizes that people often think there are two varieties, miniature and standard. In fact, the Yorkshire Terrier should not exceed 3.1kg (7lb) in weight, placing it alongside the Chihuahua as one of the world's smallest dogs. There are, however, many larger specimens which are admirably happy and healthy and make good pets.

over-popularity of some breeds and is a good family choice. The coat of the rough requires a lot of attention, however the coats of pet dogs may be clipped.

KEY CHARACTERISTICS
• **CLASS** Toy. **Recognized** AKC, ANKC, CKC, FCI, KC(GB), KUSA.
• **SIZE** Height: 17.8–20.3cm (7–8in). Weight: 2.2–5kg (5–11lb), most desirable 2.7–4.5kg (6–10lb).
• **COAT** *Brussels Griffon* Harsh, wiry. *Petit Brabançon* Soft, smooth.
• **COLOUR** Red, black or black and rich tan with white markings. FCI classifies the black, black/tan or red/black as Belgian Griffon.
• **OTHER FEATURES** Head, large in comparison to body, rounded, in no way domed, wide between the ears; eyes, black rimmed, very dark; body, short back, level from withers to tail root, neither roaching nor dipping; tail, customarily docked short, carried high.

Character and care

The Yorkie is suited to town or country living and, like most small terriers, is utterly fearless. This bossy, inordinately affectionate and lively little dog makes a fine pet. It is also a first-class show dog for those with the time to spare for intricate grooming.

KEY CHARACTERISTICS
• **CLASS** Toy. **Recognized** AKC, ANKC, CKC, FCI, KC(GB), KUSA.
• **SIZE** Height: about 22cm (9in). Weight: not exceeding 3.1kg (7lb).
• **COAT** Glossy, fine and silky.
• **COLOUR** Dark steel blue (not silver blue) extending from back of head to root of tail, never mingled with fawn, bronze or dark hairs; face, chest and feet rich, bright tan.
• **OTHER FEATURES** Small head, flat on top; medium-sized, dark, sparkling eyes; small V-shaped ears carried erect; compact body; tail usually docked to medium length.

HAVANESE

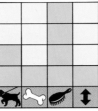

This breed is also known as the Bichon Havanese (Havanais) and as the Havana Silk Dog, because of its long, flowing coat which gives it a somewhat mystical look. It is a member of the bichon family, a group of toy dogs originating in the Mediterranean area and including the Bolognese, Maltese and Bichon Frise. Any of these might be the lesser-known Havanese's ancestor, but legend has it that it is descended from Bolognese dogs taken by some peasants from the Italian region of Emilia to Argentina. There the Bolognese were crossbred with a small poodle, thus creating a new type of bichon. Eventually this dog reached Cuba, where it became popular with the wealthy of Havana.

Character and care

The Havanese is intelligent, serious and calm rather than vivacious, inordinately affectionate and lives to please its owner. It does not require a great deal of exercise but does need considerable brushing and combing, without trimming or coiffing.

KEY CHARACTERISTICS
• **CLASS** Toy. **Recognized** FCI.
• **SIZE** Height: 20–26.5cm (10–10½in). Weight: 3.1–5.4kg (7–12lb).
• **COAT** Long, flat and soft; tufts towards extremities.
• **COLOUR** Beige, havana grey or white; solid or broad markings of these colours.
• **OTHER FEATURES** Black nose; rather pointed ears falling so that they assume a slight fold; quite large eyes, very dark, preferably black; tail carried high, curled, and covered with long, silky hair.

ENGLISH TOY TERRIER

The English Toy Terrier, developed by selective breeding from the smallest specimens of Manchester Terriers, retains many of the bigger dog's working attributes.

A long, narrow head and keenly pricked ears give alertness and dignity to a small dog.

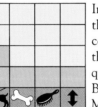

In the United Kingdom, the English Toy Terrier commenced life under that name, was subsequently called the Toy Black and Tan then the Miniature Black and Tan, and reverted to its present title in 1962. In the United States, the breed is known as the Toy Manchester Terrier.

The English Toy Terrier was bred from the Manchester Terrier. This larger but otherwise similar breed was developed from the now extinct rough-haired Black and Tan Terrier and other breeds. The Italian Greyhound and, possibly, the Whippet may also have contributed to the English Toy Terrier. The Manchester Terrier was bred to kill rats in a pit for public entertainment, and its smaller relative is an excellent ratter.

Character and care

Surprisingly rare outside the show ring today, the English Toy Terrier still retains the ability to hunt vermin and makes an affectionate and intelligent companion. It is good with children but tends to be a one-person dog. The English Toy is easy to care for, requiring little more than a daily brushing and a rub-down to give its coat a sheen. It is a reasonably tough little dog and does not have quite the same aversion to rain as its more fastidious Italian Greyhound relatives.

KEY CHARACTERISTICS
• **CLASS** Toy. **Recognized** AKC, ANKC, CKC, FCI, KC(GB), KUSA.
• **SIZE** Height at shoulders: 25–30cm (10–12in). Weight: 2.7–3.6kg (6–9lb).
• **COAT** Thick, close and glossy.
• **COLOUR** Black and tan.
• **OTHER FEATURES** Long, narrow head; dark to black eyes; ears candle flame shaped and slightly pointed at tips; compact body; tail thick at root and tapering to a point.

AUSTRALIAN SILKY TERRIER

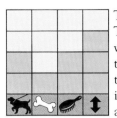

The Australian Silky Terrier, or Silky Terrier, was originally known as the Sydney Silky, and the progeny were registered under that name as recently as 1945. It owes its existence to the cross-breeding of Skye and Yorkshire terriers, and also of the Yorkshire and Australian terriers (the Australian having not only "Yorkie" but Dandie Dinmont, Cairn and Norwich terrier blood in its veins). The first breed standard was not published until 1962 although the breed was "accepted" in America three years earlier.

Character and care

The Australian Silky is a typical terrier in temperament. It is not averse to a spot of vermin hunting but offers its owners much affection. It needs good daily walks to work off its energy and regular brushing and combing – lots of attention to its coat is essential if it is to compete in the show ring.

KEY CHARACTERISTICS

- **CLASS** Toy.
  Recognized AKC, ANKC, CKC, FCI, KC(GB), KUSA.

- **SIZE** Average height: 22.8cm (9in). Weight 3.6–4.5kg (8–10lb).

- **COAT** Straight, fine, glossy.

- **COLOUR** Blue and tan, grey, blue and tan with silver-blue top-knot. Tips of hairs should be darker at roots.

- **OTHER FEATURES** Small, compactly built dog with body slightly longer than height; head medium length; eyes small, dark, round; ears small, V-shaped; tail customarily docked.

The Australian Silky Terrier probably traces its sheen back to the Dandie Dinmont, an early 19th century ancestor which contributed to the line.

Unlike that of the Yorkie (another ancestor), the Silky's coat stops short of the ground, leaving the paws visible.

PUG

Originally from China, the Pug is a Mastiff in miniature – sturdy despite its small size.

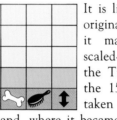

It is likely that the Pug originated in China, and it may be a greatly scaled-down relative of the Tibetan Mastiff. By the 1500s, it had been taken on trading ships to Holland, where it became popular with the royal family of the time, the House of Orange, and is often referred to as the Dutch Pug.

The breed is generally believed to have been introduced into Britain in 1688 by William, Prince of Orange, who became William III of Britain. During William and Mary's reign (1689–94) the Pug is said to have enjoyed unrivalled status. However, by the 1800s when Queen Victoria was building up her kennel, the breed had become comparatively rare in Britain. It was not until 1883 that the breed was standardized and the British Pug Dog Club was formed.

Character and care

This happy intelligent little dog is good with children, and requires only modest exercise, but the Pug should not be exercised in very hot weather. Daily grooming with a brush and a rub-down with a silk handkerchief will make its coat shine.

KEY CHARACTERISTICS
• **CLASS** Toy. **Recognized** AKC, ANKC, CKC, FCI, KC(GB), KUSA.
• **SIZE** Height: 25–27.5cm (10–12in). Weight: 6.3–8.1kg (14–18lb).
• **COAT** Fine, smooth, short and glossy.
• **COLOUR** Silver, apricot, fawn or black; black mask and ears and black trace along back.
• **OTHER FEATURES** Ears either "Rose ear" – a small drop ear that folds over and then back – or "Button ear" – the ear flap folds forward with the tip lying close to the head; very large, dark eyes; short, thick-set body; tail set high and tightly curled over the back.

POMERANIAN

This small dog is a member of the spitz family and, like other spitz, originated in the Arctic Circle. The Pomeranian derives from white spitz that existed in Pomerania, northern Germany, from about 1700. They were much larger dogs, weighing about 13.5kg (30lb), and were bred down after being imported into Britain about 100 years ago. By 1896, show classes for the Pomeranian were divided by weight, over and under 3.6kg (8lb). Then in 1915, the British Kennel Club withdrew challenge certificates for the larger variety. The American Pomeranian Club was formed in New York in 1900.

Queen Victoria was much taken with the breed and had a number of the larger variety in her kennels. This helped to make the breed very popular in Britain, but it was subsequently overtaken there by the Pekingese and today the Pomeranian is not very often seen outside show circles.

Character and care

The Pomeranian seems to have gained the reputation of being an old lady's lap-dog. While it is certainly ideal for that role, adoring lots of attention, it is also a lively, robust little dog which would walk its owners off their feet, if given the chance. This affectionate and faithful dog is good with children and makes a delightful pet. It is also a fine show dog for those with plenty of time on their hands to care for its double coat, which must be groomed with a stiff brush every day and regularly trimmed.

PAPILLON

Britain as "foreign" dogs in 1923, and had to wait another 12 years for official recognition in the United States.

Character and care

The Papillon is intelligent, usually healthy, and has proved an able contender in obedience competitions. It is fairly easy to look after, needing only a daily brushing to keep the coat shining.

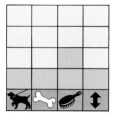

The Papillon is also known as the Épagneul Nain Continental or Continental Toy Spaniel. The name Papillon, which is French for butterfly, comes from the breed's erect ears. An identical drop-eared variety is known as the Phalène or "moth".

The Papillon has often been mistaken for the Long-coated Chihuahua, a variety it helped to produce. In fact, this toy spaniel originated in Spain and is said to be a descendant of the 16th century Dwarf Spaniel. It has been included in paintings by Rubens (1577–1640) and Van Dyke (1599–1641). Papillons were first exhibited in

KEY CHARACTERISTICS
• **CLASS** Toy. **Recognized** AKC, ANKC, CKC, FCI, KC(GB), KUSA.
• **SIZE** Height at withers: 20–28cm (8–11in).
• **COAT** Long, abundant, flowing and silky in texture.
• **COLOUR** White with patches of any colour except liver, tricolours – black and white with tan in spots over eyes and inside ears, on cheeks, and under root of tail.
• **OTHER FEATURES** Head slightly rounded; large, erect ears carried obliquely like spread butterfly wings; fairly long body with level top-line; long, well-fringed tail.

The ears which give the Papillon its name – the word means "butterfly" in French – are balanced at the other end by a gaily plumed tail.

KEY CHARACTERISTICS
• **CLASS** Toy. **Recognized** AKC, ANKC, CKC, KC(GB), KUSA.
• **SIZE** Height: not exceeding 27.5cm (11in). Weight: dogs 1.3–3.1kg (3–7lb).
• **COAT** Long, straight and harsh, with a soft fluffy undercoat.
• **COLOUR** All colours permissible, but free from black or white shadings; whole colours are white, black, brown, light or dark blue.
• **OTHER FEATURES** Head and nose soft in outline; medium-sized eyes; small, erect ears set not too low down or too wide apart; short back and compact body; tail set high, turns over back and is carried flat and straight.

PEKINGESE

By the early 19th century, Pekingese were so prized by the Chinese Imperial court that no commoner was allowed to own one.

Character and care

The Pekingese is a thickset, dignified little dog with a mind of its own and is good with adults and children. Intelligent and fearless, it does not mind walking across a muddy field but its ideal role is that of a pampered, sole companion. It requires considerable brushing and combing.

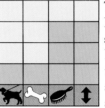

The origins of the Pekingese may trace back some 1500 years. Believed to be a close relative of the Lhasa Apso and Shih Tzu, they were said to combine the nobility of the lion with the grace and sweetness of the marmoset. Favoured by the 19th-century Chinese Imperial court, they were kept in their thousands in extraordinarily privileged circumstances. The Pekingese first arrived in Europe, and subsequently the United States, when British Army officers raided the Summer Palace in Peking following the Boxer Rebellion of 1860. Five Imperial Pekingese looted from the women's apartments were brought back to England. One of these dogs, appropriately christened "Looty", was presented to Queen Victoria. It lived until 1872.

Miniature dogs of the Pekingese type have been known in China since the T'ang dynasty of the 8th century.

KEY CHARACTERISTICS
• **CLASS** Toy. **Recognized** AKC, ANKC, CKC, FCI, KC(GB), KUSA.
• **SIZE** Weight: dogs, not exceeding 5kg (11lb); bitches not exceeding 5.4kg (12lb).
• **COAT** Long and straight, double-coated with coarse top coat, thick undercoat; profuse mane and feathered tail.
• **COLOUR** All colours and marking are permissible and of equal merit, except albino or liver. Particolours should be evenly broken.
• **OTHER FEATURES** Wide, flat head with shortened muzzle and deep stop; flat face; prominent round eyes; feathered ears carried close to head; thick chest and neck, short body with slightly rolling gait; tail set high and curving over back.

JAPANESE CHIN

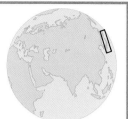

The Japanese Chin probably shares a common ancestor with the Pekingese and the Pug.

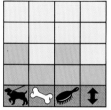

There are two theories on the origin of the Japanese Chin or Japanese Spaniel. One is that it derives from Pekingese-like dogs brought to Japan by Zen Buddhist monks in the AD500s, and the other that it descends from a lap-dog sent as a present in AD732 to the Emperor of Japan from Korea. It is not dissimilar to the Pekingese, but is longer in the leg and lighter. Whatever its ancestry, for more than 1000 years this little dog was a favourite of Japanese emperors who decreed that it should be worshipped. It is said that smaller Chins were sometimes kept in hanging cages like pet birds.

Two Japanese Chins were presented to the British Queen Victoria by Commodore Perry, an American naval commander, on his return from the Far East in 1853. The breed first made an appearance in the British show ring in 1862 and, some 20 years later, started being exhibited in the United States.

Character and care

Bearing some resemblance to the King Charles Spaniel, the Chin is a popular show dog but less often kept as a pet. This is attractive and hardy little dog that is good with children. It requires an average amount of exercise and little grooming, except for a daily going over with a pure-bristle brush. Like other flat-nosed breeds, it must not be over-exerted in hot weather lest it should suffer breathing difficulties.

KEY CHARACTERISTICS
● **CLASS** Toy. **Recognized** AKC, ANKC, CKC, FCI, KC(GB), KUSA.
● **SIZE** Weight (ideal): 1.8–3.2kg (4–7lb).
● **COAT** Profuse coat; long, soft and straight.
● **COLOUR** White and black or white and red and white (all shades, including sable, lemon and orange); never tricolour.
● **OTHER FEATURES** Large round head in proportion to size of dog; short muzzle; small ears, set wide apart; large dark eyes square, compact body; well-feathered tail set high and curling over back.

Also once revered by the nobility, the Chin is longer in the leg than the Pekingese, and lighter in colour.

KING CHARLES SPANIEL

This toy breed owes its name to the affection King Charles II developed for its ancestors.

Smaller than the Cavalier, the King Charles has a distinctly domed head and deep stop.

In the United States and Canada, this popular breed is known as the English Toy Spaniel and the name "King Charles" is given to the Black and Tan variety only.

Although the King Charles Spaniel is generally thought of as a British breed, its history traces back to Japan in 2000BC. The slightly larger Cavalier King Charles Spaniel (see page 229), which has the same origin, became very popular at court in 16th century England. Then the fashion came about for short-nosed dogs, and the King Charles Spaniel emerged. It is said that King Charles II (1630–85) was so devoted to these little spaniels that he would frequently interrupt affairs of state in order to fondle and play with them, and there is a law in England, yet to be rescinded, that enables a King Charles Spaniel "to go anywhere".

Character and care

This little spaniel makes a delightful pet, being good with children, full of fun, and able to adapt its exercise requirements to its owner's capabilities. The King Charles should be brushed every day with a bristled brush, and it is advisable to keep the area around its eyes clean with eye wipes.

KEY CHARACTERISTICS

- **CLASS** Toy.
  Recognized AKC, ANKC, CKC, FCI, KC(GB), KUSA.

- **SIZE** Height: about 25cm (10in). Weight: 3.6–6.3kg (8–14lb).

- **COAT** Long, silky, straight coat. Slight waviness permissible.

- **COLOUR** Black and Tan – raven black with bright tan markings above eyes, on cheeks, inside ears, on chest and legs and underside of tail, white marks undesirable. Ruby – solid rich red, white markings undesirable. Blenheim – rich chestnut markings, well broken up, on pearly white ground; markings evenly divided on head, leaving room for lozenge spot between ears. Tricolour – black and white, well spaced and broken up with tan markings over eyes, cheeks, inside ears, inside legs, on underside of tail.

- **OTHER FEATURES** Large domed skull, full over eyes; deep, well defined stop; low-set ears, long and well feathered; wide, deep chest; well feathered tail, carried above level of back (docked in the US).

CAVALIER KING CHARLES SPANIEL

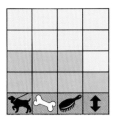

The Cavalier King Charles Spaniel originated in Japan, and there is a resemblance between it and the Japanese Chin or Spaniel. The Cavalier is very similar to the King Charles Spaniel (see page 228), but while the King Charles has an apple domed head, the slightly larger Cavalier is almost flat between the ears and its stop is shallower. Both breeds were named after Charles II (1630–85) and the Cavalier was the original favourite. It was doubtless this breed the famous diarist, Samuel Pepys (1633–1703), was referring to when he complained that King Charles II devoted more time to his dogs than he did to affairs of state.

Today, the Cavalier is one of the most popular pet dogs in Britain and America (although it is not recognized as a separate breed in the United States).

Character and care

This breed is an admirable choice of family pet, being good natured and fond of children. While it is allocated to the toy group, it is among the largest of the toys and enjoys a fair amount of exercise. It should be groomed every day with a bristle brush.

KEY CHARACTERISTICS
● **CLASS** Toy. **Recognized** ANKC, CKC, FCI, KC(GB), KUSA.
● **SIZE** Weight: 5.5–8kg (12–18lb).
● **COAT** Long and silky, free from curl.
● **COLOUR** Black and Tan – black with bright tan marks above eyes, head, chest, legs, underside of tail; white marks undesirable. Ruby – rich red, white markings undesirable. Blenheim – chestnut markings, well broken up, on white ground; markings evenly divided on head, lozenge between ears. Tricolour – black and white, well spaced and broken up, with tan markings over head, inside legs, on underside of tail.
● **OTHER FEATURES** Flattish skull; long ears, set high; large, dark eyes; short-coupled body; long, well feathered tail.

A well tapered muzzle, flat head and shallow stop distinguish this breed from the King Charles Spaniel.

Also a favourite of Charles II, the Cavalier has a fairly flat skull with high-ears. The body is long, with a feathered tail.

CHIHUAHUA

The Chihuahua, the smallest dog in the world, is named after the state of Chihuahua in Mexico and is believed by some to have been a sacred dog of the Aztecs. However, a dog not unlike the Chihuahua may well have existed in Egypt some 3000 years ago. In 1910, a zoologist, K. Haddon, described the mummified remains of a little dog in an Egyptian tomb which had the soft spot in the skull, common in the breed. Chihuahuas have been known in Malta for many centuries, having arrived there from North Africa around 600BC, and a Botticelli fresco (c. 1482) in the Sistine Chapel in Rome includes the likeness of a pet that is clearly a Chihuahua. Such early Chihuahuas were slightly larger and had bigger ears than modern ones, which may be the result of a cross with the hairless Chinese Crested Dog.

Character and care

There are two varieties of Chihuahua, the Smooth-coated and Long-coated, the latter having long hair of soft texture, which is either flat or slightly wavy. At one time, it was normal for Long-coated and Smooth-coated to interbreed and both varieties would appear in the same litter, but such interbreeding is no longer permitted. The first Chihuahua to be registered in the United States was "Midget" in 1904, and the breed went on to become enormously popular there. In Britain a Chihuahua was still a comparatively rare sight in the 1950s, but now it draws large entries in show classes.

The Chihuahua is an exceedingly intelligent dog, that is affectionate, possessive, and makes a good watchdog in miniature. Despite being generally thought of as a lap dog, it can walk as far as most owners would wish. Care must be taken on outings that it does not start a fight because it seems to imagine that it is

Although the Chihuahua, the world's smallest dog, is named after the Mexican state, its origins remain uncertain; dogs of this type were known in Egypt 3000 years ago.

At one time the two varieties of Chihuahua – Long-coated and Smooth-coated – were allowed to interbreed, but this is no longer acceptable.

enormous when confronted with other canines. The breed is inexpensive to keep, and both long-haireds and short-haireds are fairly easy to groom, requiring only daily combing and brushing with a soft brush.

KEY CHARACTERISTICS
• **CLASS** Toy. **Recognized** AKC, ANKC, CKC, FCI, KC(GB), KUSA.
• **SIZE** Height: 16–20cm (6.3–7.9in). Weight: up to 2.7kg (6lb)
• **COAT** Long coat: long and soft to touch, slight waviness permissible; smooth coat: short and dense, soft to touch.
• **COLOUR** Any colour or mixture.
• **OTHER FEATURES** Apple-domed head; large flaring ears; large, round eyes that do not protrude; level back; medium length, high set tail, curved over back.

ITALIAN GREYHOUND

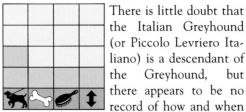

The Italian Greyhound may have been the first breed to have been developed exclusively as a companion or pet.

There is little doubt that the Italian Greyhound (or Piccolo Levriero Italiano) is a descendant of the Greyhound, but there appears to be no record of how and when it was reduced in size. The Greyhound is one of the most ancient breeds in the world, depicted in paintings on the tombs of the Egyptian pharaohs, and there are drawings of smaller Greyhounds dating back to Egyptian and Roman times.

The Italian Greyhound Club has existed in Britain since 1900. At the end of the Second World War, fresh blood was introduced from North America and the Continent, and there are now many excellent examples in the show ring in Europe, USA and Canada.

Character and care

The Italian Greyhound is a delightful and affectionate housepet, which is easy to train, rarely moults and is odourless. Indeed, it was recently publicized as the ideal pet, a statement which caused considerable concern among breeders, who feared that breed members might fall into unsuitable hands. Such concern is justified because this dainty little dog is very sensitive. It feels the cold, can be wounded by harsh words, and its legs are all too easily broken. The breed enjoys a fair amount of exercise, but must have a warm coat in wintry conditions. It is easy to groom, a rub-down with a silk handkerchief making its coat shine.

KEY CHARACTERISTICS
• **CLASS** Toy. **Recognized** AKC, ANKC, CKC, FCI, KC(GB), KUSA.
• **SIZE** Height at withers: 32–38cm (12½–15in). Weight: 2.5–4.5kg (5½–10lb).
• **COAT** Short, fine and glossy.
• **COLOUR** Solid black, blue, cream, fawn, red or white, or any of these colours broken with white; white broken with one of above colours; black or blue with tan markings, or brindle, not acceptable.
• **OTHER FEATURES** Long, flat and narrow skull; slight stop; rose-shaped ears, set well back; large, expressive eyes; hare feet; low-set long tail, carried low.

The Italian Greyhound appears to be delicate, but it enjoys chasing small prey and can leap nimbly to catch a bird in flight. The elegant, finely chiselled head and muzzle of the Italian Greyhound make it an appealing dog to show.

MINIATURE PINSCHER

The Miniature Pinscher is a compact, well-proportioned toy dog, whose self-confidence belies its size.

The broad chest and muscular legs enable the feet to be lifted high in the characteristic hackney gait.

The Miniature Pinscher, or Min Pin as it is commonly called, is known in its native Germany as the Zwergpinscher. It is not, as many believe, a small Doberman, having existed for many centuries. Its ancestor is the German Pinscher to which Italian Greyhound and, it is thought, Dachshund blood was added. A painting, *The Peasant Family*, dated 1640 and currently in the Louvre, Paris, includes the likeness of a dog similar to the Miniature Pinscher.

The breed was officially recognized in Germany in 1870 and has achieved great popularity in a number of European countries. The Miniature Pinscher Club of America was formed in 1929, and the breed still has a much larger following there than in Britain.

Character and care

The Min Pin has an attractive hackney (high-stepping) gait. It makes an ideal pet for town or country, being affectionate and intelligent, and rarely moulting. The breed enjoys obedience work and exercise, often following a scent. It is easy to groom, requiring little more than a daily brush and a rub-down with a silk handkerchief or piece of chamois leather to make its coat shine.

KEY CHARACTERISTICS
• **CLASS** Toy. **Recognized** AKC, ANKC, CKC, FCI, KC(GB), KUSA.
• **SIZE** Height at withers: 25.5–30cm (10–12in). Weight: 4.5kg (10lb).
• **COAT** Hard, smooth, short coat.
• **COLOUR** Black, blue or chocolate, with sharply defined tan markings on cheeks, lips, lower jaw, throat, twin spots above eyes and cheeks, lower half of forelegs, inside of hind legs and vent region, lower portion of nodes and feet.
• **OTHER FEATURES** Tapering narrow skull; small, erect or dropped ears set on high; bright dark eyes; compact, square body; tail set high, level with topline, often docked.

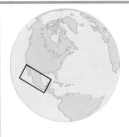

MEXICAN HAIRLESS DOG

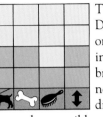

The Mexican Hairless Dog or Xoloitzcuintli is one of the oldest breeds in the world. It was brought to Mexico from north-east Asia by nomadic ancestors of the Aztecs, but possibly originated as far away as Turkey, where there is another naked breed, the Turkish Greyhound. Earlier inhabitants of Mexico, the Toltecs, kept the Chihuahua in their temples for religious purposes. Once the Aztecs had conquered the Toltecs, the Chihuahua and Mexican Hairless lived in the temples side by side and their interbreeding may have produced the Chinese Crested Dog (see right). The Mexican Hairless was also highly valued as a hot-water bottle, having a higher than average body temperature of 38.6°C (101.5°F). It is in danger of extinction, although there are a few breeders in North America. It is recognized by the Mexican Kennel Club and the Canadian Kennel Club but not by those in the USA.

Character and care

This most loving, intelligent dog has a good temperament, and requires only a moderate amount of exercise. Being virtually naked, it needs regular bathing and massaging with baby cream to keep its skin soft and supple. It is a natural vegetarian, but easily converts to a meat diet.

Note: This breed must be protected against sunburn.

KEY CHARACTERISTICS
• **CLASS** Toy. **Recognized** CKC, FCI.
• **SIZE** Height: about 40.5–51cm (16–20in), but may be smaller.
• **COAT** May have tuft of hair on head, tip of tail and between toes, otherwise smooth skin.
• **COLOUR** Skin may be a variety of colours, solid or mottled.
• **OTHER FEATURES** Absence of premolar teeth; sweats through skin; long, tapering tail; hare feet, prehensile leading to endearing habit of gripping owner and objects with its feet.

CHINESE CRESTED DOG

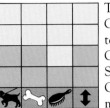

The almost hairless Chinese Crested is said to have originated in China and been taken to South America in Chinese sailing ships many centuries ago. However, there have been hairless dogs in many countries of the world, including Africa and Turkey, and some think the Chinese Crested may be the result of the mating of a Mexican Hairless Dog (Xoloitzcuintli) with the Chihuahua. Certainly the mating of a Chinese Crested with a Chihuahua can produce a completely hairless dog.

Until 1966, an elderly lady in the United States owned the only remaining examples of the Chinese Crested Dog in the world. Four of these were introduced into the United Kingdom and the breed is now thriving in both countries. In Britain it attracts large show entries and received championship show status in the 1970s.

The Chinese Crested has no coat except for a flowing crest or mane, and hair on its feet and gaily carried, plumed tail. However, in almost every litter, there are some haired pups which grow into luxuriantly coated

For show purposes, the hair on the Chinese Crested may be long or short, but a full crest on the head and a full plume on the tail are preferred.

The Powder Puff Chinese Crested Dog takes its name from the silky double coat, which makes its ears drop forward.

adults resembling little sheepdogs. These are known as Powder Puffs and have won the right to be exhibited in the show ring alongside their hairless siblings.

Character and care

This affectionate little dog makes an excellent pet for those who appreciate its loving nature and are not put off by its exuberance. It is frequently hyperactive, playing tirelessly and leaping about in circles in anticipation of the tiniest crumb of food. The Chinese Crested adores food, its body feeling hotter to the touch after it has eaten, and rations should be increased in the winter months. Its paws will grip in an endearing, almost human fashion. Ideally, it should be bathed about every three weeks and have its skin massaged with cream. Whiskers, and any straggly odd hairs, should be removed for the show ring.

This breed can adjust to warm or cold climates but should *never* be kennelled out of doors and must be protected against sunburn.

KEY CHARACTERISTICS
● **CLASS** Toy. **Recognized** AKC, ANKC, CKC, FCI, KC(GB), KUSA.
● **SIZE** Height: dogs 28–33cm (11–13in), bitches 23–30.5cm (9–12in). Weight: not exceeding 5.5kg (12lb).
● **COAT** *Chinese Crested Hairless* Tuft of long, soft hair only on head, feet and tail. *Chinese Crested Powder Puff* Double, long, straight outer coat, soft silky undercoat.
● **COLOUR** Any colour or combination.
● **OTHER FEATURES** Slightly rounded head and skull; low-set erect ears; dark eyes; body may be racy and fine-boned (deer type) or heavier (cobby type); slender tapering tail set high and carried forward over the back in motion.

RARE BREEDS

NON-SPORTING

The **MAJORCAN BULLDOG** is also called the Perro de Presa Mallorquin. This bulldog comes from the island of Majorca in the Spanish Balearic Isles. With the same massive head, "rose" ears and wide chest, it is an obvious relative of the English Bulldog but has a longer neck and its tail is longer and slightly curved. Its colour is brindle with white markings, the less white the better. Like its English counterpart, it was developed for bull-baiting and dog fighting, and became relatively rare when the popularity of these "sports" diminished.

This powerful, courageous dog makes a splendid guard. Like most bulldogs, it is good natured, requires only a daily brushing with a bristle brush, and the minimum of exercise, and is, alas, generally short lived.

WORKING

BROHOLMER, which derives from a Mastiff imported from England, was a favourite of the Danish court from the 16th century. The breed was standardized in 1886 by Count Niels Frederik Sehested of Broholm-Funen, and, as well as being regarded as the national breed, it became a popular working and cattle-droving dog. However, its popularity waned after the First World War and it was feared extinct. A nationwide search was launched in 1974, and, on some isolated farms in the north of the country Broholmers were found which conformed to the standard. The breed was approved by the FCI in 1982 and it can now be shown internationally.

DOGO ARGENTINO or Argentinian Mastiff is used in its native land for hunting puma and other big game, and as a guard. It is a large dog, with a broad skull, deep chest, and loose skin around the neck, characteristic of fighting dogs. It is all white, with a short, smooth coat.

This powerful, loyal, courageous dog is claimed by owners to be trust-worthy. However, it is on the British list of potentially dangerous dogs, and requires space, liberal exercise and very knowledgeable handling.

ITALIAN SPITZ is also known as the Volpino Italiano, the Cane de Guirinale and in Tuscany, where it is particularly prevalent, as the Florence Spitz. The Italian Spitz is so similar in appearance to the German Spitz and the Pomeranian that few people other than breed experts can tell them apart. However, the Italian Spitz's eyes are slightly bigger, its ears longer and its skull rounder. It is not known whether the Italian Spitz is a descendant or ancestor of the German Spitz but it has certainly been established in its native land for centuries. It was once a very popular companion dog in Italy, but its numbers have now dwindled.

This loyal, small dog is affectionate towards its owners but somewhat suspicious of strangers and so makes a good watchdog. It is apt to bark a lot, if unchecked. It does not need a great deal of exercise, but its coat requires regular brushing.

KARELIAN BEAR DOG or Karelsk Bjornhund is a member of the spitz family, closely related to the Russian Laika. It is named after the area of Karelia in Russia near the Finnish border. However, its development was mainly carried out in Finland in the 1930s, and it was recognized by that country's Kennel Club in 1935, and by the FCI in 1946. It is a medium-sized breed, and its colouring is black and white. Its tail curls over the back in the characteristic style of the spitz and it has a harsh upper coat and a softer, dense undercoat. It was bred to hunt bear, elk and other large game, and is said to have a flair for locating its quarry and to display great courage when confronting it. It also has a somewhat sullen, quarrelsome nature, preferring its own company and that of its master to canine companions, and so usually hunts singly. This may explain why it is not as popular outside its homeland as other Finnish breeds.

A powerful and temperamental hunter, the Karelian Bear Dog is good at the job for which it was bred, loyal to its master and a fine guard. It can be aggressive towards other dogs, needs firm control and is not suitable as a pet. The breed is generally housed outdoors. It needs considerable exercise and daily brushing. The coat is black and white.

LAIKAS A number of breeds of Laika are recognized in Russia, including the Russian-European, the West Siberian and the Karelian. All are members of the spitz family and are barkers (the name means barking dog). They are used against large and small game and will bark after cornering the quarry to allow the approach of hunters with their guns.

The Laikas may also be kept for purposes other than hunting. The Russian-European Laika, closely related to the Karelian Bear Dog, is probably best known in the West as the dog which was shot into space in Sputnik 2 in 1957. This breed and the West Siberian Laika are both medium-sized dogs and are sometimes used as farm dogs and guards. All three have rough, thick coats, and curled tails. The smaller Karelian Laika, which is found near the Finnish border and resembles the Finnish Spitz, may be used for sledge hauling and herding cattle.

These lively, energetic spitz dogs have a good temperament and may fill a variety of roles, including that of housepet and guard. They need plenty of exercise and food and regular grooming with a brush.

LUNDEHUND is also known as the Norwegian Puffin Dog or Puffin Hound (*lund* is Norwegian for puffin). It is a spitz variety, deriving from the Miniature Elkhound, and has existed for centuries on two islands off the coast of northern Norway. There, its flexible body allowed it to explore the nooks and crevices in the rock where puffins nest. In the past, the dog's task was to retrieve puffins' eggs and the birds themselves, which were eaten by the islanders. The breed has been recognized in Scandinavia since 1943 but is little known outside its native land and few, if any, specimens have been exported. It is a smallish dog with a

The Lundehund is a specialized hunter which can climb steep sea cliffs and reach into narrow crevices to find hidden puffins' nests.

rough, dense coat, and its colour is black, grey or various shades of brown with white. It has five (rather than the usual four) functional toes on each foot. The cartilage in the upper parts of its ears can meet and shut when the ears are partly raised, which may prevent water entering and damaging the ear.

The alert, active Lundehund is a good hunter and is also said to make a faithful companion. It needs daily brushing and plenty of exercise.

PORTUGUESE WATCHDOG is also known as the Cão de Castro Laboreiro. This breed originated in the mountains in the north of Portugal. It is a mastiff-type dog which served as a protector of livestock, even doing battle with wolves. It is now also used as a watchdog and in police work. It is wolf grey, dark fawn or brindle in colour, and has a short, rough coat.

The Portuguese Watchdog is faithful, agile, hardy, intelligent, and makes a splendid guard. It needs considerable exercise but minimal grooming, and does best when given a job to do.

SLOVAKIAN KUVASZ has worked for centuries as a flock guard in the Carpathian mountains in eastern Slovakia, but it is now relatively rare. It is rather similar to the Hungarian Kuvasz (see page 59) and to the ancient **Polish herding breed,** the Polish sheepdog or Owczarek Podhalanski, both of which also occur in the vast Carpathian range which includes the Tatra mountains. Indeed, although their respective countries consider them separate breeds, the three may, in fact, be varieties of the same breed. The Polish and Slovakian types are sometimes called "Tatry" dogs after the mountain range that stretches between both countries.

The Slovakian Kuvasz is quite tall, white or ivory white in colour, and has a straight or wavy medium coarse coat with a fine undercoat. It has a distinctive, perfectly proportioned head, a mane extending to and covering its chest, and a low-set tail.

The Slovakian Kuvasz is a loyal, efficient guard and tends to be kept for that purpose rather than as a domestic pet. It is lively, alert and known to have extremely acute hearing. It needs plenty of exercise and a daily brushing to keep it in good condition.

SWEDISH GREY DOG or Grähund is a medium-sized dog of the spitz type, fox-like in appearance and extremely energetic, with its tail curled characteristically over its back. It has a moderately long top coat and soft undercoat and occurs in all shades of grey. Like all the spitz breeds, it doubtless originated in the Arctic Circle. The Swedish Grey Dog has been used in its native land for hunting elk, and in America against raccoon and lynx.

This good-natured, lively, confident dog ideally combines the roles of hunter and family pet, provided that it receives a good daily brushing and plenty of exercise. It will not be comfortable in an over-heated house and is usually happiest when kept in an outside kennel.

HERDING

ARMANT This rare breed, also called the Ermenti or Egyptian Sheepdog, is believed to descend from local dogs crossed with French dogs that accompanied Napoleon's army during his Egyptian campaign of 1798. The resultant dog resembles a small collie with a long, rough grey coat, evident moustache and snipey muzzle. Named after the village of Armant (Ermenti), in northern Egypt, it has been used as a herding dog and also as a guard. The Armant is suspicious of strangers and makes an excellent guard but would probably not be suitable as a household pet. It needs regular brushing and exercise.

The breed received some prominence prior to the Second World War when an Armant was brought to Berlin by the Egyptian ambassador. The breed is rarely seen outside Egypt and has yet to appear in the international show ring.

ATLAS DOG Also known as the Aidi or Chien de l'Atlas, this collie-type herding dog is a Moroccan breed about which very little is known. It is prized in its native land as a flock guard protecting against predators, and also works as a drover and watchdog. It has considerable strength and mobility, and a long, thick coat which is said to give it protection against intense heat and cold, and against attackers. The

Atlas Dog is a sensitive, lively, muscular guard which is unlikely to be kept in the home.

BERGER DE BRESSE and BERGER DE SAVOIE
are robust, reliable, medium-sized working sheepdogs with fairly long bodies and tails curled at the tip. They are light or dark grey, with darker hairs, or are patched blue or brown. Their coat is thick, coarse and short on the head, longer on the body and tail. They have a ruff around the neck. They are named after the regions of eastern France in which they were developed, Bresse being a fertile area east of the Saône River and Savoie lying in the northern Alps.

Like all French sheepdogs, these Bergers are good companions and guards as well as being hardy, reliable workers. There is no reason why they cannot be kept as house-pets provided that they are given sufficient exercise and are adequately groomed, but they do benefit from having a task to perform.

BERGER DU LANGUEDOC
This entry should really be headed Bergers du Languedoc because, although usually grouped under one name, there are five types of sheepdog from the southern French province of Languedoc. They are also known as the Farou, Berger de la Camargue, Berger de la Grau, Berger des Carrigues and Berger du Larzac. All are small to medium-sized working sheepdogs with a variety of coats. They are fawn or black and fawn.

The Languedoc sheepdogs are strong, hardy, reliable, generally good tempered, and easy to train. They may be kept as companions provided they are given adequate exercise and are not kept in confined quarters. They need regular brushing.

BLUE LACY
Little known outside the American South, the Blue Lacy is thought to be the descendant of wild pariah dogs crossed with herding and droving dogs. It is used for herding and driving sheep and cattle, and will also guard most types of farm stock. It is black and tan, tan, yellow, cream and gun-metal grey, its coat carrying the much sought

after "blue" gene. Colours are usually solid, but may be bicolour or tricolour.

This dog is a natural herder, easy to train and makes a tireless worker. Since it is also reliable and has a good temperament, there is no reason why it cannot be kept in the home provided that it is given a job of work to do. It needs regular exercise and grooming.

CATALONIAN SHEPHERD
Also known as the Catalan Sheepdog, Perro de Pastor Catalan or Gos d'Atura, this breed is native to the province of Catalonia in Southern Spain. It is probably a descendant of a number of European herding dogs, particularly those of the Pyrenees area. There are two varieties of this sheepdog, differing only in coat: the Gos d'Atura, which has a long slightly wavy coat, and the rarer d'Atura Cerdà, which has a short smooth coat. Its legs and paws are fawn to tan while the rest of its body is black and white. Tan, grey and white marks are not allowed.

The Catalonian Shepherd is popular in its native land, where it is an able herder and inspires confidence in the animals it moves. It has also proved to be a fine army, police and guard, and a stalwart companion.

This intelligent sheepdog of gentle expression is said by some to have a nervous temperament. It makes a good companion and can be kept in

the house, but does best when given a job to do and wide, open spaces. It should have plenty of exercise and needs daily brushing.

CHARPLANINATZ
(or Šar Planina), the Yugoslavian Sheepdog, is an ancient breed particularly widespread in the mountainous areas of the Adriatic. It is thought to descend from the dogs which migrated westwards with shepherds in ancient times and then interbred and changed as they adapted to the requirements of work and climate. It may also have links with the ancient Roman Molossus.

The Charplaninatz is sometimes used as a herder or drover, but is kept mainly as a flock guard. It was imported into the US in the 1970s and is now widely used in America and Canada as a stock dog. Devoted to its owners and a dedicated guard, the breed remains principally a working dog and is unlikely to be kept as a domestic pet. The Charplaninatz is courageous and enormously strong. It has something of the wolf about it, with its long, dense iron-grey coat and wolf-like howl.

An energetic herder, the Schapendoes has a roguish, unkempt appearance that belies its steady temperament.

KARST SHEPHERD also known as the Krasky Ovcar, Croatian or Istrian Sheepdog, is a medium-sized, capable flock guard with exceptionally well-developed muscles and a strong constitution. It has a noble head, a medium-length coat with abundant undercoat, and is iron grey in colour. It has worked for centuries in the Karst area, which includes the Istrian peninsula, in the north-west of the former state of Yugoslavia, but is little known outside its country of origin.

This shepherd is courageous, vivacious, loyal and obedient, and makes a fine companion and guard. However, it is not a good choice for the inexperienced dog owner, as it is suspicious of strangers, hard to win over, and ready to defend its owners if it believes them to be under threat. It needs plenty of exercise and food and daily brushing.

PORTUGUESE SHEEPDOG or Cão da Serra de Aires is an ancient breed which comes from the south of Portugal. It is a versatile working dog, which makes a fine guard, but is mainly used for herding and driving livestock. It is a medium-sized, strong dog with a deep chest, long body and tail. It is yellow, brown, grey, fawn, wolf grey or black in colour, and has a long, rough, goat-like coat with a tendency to curl.

This tough, active, intelligent dog is an instinctive herder, devoted to its owners and wary of strangers. It needs plenty of space, considerable exercise, and is best suited to a working life.

RAFEIRO DO ALENTEJO This Portuguese herding dog of ancient lineage originates from the Alentejo province south of Lisbon. It is a mastiff-like dog with a bear-like head, which slightly resembles a light short-haired Saint Bernard. It has a short or medium-length sleek coat, and its colour can be black, grey, brindle, cream or fawn with white markings. It may also be white any of these colour markings. The Rafeiro do Alentejo's job in life has always been to guard flocks and herds from predators. It is little known outside its country of origin

and has yet to make an appearance in the international show ring. This massive, powerful, sober dog is an alert and somewhat aggressive guard. It is readily trained but needs plenty of space and exercise, is rather self-willed and is not suitable as a housepet. It should be groomed with a bristle brush and slicker.

SCHAPENDOES or Dutch Sheepdog (distinct from the Dutch Shepherds, see page 101) closely resembles the Bearded Collie. This is not surprising since this ancient breed is thought to share common ancestry with the Bearded Collie, as well as with the Puli, Bergamasco and Briard. It is an appealing shaggy dog with a long, low-set tail, and a long, harsh coat and a smooth undercoat. The Schapendoes has herded flocks for centuries and is still sometimes used in this role today. However, it is now more widely kept as a household companion and guard in the Netherlands, where it is very popular. The breed has been established since the 1880s and was recognized by the FCI in 1970 but is still little seen outside its country of origin.

This good natured, lively, intelligent dog is easily trained and generally reliable with children. Its coat needs daily brushing, and it should have plenty of exercise.

GUNDOGS

AUVERGNE SETTER or Braque Bleu d'Auvergne comes from the Auvergne province in the south of central France. This tough elegant gundog resembles the English Pointer and the German Short-haired Pointer, both of which are descendants of the Spanish Pointer. The French did produce quite a number of breeds by crossing the Spanish Pointer with various hounds, the short-haired ones becoming known as Braques. However, the Auvergne is often said to be an indigenous breed, or one that evolved through cross-breedings with the old French Setter. Others are convinced that the Braque is descended from dogs

introduced into the Auvergne in 1798 by the Knights of Malta.

This large setter has a white coat with black on the head and ample black ticking to create a blue effect, and has a short, glossy coat.

It is an intelligent and sensitive dog. It requires a lot of exercise, and regular grooming.

CZECH COARSE-HAIRED SETTER seems to have been developed by crossing the rather similar German Wire-haired Pointer or Drahthaar and Wire-haired Pointing (or Korthals) Griffon and breeds, such as the Pudelpointer, with the German Short-haired Pointer.

In all respects other than coat and colour, this breed is like the German Short-haired Pointer. Its coat has three layers, a short, dense undercoat (absent in summer), a close-lying top coat and longer guard hairs.

DRENTSE PARTRIDGE DOG or Drentse Partrijshond originated in the Drentse province of north-east Netherlands, where it has existed for more than 300 years. It is a medium-sized dog with a sleek, close-lying coat that is white with brown or orange markings. It bears some resemblance to the German Long-haired Pointer (Langhaar) but has a shorter head and muzzle. This fine pointer and retriever has keen scenting ability and is used, as its name suggests, for hunting partridge and other birds and small game. It is little known outside its native land, where it is a great favourite as an all-purpose gundog and a competitor in field trials.

Good natured, trustworthy and easy to train, the Drentse Partridge Dog is popular in the Netherlands both with sportsmen and as a family pet. It needs plenty of exercise and a good daily brushing.

OLD DANISH POINTER or Bird Dog is known in its native Denmark as the Gammel Dansk Honsehund. It was bred in the 17th century from Spanish dogs, including the Spanish Pointer, and possibly local dogs. A strong, rugged animal, well suited to the flat terrain of Denmark, it is used as an all-purpose gundog. The breed's popularity waned and it almost became extinct in this century, but fortunately it was revived and was recognized by the Danish Kennel Club in 1962. It is now firmly re-established in its country of origin, but little known elsewhere.

This dog's body is longer than its height at withers, and it has a fairly short head, a well-developed muscular body, a medium-length tail, thick at the root, and a dense, tight coat. Its colour is white with light or dark liver markings.

The Old Danish Pointer is calm and friendly, easy to train, and makes a good, versatile gundog, that can also be kept as a family pet. It needs a regular rub-down with a hound glove and lots of exercise.

PONT-AUDEMER SPANIEL is also known as the Épagneul Pont-Audemer. This spaniel originated in north-west France and is named after a town in Normandy. It is thought to have been developed in the 18th century through the crossing of an old French spaniel and the Irish Water Spaniel. The resultant dog is a fine hunter and swimmer, particularly adept at working in swampy ground. Unfortunately it has become rare, even in its country of origin.

The Pont-Audemer is an attractive dog with dark, amber eyes, a kindly far-seeing expression and a docked tail. Its long coat is slightly wavy and the ears have long, curled fringes which joint the dog's topknot to form a curly halo around its short-haired face. It is chestnut with or without grey markings.

This appealing, lively, intelligent dog is known to be an excellent hunter of feathered game over wet and marshy terrain. It happily combines the roles of sportsman's dog and family pet. It needs daily brushing, and handstripping or clipping for a show.

The **SMALL-SIZED FRENCH SETTER**, also known as the Braque Français de Petite Taille, was bred down from the French Setter or Braque Français (see page 133). Thought to originate in Gascony, south-west France, it is an almost perfect scaled-down version of the

The curled tail of the Wetterhoun suggests that this breed descends from Nordic spitz-type stock as well as from the European water dog.

French Setter, but differs slightly in head shape and colour. Like its larger counterpart, it is an ancient breed, which has been used as a hunting and tracking dog in France for centuries. It has considerable powers of endurance and is capable of working over all types of terrain.

The small-sized French Setter is a robust, intelligent, good natured dog, which makes a first-class hunter and retriever, and combines this role admirably with that of family pet. It requires a daily brushing and can cope with limitless exercise.

SPANISH POINTER The modern Spanish Pointer (Burgos Setter, Perdiguero de Burgos), native to northern Spain, is a descendant of the old Spanish Pointer, which is thought to be an ancestor of all pointing dogs. This large, well-built dog will work on any terrain, under any climatic conditions, and can cope with feathered as well as other game. In colour

it is white with liver flecks or ticks, or dark liver with white markings, and it has a short, smooth coat.

The Spanish Pointer is a capable, eager and reliable dog of good temperament. In common with other pointers, it will happily combine the role of sporting companion and family pet. It needs plenty of exercise and its short, fine coat requires regular, moderate grooming.

WETTERHOUN or Dutch Water Spaniel originated in the Friesland province of the Netherlands. It was bred from otter-hunting dogs for use against the otter and other water game. It is a fearless hunter with a dense, tightly curled coat, which enables it to withstand harsh climatic conditions. It is medium sized, and occurs in black, brown or blue, with or without white. The Wetterhoun has been known in its native Holland for centuries, but was not recognized by the Dutch Kennel Club until 1942.

This intelligent hunter is a somewhat aggressive animal, widely used as a guard and farm dog in Holland. It needs firm and kindly handling. It needs a lot of exercise and regular grooming, and is best kept kennelled out of doors.

WOOLLY-HAIRED GRIFFON or Long-coated Pointing Griffon or Griffon à Poil Laineux is also referred to as the Boulet Griffon after Emanuel Boulet, a French industrialist who developed the Woolly-haired Griffon in the 19th century with the aid of Leon Vernier. The resultant breed looks like a cross between the Wire-haired Pointing Griffon (Korthals Griffon) and the French Setter or Braque. It is the same size as the Korthals Griffon with the head of a pointer and a coat similar to the Braque's but silkier and softer, like that of the Afghan Hound. Its colour is a dull brown, described as dead-leaf. Boulet's dog and bitch, Marco and Myra, became international champions and are in the pedigrees of most of today's Woolly-haired Griffons.

This gentle, obedient griffon is a good all-purpose gundog with keen scenting ability and great powers of endurance. Its good temperament also makes it a fine household pet. It needs plenty of exercise and daily grooming with a brush and comb.

The Woolly-haired Griffon is a slightly smaller, long-coated version of the Wire-haired Pointing Griffon.

HOUNDS

AUSTRIAN COARSE-HAIRED HOUND or Styrian Rough-haired Mountain Hound is also known as the Steirischer Rauhaarige Hochgebirgs Bracke or Peintinger Bracke. Originating in Styria, a southern province of Austria, it was developed in the late 1800s from the German Hanover Hound and various other Austrian and Istrian coarse-haired breeds. The aim was to produce a dog tough enough to hunt on Austria's high mountains, and this breed is particularly noted for its hardiness. It is a medium-sized, muscular and strongly built hound with drop ears and a curved, sabre-style tail with a small tuft of hair on the tip. It has a rough coat, and occurs in red, pale yellow or fawn; a small white spot on the chest is acceptable. It is kept only for hunting, and is greatly valued as a boar hunter. It has considerable powers of endurance and a magnificent cry.

The good natured, intelligent and appealing Austrian Coarse-haired Hound is readily trained and a popular and willing worker. It is gentle and faithful, but it retains a strong hunting instinct and is not suited to being kept as a household pet. It requires a lot of exercise and the coat needs daily brushing.

The **AUSTRIAN HOUND**, Brandl Bracke or Österreichischer Bracke is a medium-sized dog little known outside its country of origin. In Austria it is highly valued for its ability to follow a cold scent, and is also used to hunt small game. It is thought to be descended from Celtic hounds and to be related to the Jura Hounds and Bloodhound. It is very similar to the Tyrolean Hound, differing only in size, colour and length of coat.

The fine-looking Austrian Hound has a sturdy body, domed skull, long head and tail, and a smooth, glossy coat. It is solid red or black with flame markings, and a small white spot on the chest is permissible.

It is used for hunting all types of game, and is sensible and obedient. It requires a lot of exercise, and regular brushing.

BALKAN HOUND or Balksanski Gonič is a sighthound from the former country of Yugoslavia, bred to suit particular tasks and climate. Its ancestors were brought to Europe by the Phoenicians.

This is a medium-sized breed with a short, coarse, dense coat. It is fox red with a black saddle or mantle extending to the base of the head. It is used to track over rough ground for small and large game, including hare, fox and deer.

This good natured breed is strong and untiring, hard-working, and has a high-pitched voice, making it an excellent tracking dog. It requires a lot of exercise.

BANJARA GREYHOUND This breed is associated with the Banjara people of the state of Rajasthan in north-west India. It is a sighthound, and is used as a hunting and coursing dog. It is rough-coated, muscular, and its colours are brindle, grey, wheaten or sandy.

The Banjara are ancestors of the European Romanies, and their small greyhounds could have contributed to the development of the Lurcher (page 251). Like the Lurcher, the Banjara Greyhound is a mixture, and a pure Banjara would be unique. The breed is not officially recognized, and is not known outside India.

BASSET ARTÉSIEN NORMAND
is a descendant of short-legged hounds once native to the Artois and Normandy in northern France. The hound experts, George Johnston and Maria Ericson, report that there were dwarfed versions of the bicoloured Artois and the tricoloured Normand, and these were interbred, merging over time into the dog we now know as the Basset Artésien Normand. The breed was given its modern name in 1911.

The Basset Artésien Normand is a long-bodied dog, the length of which exceeds its height, making it easier for it to work in thickets. It is either bicolour – orange and white – or tricolour – white with tan head, black back and extremities. The breed is used to hunt rabbits and other small prey and has a keen following throughout much of Europe but is little known in the United Kingdom.

The Basset Artésien Normand retains a strong hunting instinct and still fulfils its traditional role in its native land. It is not suitable as a domestic pet.

BAVARIAN MOUNTAIN DOG
This German breed is also known as the Bavarian Schweisshund or Bayerischer Gebirgsschweisshund. It was bred in the 1900s because the Hanover Hound, although an excellent tracking dog (see page 161), was found to be too heavy to work successfully in the Bavarian mountains. So the Hanover was crossed with the Tyrolean Hound (a relative of the old Bavarian Hound) to produce a lighter, more agile animal, but with the same keen nose.

It has a strong, somewhat fine body and has long pendent ears. It has a thick, rough, close-lying coat, and comes in deep red, red tan, fawn to wheaten, red grizzle or brindle. The Bavarian Mountain Dog is used to hunt deer and to track down wounded game through heavy cover.

This intelligent, lively, muscular dog is suitable for working free, or on a line, in the mountains. It has a calm, steady temperament and is a favourite with deer hunters and gamewardens, and is not kept as a housepet. It should be groomed with a hound glove.

The BLACK FOREST HOUND
(Slovakian Hound, Slovensky Kopov) is of ancient origin and is the only hound native to Slovakia. It was not a recognized breed until after the Second World War but since then efforts have been made to preserve and perpetuate its characteristics. It is medium-sized, black with tan markings, and has a thick, close-lying coat. The breed has strong hunting instincts, first-class scenting abilities, a well-developed sense of direction, and also makes a good guard. When tracking, it is single-minded and will follow a trail for many hours, barking loudly. It is now used mainly for hunting the European wild boar.

This affectionate hound has a lively personality and immense courage but is extremely independent and needs rigorous training. It is unlikely to be kept as a housepet.

BLUETICK COONHOUND is
similar in appearance to the American Foxhound and is descended from various foxhound types crossed with French hounds such as the Gascony Blue hounds (page 169), the Porcelaine (page 162) and the Saintongeois (page 245). For a time it was registered, along with various other types of hounds, as an English Coonhound, but in 1945 the Bluetick Coonhound was registered as a separate breed in order to resist attempts to make it faster and more like a foxhound.

It is a quite tall hound with a smooth, short, slightly coarse coat. Its colour is white, thickly ticked (spotted) with dark blue, with fawn markings on the head and ears. It is a free tonguer on trail, with a bugle voice when trailing, which may change to a steady chop when running, with a steady, coarse chop at the tree. It is obedient and has great powers of endurance. It should be kennelled out of doors, and given plenty of exercise.

BOSNIAN COARSE-HAIRED HOUND or Basanski Ostrodlaki Goniči-Barak is a native of Bosnia in the north of the former state of Yugoslavia. This powerful hunter has a thick, tapering tail and a trunk

only slightly longer than its height at withers. It has long, coarse hair over a dense undercoat giving it an appealing shaggy appearance and enabling it to be used over rough ground and in bad weather. It occurs in wheaten yellow, reddish yellow, grey or blackish; bicolour and tricolour are acceptable, as are white areas on the head, dewlap, chest, lower limbs and tail tip.

It has a serious expression, but is said to be both a playful dog and one that is courageous with great powers of endurance. It can be used against all manner of game, but is gentle in the home. It requires a lot of exercise and daily grooming.

BRAZILIAN TRACKER or Rastreador Brasileiro was developed from the American Foxhound and the Coonhounds, the Black and Tan, the Treeing Walker and the Bluetick. The aim was to produce a hardy tracker of the jaguar with great powers of endurance and the ability to work over most types of terrain. The breed has a short, dense coat, quite rough to the touch, a fairly long head, long pendulous ears and dark eyes. It has Foxhound, Treeing

The powerful Basset Artésien Normand is a popular European hunting breed which gave rise to the Basset Hound.

Walker, Bluetick or Black and Tan Coonhound markings – that is, blue merle, white with black or tan patches, or black and tan.

Despite being a keen jaguar hunter and a superb tracking and hunting dog, the Brazilian Tracker is a good natured animal without any history of aggression towards people.

DREVER or Swedish Dachsbracke is one of the most popular dogs in Sweden but is little seen outside its native land. It was developed by mating German Dachshunds with Swedish hunting dogs, and is of moderate size, with a rectangular body shape and expressive eyes. It has a smooth, thick coat, and all colours are acceptable although white should always be well in evidence in front, on the side and behind. The Drever is famed for following fox, hare, deer and even wild boar and, possessing a good voice and keen nose, will drive its prey towards the guns. It began life with the German name, Dachsbracke, and was given its current name when recognition was sought. The breed was recognized by the Swedish Kennel Club in 1949 and by the international body, the FCI, in 1953. It is not, however, recognized by Kennel Clubs in Britain or the United States.

The Drever is a favourite hunting and popular show dog in Sweden. Being intelligent, devoted and of equable temperament, it also makes a splendid family pet provided that it receives plenty of exercise and a good daily brushing.

DUNKER or Norwegian Hound is named after its originator, Wilhelm Dunker, who crossed the Russian Harlequin Hound with other hounds. The resultant dog is renowned for its endurance and staying power rather than its speed, and is used mainly to hunt hare. It has a straight, strong but not too long body and deep chest, a tail reaching to the hocks or a little way beyond, and a close, hard coat. Its colouring is black or blue merle with fawn and white markings. A popular hound in its native Norway and throughout Scandinavia, the breed is little known elsewhere and is not recognized by the British or American Kennel Clubs.

The Dunker is reputed to be a confident and affectionate dog, which is trustworthy and loyal to its master. This powerful hunting dog is not normally kept as a housepet.

ENGLISH COONHOUND Like other coonhounds, the English Coonhound is descended from English hounds crossed with other hound types. All coonhounds apart from the Black and Tan and Redbone (see page 149), which achieved breed status early on, were originally registered as English Coonhounds. The breed included a variety of types of hounds with both fast and slow, patient styles of hunting. They were used against a variety of game, but particularly fox and raccoon. During the 20th century, types such as the Bluetick (page 244) were classified as separate breeds in order to preserve their distinct qualities.

The modern English Coonhound is a medium-sized dog with a short, hard coat. Its colour is usually redtick – white with red patches and red ticking (specks) in the white areas – although other colours are allowed. It is a fast and efficient hunter, and is popular with sportsmen and in the competition ring. It should be kennelled out of doors, and requires a lot of exercise.

FINNISH HOUND This is also known as the Finnish Stövare and, in its native Finland, as the Suomenajokoira. It is a medium-sized hound with a fairly lean, noble head and a medium-length, thick dense coat. Its colour is black and tan with white markings on the head, neck, chest, feet and tail tip. The breed was created by a Finnish goldsmith named Tammelin who carefully mixed German, Swiss, English and Scandinavian hound blood. The breed has been known since 1700 and became popular in Finland at the end of the 19th century. The Finnish Hound is a popular dog in its native land, where it is famed as a hunter of fox, hare, moose and lynx, but is little known elsewhere.

The Finnish Hound is a good natured animal but is known to have a mind of its own and has a strong hunting instinct. Although it may be kept indoors outside the hunting season in its native land, it is chosen for its hunting abilities rather than as a household companion. It requires a lot of exercise and a regular grooming with a hound glove.

The **GASCONS-SAINTONGEOIS, GREAT AND SMALL** The Great (Grand) Gascon-Saintongeois is a powerful coursing dog, which is also known as the Virelade after its creator in the 1800s, Baron Joseph de Caryon Latour de Virelade. His aim was to produce a dog that combined the qualities of those fine hunting breeds, the Ariégeois, the Great Gascony Blue and the now extinct wolf-hunter, the Saintongeois. He achieved an animal with a very sensitive nose for tracking, strong enough to hunt large game such as the wolf and the roebuck, and also able to function as a gundog. The Small (Petit) variety was developed in south-west France to hunt hare. Henri de Caryon, Baron de Virelade's nephew, attempted to improve the breed by introducing blood from Bordeaux, but little information is available.

Their short dense coat is predominantly white with black markings. They also have some brown markings on the head, and a grey-brown patch on the thigh.

Today, the Gascons-Saintongeois are rare in France and little seen outside their country of origin.

GREEK GREYHOUND is also known as the Albanian Greyhound. This breed resembles the Saluki (see page 182). It is a hardy coursing dog, which is now extremely rare. It has a short, close coat with fringed ears and tail. It can be any colour.

The Greek Greyhound is a faithful hunting companion, but so rare that it is unlikely to be kept as a housepet. It would require plentiful exercise, and grooming with a soft brush and a brisk rub-down with a towel or hound glove.

HALDENSTÖVARE is named after the town of Halden, in Norway, where it was developed through crossings of local hounds with imported hounds from France, Britain, Germany and, probably, Russia. It is a strong, long-bodied hound of considerable endurance, which can chase game at speed even across snow. It has a medium-sized head, a straight and strong back, broad loins, and a rather thick tail that is carried fairly low. Its colour is white with black markings and brown shading on the head and legs and between the white and black areas. This breed is popular in its native country but little known elsewhere.

The Haldenstövare is a loyal, gentle and affectionate animal. Since it is unusual for Scandinavian hounds to be kept in packs it doubtless generally lives in the home. It requires a lot of exercise and a regular rub-down with a hound glove.

HELLENIC HOUND The Hellenic Hound (Greek Harehound) is a tracking dog of ancient Greek origin. In its native land, it works singly, or in packs, over virtually any type of terrain, often in rocky areas inaccessible to people. It has considerable scenting powers, and a pleasant, resonant bay. It is medium sized, with a short, dense coat, and its colour is black and tan.

This strong, intelligent hound is little known outside Greece and is unlikely to be kept as a housepet there. It requires abundant exercise and grooming with a hound glove.

HYGENHUND This fine Norwegian hunting dog takes its name from a Norwegian breeder Hygen, who developed it in the 1800s. He crossed the German Holsteiner with various other hounds to produce a dog with great staying power, able to hunt over snowy terrain. The Hygenhund was subsequently crossed with the lighter and less regal Dunker, and efforts were made to register the progeny under the name of Norwegian Beagles. These failed, however, and the Hygenhund and Dunker remain separate breeds. The Hygenhund is still used in Norway but is not numerous there and is rarely seen outside Scandinavia. It is a medium-sized dog with a broad head, dark or hazel-coloured eyes, long, deep chest, and a straight, dense, glossy coat that is slightly rough to the touch. It is chestnut or yellow ochre, with or without black shading, or black and tan. All these colours may be combined with white. It can also be white with tan to yellow markings or spots, or with black and tan markings.

This reliable, affectionate dog is a dedicated hunter with considerable powers of endurance. It requires a lot of exercise and needs a regular rub-down with a hound glove.

ISTRIAN HOUNDS There are two varieties of Istrian Hound or Istrishi Gonič, which differ only in coat. The short-haired (Kratkodlaki) has a short, dense coat, not unlike that of the Pointer, while the Wire- or Rough-haired (Resati) has long, straight, coarse hair over a dense, woolly undercoat. They have a long, narrow head, straight, broad back and medium-length tail. Their colour is snow-white with orange markings on the ears. Markings may also appear on the body, particularly at the root of the tail. Both are ancient breeds native to Istria, a peninsula in the north-west of the former state of Yugoslavia, and are seldom seen outside their land of origin. Possessing a keen sense of smell, the Istrian Hounds locate their quarry by scent and drive it to the guns. They are used to hunt fox and hare, and are also useful tracking dogs.

The Istrian Hounds have great powers of endurance, and are known to be active, friendly and easy to train. They are gentle in the home and happy to combine the roles of sportsman's dog and family pet. The Short-haired should be groomed with a hound glove, the Wire-haired with a wire brush.

KANGAROO HOUND resembles a heavily built Greyhound and is sometimes called the Australian Greyhound. It was developed in the mid-1880s by Australian settlers who wanted a dog that was keen-eyed and fast enough for coursing kangaroos and wallabies, yet powerful enough to hold the quarry when caught. They set about producing such a dog by crossing the English Greyhound and the Irish Wolfhound. The result was a large, tough sighthound, well able to chase and overpower a kangaroo, with a short, harsh coat, resembling that of the Wolfhound. Its colours are brindle, pied, black, tan and white, or black and tan. However, as its quarry became scarce the Kangaroo Hound dwindled in numbers. Although there are said to be some specimens on remote stations, it appears to be a dying breed and may even be extinct.

LEVESQUE is named after its originator, Rogatien Levesque, who embarked on creating this hound and versatile gundog in 1873. He mated a Great Gascony Blue bitch with a rough-coated Foxhound, and the pups in the two litters produced were crossbred with the Virelade. The resultant progeny were then crossed with the Gascon Saintongeois-Vendéens. There was a considerable stir in Paris when a pack of Levesque was first displayed there. Despite all the crossings, the Levesque now breeds very true to type.

The Levesque is a good-natured hound with light chestnut eyes and an expression which has been described as both sweet and intelligent. It has a smooth, strong, close coat, and occurs in black and white only, although it has a purplish tint on its back. Like all hounds it requires a lot of exercise and regular grooming.

MAJESTIC TREE HOUND This scenthound is used in the American Deep South for hunting big cats and other large game. It was developed recently for this purpose by American enthusiasts, who crossed the Bloodhound with other large hounds. The resultant dog is large, rather ponderous, with an excellent nose, fine voice and great powers of endurance. It has a short, thick, dense coat, loose folds of skin around its face and neck, and can be any colour or combination of colours.

Like its relative, the English Bloodhound, the Majestic Tree Hound is affectionate, good natured and can be kept as a pet by those who have the space to allow it to run and neighbours who do not object to

The Steinbracke (see page 248) can be readily identified by the typical white markings on the head, chest, legs and tip of the tail.

its melodious voice. It should be groomed with a hound glove.

MOUNTAIN CUR This little-known American breed is descended from dogs brought to the United States by European settlers and, possibly, native pariah dogs. It is reminiscent of the now extinct English Drover's dog or Cur, which may have played a part in its ancestry. The Mountain Cur is a strong, stocky hound, able to work over difficult terrain. It is skilled at treeing game and is also a good tracker, which seldom gives tongue, and makes a fine guard.

The Mountain Cur is a tough, courageous dog, capable of doing battle with big game. It does not have a very affable temperament, and is suited to a rugged working life, not the suburban fireside.

PLOTT HOUND The Plott Hound is a medium-sized hound descended from hounds brought to England from Germany by the Plott family in the 18th century, which were crossed with English and other types of hounds. It has bred true in North Carolina for 200 years. It has a short, harsh, close-lying coat, and is tan-pied with black saddle. It has been used to hunt all types of game, including wolf, puma, coyote, wild cat, red deer, bear, boar and smaller game. It is a tough and persistent hunter, quite able to stand up to its prey. It is best kept kennelled out of doors, and needs plenty of exercise.

POSAVATZ HOUND or Posavski Goriči is a vigorous hound named after the Posavine area around the Sava river in the north of the former state of Yugoslavia. Little known outside its country of origin, it is used there for hunting small game and deer. This medium-sized breed has a thick, dense coat, dark eyes with a "wide awake" expression, and a long, narrow head with pendulous ears rounded at the tips. Its short tail should not reach below the hocks, and the length of the body should be 4–7.5cm (1½–3in) more than the height at withers. It has a short, thick coat, usually reddish. However, it may be wheaten yellow to fawn, but without darkening to deep chocolate brown. White is allowed on the head, chest, feet and tail.

Highly regarded in its native area, the Posavatz is swift, obedient and affectionate towards its owners. It needs lots of exercise, and should be groomed with a hound glove.

RUSSIAN HOUNDS and **ESTONIAN HOUND** There are three breeds of hound recognized in Russia: the Russian (Drab Yellow) Hound, the Russian Particolour (Harlequin or Piebald) Hound and the Estonian Hound. The Drab Yellow, which was standardized early in this century, is an indigenous Russian breed. Fox-hound blood was added to the Russian Hound to produce the Particolour which is tan, sometimes with a black saddle, and with white or yellowish markings. Both these hounds are used for hunting fox, hare and sometimes badger, and are extremely popular in their native land.

The Estonian Hound, which is black with fawn markings, has a more elongated body and longer ears then the Russian Hounds and is comparatively rare. The two Russian Hounds are medium sized and similar in conformation, except that the ears and tail of the Particolour are shorter. The Estonian's body is twice as long as its height, and it looks rather Basset-like. All three have short, dense coats.

These are fine scenthounds, being of good temperament with keen noses and great endurance. They will hunt in a pack or singly and require abundant exercise. They should be groomed with a hound glove.

SCHILLER HOUND or Schiller-stövare is named after the Swedish breeder, Per Schiller. He developed it in the late 1880s using local Swedish dogs crossed with hounds from Austria, Germany and Switzerland. The resultant Schiller Hound is believed to be the fastest of the Scandinavian hounds. This powerful, medium-sized dog has a short coat, and is black with reddish brown or yellow markings. Sturdy as well as swift, it is hunted singly and is also used as a tracking dog. The breed was recognized in 1952, and is now one of the most popular hunting dogs in Sweden.

This is an excellent hunting dog and faithful to its owner, but is not suitable for keeping as a housepet. It requires abundant exercise and grooming with a hound glove.

The **SMALL BLUE GASCONY GRIFFON** or Petit Griffon Bleu de Gascogne combines the qualities of both the Griffon – or rough-coated hound – and the Small Gascony Blue from which it was bred. It is a rustic looking, solidly built, low-slung

French hound which is similar in appearance to the Small Gascony Blue apart from its smaller size, shorter muzzle and ears, and a dry coat that is harsh to the touch. Its coat is white with black markings and specific tan markings. The Small Blue Gascony Griffon is now extremely rare.

It is a hard-working, tireless hunter with a good nose, and is used for hunting hare. It is not suitable for a family pet. Like all hounds, it requires a lot of exercise. It needs daily grooming with brush and comb to prevent its coat matting.

The **SMÅLAND HOUND** or Smålandstövare is indigenous to Sweden and named after the densely forested southern Swedish province of Småland. There and elsewhere it is used singly to hunt game, mainly fox and rabbit. The Småland is a light, medium-sized dog with a keen sense of smell. Although an ancient breed, it was not recognized until 1921 and the standard was revised in 1952. It is a powerful, medium-sized breed, has a short smooth coat, and is black with tan markings. It can be born with either a long or short tail.

The breed is calm and reliable, and devoted to its master. It is not suitable as a housepet. The Småland needs abundant exercise and should be groomed with a hound glove.

SMALL GASCONY BLUE or Petit Bleu de Gascogne was bred down from the Great Gascony Blue to hunt smaller game. Its ancestor is one of the most ancient hunting dogs in France. The Small Gascony Blue differs from its larger relative only in size and in having a finer head and thicker ears than those of the Great Gascony Blue. The Small has a keen sense of smell and is used mainly against hare, but is now rarely seen outside its native south-west France.

SPANISH HOUNDS There are two varieties of Spanish Hound or Sabueos Español, the Large (de Monte) and Small (Lebrero), which differ only in size and colour. Both are descended from hounds brought by the Celtic people in the 1st

millennium BC. These long-bodied, short-legged dogs have keen noses. They have long heads and wrinkled foreheads, and a fine coat. The Large is white with patches of black or deep orange. The Small is the same except that patches may cover almost the entire body excepting the neck, chest, feet and muzzle. At one time they were used in packs for tracing game and, later, also drove quarry towards the gun. Today they are still used for tracking, but mainly by the police, and as guard dogs.

These fine hounds have considerable endurance and perseverance on the trail, but can be self-willed and need firm training. They require a lot of exercise, and should be groomed with a hound glove.

STEINBRACKE is a medium-sized German hunting and tracking dog that is used against small game. Less common than other breeds within the bracke group, it is one of a number of old hounds of similar type that once existed in Germany. The German hound club produced a brief standard for the Steinbracke in 1955 which was accepted by the FCI. The breed bears some resemblance to the Westphalian Dachsbracke, but is much longer in the leg and squarer in outline. It has a long, very dense,

The Tawny Brittany Griffon is an ancient European breed which was developed to guard flocks from predators.

hard coat, and is always tricolour.

The Steinbracke is a lively, friendly dog requiring plenty of exercise and grooming with a hound glove.

STEPHENS' STOCK, one of five varieties of mountain cur found in the Deep South of the United States, is similar in type to but smaller than the Mountain Cur. Also known as "Little Black", this hound was developed to hunt small game by the Stephens family in the mid to late 1800s. It was not until 1970, after 100 years or so of breeding true, that it was described, and it is not yet recognized by any kennel club. It is fairly small with a strung-up, sinewy appearance, a small head with narrow muzzle and rat's tail. It is black and has a short coat.

Stephens' Stock is essentially a working dog and is greatly favoured by hunters, being quick, courageous and fairly easy to train. It may be kept in the home provided that it has adequate space, plentiful exercise and, above all, is used for the job for which it was intended.

TAWNY BRITTANY GRIFFON or Griffon Fauve de Bretagne is a medium-sized, muscular, well-boned hound, with a rustic appearance, hard, fawn-coloured coat, expressive eyes, pendulous ears and a very coarse coat. This ancient breed was reputedly used for wolf hunting in the Middle Ages. Tawny Griffon packs were disbanded in the breed's native Brittany after 1885 when their quarry had become extinct. It

was saved from extinction itself by a few breeders and is now used in its native land to hunt wild boar and fox but is still comparatively rare.

TRANSYLVANIAN HOUND

The Transylvanian Hound (Hungarian Hound, Erdeliy Kopo) traces back to hounds brought by the Magyars when they invaded the Carpathian region in the 9th century. It originated through the crossing of the Magyar hounds with local dogs and thereafter with Polish dogs. The result was a versatile hunting dog able to cope with the dense forests and extremes of climate in the Carpathian mountains. It was once used by Hungarian royalty to hunt wolves and bears. Today there are two varieties, the Large being used to hunt wild boar, deer and lynx, and the Small, fox and hare. The Large is a medium-sized dog, with a medium-length, straight, dense coat, black with tan markings. The Small is slightly smaller, with a short, straight, dense coat, brown-red, with slightly lighter markings towards the belly. Both have fairly long bodies, nearly square in outline, and long tails set on low.

The Transylvanian is a tireless, obedient hound which is brave and easy to train. It requires boundless exercise and should be groomed with a hound glove.

The **TREEING TENNESSEE BRINDLE** This smaller coonhound was, like the other coonhounds, bred from crosses between English and other types of hounds. It is an excellent tracker, fearless and fast, and is used against game such as raccoon and squirrel. It is also intelligent and affectionate and makes a good hunting companion. It should be kennelled out of doors, and needs plenty of exercise.

The **TREEING WALKER COONHOUND** is of definite foxhound type, descending from the English Foxhound (page 176) crossed with other hounds. This medium-sized hound has a good treeing ability, and although it is used for hunting all types of game it is particularly suited to raccoon and opossum. Its short,

smooth, harsh coat occurs in a variety of colours – black, brown, red, white, black and white, red and white or other combinations. It preferably has a clear, ringing, bugle voice on a cold trail, changing to a chop or turkey mount on a running trail. It has a deep, throaty, loud chop mouth at the tree. It is persistent and obedient, and is popular for use in field trials. It should be kennelled out of doors, and needs plenty of exercise.

Another coonhound breed, the Trigg Hound, is very similar to the Treeing Walker Coonhound.

TYROLEAN HOUND or Tiroler

Bracke was bred by hunters in the Tyrol province of Austria from a number of local hounds. It is a long-headed dog with a long, slightly curved tail, a smooth or wiry short coat and an expression similar to that of the Austrian Coarse-haired Hound. It can be black, red or fawn yellow, or tricolour (black and tan with white markings). There are two varieties of the breed, which are identical except for size and are often described as Standard and Miniature. Both are used against fox and other game in the Tyrol's high mountains. Possessing an excellent nose, the Tyrolean Hound locates quarry for the hunters and is particularly good at tracking wounded game in dense cover.

This versatile hunter is well adapted to harsh mountain climate and terrain, and is capable of great endurance. It is an intelligent, trustworthy, and obedient dog. It is usually kept kennelled out of doors. It needs considerable exercise and does best in the role of hunting companion. It should be groomed with a hound glove.

WALKER HOUND was bred from

the American Foxhound (page 177) and crossed with hounds imported from England. It is used as a pack hound after various types of game. It is a medium-sized hound with a short, hard, close coat, and is usually black with tan spots above the eyes, but it may be any foxhound colour.

YUGOSLAVIAN MOUNTAIN HOUND (Planinski Gonič) and the Tricolour Hound (Tribarvni Gonič) occur in the southern mountainous part of the former state of Yugoslavia. Similar in size with rectangular bodies, the Tricolour is slighter than the Mountain Hound. The Tricolour is black or yellowish black, pale yellow to tan and white, and has a short, dense, glossy coat. The Mountain Hound is black with rust-coloured markings, and has a thick, flat, slightly coarse coat with an abundant undercoat. Both are used to hunt hare, fox, deer and other game and are untiring and diligent in pursuit. They are little known outside their country of origin where they are uncommon.

These strong, compact, attractive-looking hounds are calm, gentle and of good temperament. They require plenty of exercise and daily grooming with a hound glove.

TERRIER

AMERICAN STAFFORDSHIRE

TERRIER (Pit Bull Terrier, Yankee Terrier) is descended from the English Staffordshire Bull Terrier, which is the result of a mating between the Old English Bulldog and an English Terrier. This strong dog had reached the United States by 1870, where it was used, as in Britain, to fight other dogs in pits. It was recognized by the American Kennel Club as the Staffordshire Terrier in 1935, the name being revised in 1972 to American Staffordshire Terrier. By this time, the "sport" of dog fighting had long since waned, and the breed had been developed into a companion dog.

The American Kennel Club did, at one time, allow the American Staffordshire Terrier and the Staffordshire Bull Terrier to be exhibited together and even crossbred. However, the American Staffordshire was bred to be a larger, heavier dog than its English relative and it is now a quite different breed. The ears on its massive head may be cropped.

An American Staffordshire from a reputable breeder should, like its

Sturdy and fearless, the American Staffordshire Terrier rewards firm handling with unswerving loyalty.

English relative, be affectionate and trustworthy towards its owner and a fine guard. Owing to its ancestry, it is likely to be aggressive to other dogs and to need firm control. However, some irresponsible breeders and owners have encouraged the dog's aggressive tendencies, making this breed widely feared. There are very strict laws on the keeping of American Staffordshires in the United Kingdom, and it is forbidden to breed them there. It needs a lot of exercise and regular grooming.

AUSTRIAN SHORT-HAIRED PINSCHER Also known as the Österreichischer Kurzhaariger Pinscher, this terrier is an old breed native to Austria. It is little known elsewhere and there appears to be some confusion about what constitutes a good specimen. However, it is generally a medium-sized dog with a short neck, sturdy broad-chested body and short, smooth coat. The tail is short and curled up over the back or docked, and the ears on the pear-shaped head may be erect, semi-erect or dropped. It has

a short coat, and is fawn, golden, red, or black and tan, sometimes with brindle markings; white markings are common. It is said to be a fearless hunter and, in true terrier fashion, will readily go to ground after quarry.

This brave, vivacious and noisy dog makes a good guard but is best suited to an active country life and to being kennelled outside. It needs plenty of exercise and grooming with a bristle brush.

TOY

PERUVIAN INCA ORCHID or Moonflower Dog is an ancient hairless breed native to Peru. Prized by Inca nobility, this deer-like dog is still kept as a pet in Peru and has been exported to North America, Europe and other parts of the world. In common with most other hairless breeds, it also exists as a coated variety, which may occur in litters of hairless parents. It may have a tuft of hair on its head, but otherwise it has smooth skin. The coated variety has long silky hair. It can be pale pink, cream or white, solid or mottled in any colour. It has a high body temperature, an absence of pre-molar teeth, and prehensile hare feet that can grip objects.

The Peruvian Inca Orchid is a calm, sensitive dog and makes a loving, devoted companion. It needs only a moderate amount of exercise, and its skin should be massaged with cream or oil to keep it supple. This breed must be protected against the cold and against sunburn.

UNCLASSIFIED

CAROLINA DOG Occurring in the Deep South of the United States, this dog is a descendant of Pariah-type dogs (see p. 8), which probably migrated from Asia to North America thousands of years ago. It is a medium-sized, lightly built animal with a yellow coat that has earned it the nickname "Old Yeller". It is doubtful whether anyone outside the Deep South would ever have seen the Carolina Dog had it not starred in the Walt Disney film *Old Yeller*, made in 1957.

The Carolina Dog tends to be slightly more friendly than many Pariah-type dogs and some are kept as companions and have even been trained to the gun. However, it is really a wild dog, which must be reared carefully by humans from a very early age if it is to be domesticated and trained, and so it is not the ideal choice of pet.

DINGO The Australian Dingo is a Pariah-type dog which, according to the late Dr Erich Schneider-Leyer, occupies a position between ancestral dogs and the Pariahs. It is thought to have migrated to Australia with Aborigines over 20,000 years ago. The Aborigines tamed some and used them as hunting dogs but most remained wild. Operating singly or in packs, the Dingo is an efficient hunter and, when Europeans arrived, it started preying on rabbits, sheep and other imported livestock as well as native animals. So it was killed on sight and continues to be persecuted but still survives. It is medium sized, with a short, thick coat, and is usually reddish to pale fawn, sometimes with black on the back. Black, white or cream, solid or patched, can also occur.

The Dingo is a naturally suspicious, alert and extraordinarily intelligent animal. It can be reared by humans from a young age and trained gently but it basically remains a wild dog.

JINDO or Korean Dog is an excellent runner, able to bring down a rabbit or other quarry at amazing speed. It is named after Jindo island in Korea, where in the past this ancient breed was used in the hunting season against small animals and wild boar. At other times of the year it earned its keep as a watch dog. It is powerfully built, has a straight coat, and is usually red-brown in colour with light markings. It is something of a wild dog and, although the occasional litter has made its way overseas, the breed is not recognized by the FCI.

This beautiful dog is, unfortunately, proud, dominant and fairly difficult to train, the bitch being slightly more amenable.

LURCHER The English Lurcher is not a purebred dog but is of definite type, usually having a member of the greyhound family as one of its parents. It is thought to have been developed because, at one time in England, only those of noble blood were permitted to own a Greyhound. So Greyhound crosses were made to produce an efficient hunting companion for commoners and a popular poacher's dog. Possibly the best Lurchers result from a Greyhound/working Collie cross. Saluki, Deerhounds, Afghan Hounds and Borzoi are a few of the other members of the Greyhound family used. Its coat can be rough or smooth and it should look like a relative of the Deerhound or Greyhound.

The Lurcher is generally an obedient dog, which makes an excellent coursing hound and hunter, and will combine this role with that of a faithful and affectionate family pet. It needs plenty of exercise and a daily brushing.

NEW GUINEA SINGING DOG is a wild dog native to the large island of Papua New Guinea near Australia. Probably descended from early domesticated dogs of the southern hemisphere, it is a medium-sized Pariah, similar in type to the Dingo and named after the surprisingly melodious sound of its howl. It has a broad head, a short, smooth coat with plumed tail, and is red, with or without white markings. It existed in the wild state mainly in mountainous areas of its island home but is becoming increasingly rare there and, to the writer's knowledge, most surviving specimens are to be found in zoological parks.

This tough, efficient hunter may be approached and, on occasions, handled by humans. However, like the Dingo, it is a wary dog of uncertain temperament and must always return to the wild.

TELOMIAN This is a smallish Pariah dog, indigenous to Malaysia. It bears some resemblance to the

The Lurcher may have originated in Ireland. It is an excellent poacher's dog, able to run down prey swiftly and silently.

Basenji (see page 148), with which it shares a number of characteristics, including facial wrinkles and a yodelling rather than barking vocalization. It is medium-size with a short, smooth coat, and is sable with areas of white, sometimes speckled. The Telomian has been kept for centuries by the native inhabitants of Malaysia. They often lived in houses on stilts and the dog is said to have climbed a ladder to reach its human family's home at night. It hunted small game and otherwise existed on a mainly vegetarian diet. Perhaps because of a change in diet, specimens are now believed to be attaining a greater height.

The Telomian is gradually becoming known in Europe and North America, but has yet to be recognized by any kennel club.

Although the Telomian is intelligent, courageous, and basically of good temperament, and has lived with humans in Malaysia, it remains a semi-wild dog and so may not be a good choice of family pet. It must be reared by humans from an early age and carefully handled, if it is to be a companion, and does not like to be confined.

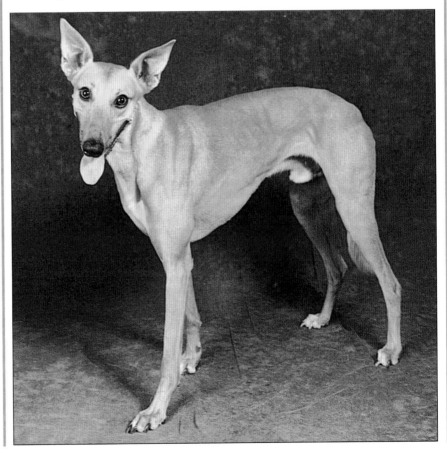

INDEX

CREDITS

Quarto Publishing would like to thank all the owners who kindly allowed us to photograph their dogs for inclusion in this book.

Additional photographs were supplied by: Ace 7cl (Bo Cederwall), 176 (Lazlo), 20cr (J. Stathatos), 85b (Paul Steel), 7l (Paul Thompson), 20bl; Val Connolly 251; Marc Henrie 6, 7cr, 15, 20tl, 21, 23r; Jacana 154b, 157, 168, 237tr, 248 (Axel), 154t (Jean-Paul Ferrero), 156 (Frederic), 128, 236r, 244 (Jean-Michel Labat), 162 (Elizabeth Lemoine), 155, 160, 179 (Mero), 138; Robert & Eunice Pearcy 177b & t, 236c; Pictor 8, 18l; Unicorn Stock Photos 7r (Betts Anderson), 20br, 22 (Christian Mundt), 23c & l (Perry Murphy), 20cl (Alon Reininger); Wim Van Vugt 57c, 95b, 145, 199r, 239, 240, 242, 243, 247, 250.

Key: b bottom, c centre, l left, r right, t top

All other photographs are the copyright of Quarto Publishing.